THE
MAD
ENTREPRENEUR

PHILIP J. ROMANO

To my son, Sam. Of all the experiences I've had in my life, the best one has been to be your dad. This book is dedicated to you.

Acknowledgement

I want to thank my ever-patient co-writer Steve McLinden for sharing my enthusiasm for this book, organizing my often random thoughts and pulling together everything into one cohesive unit. Steve co-authored my best-selling first book, *Food for Thought: How the Creator of Fuddrucker's, Romano's Macaroni Grill, and eatZi's Built a $10 Billion Empire One Concept at a Time,* and has an uncanny ability to write in my voice. Steve, 63, is a little younger than me and will co-write my third book...if he lives long enough!

Steve McLinden is an Arlington, TX-based writer who also co-wrote books with sportscaster Pat Summerall, *Summerall: On and Off the Air,* and educator Stedman Graham. *Diversity: Leaders Not Labels -- A New Plan for the 21st Century.* McLinden is contributing editor of *Shopping Centers Today* magazine.

Contents

Prologue:

SETTING THE TABLE

I'm MAD when I wake up, I'm MAD all day, and I'm MAD when I go to bed. I do my best to make people MAD, too and encourage them to make others MAD. There's no need to enroll me in an anger management class, and no, I haven't gone off the deep end, although I have been called the "mad scientist" of the restaurant industry. The acronym MAD I'm using stands for "Making a Difference."

Making a difference gets me going every morning. When I wake up, I ask myself, "How can I make a difference in my life today? How can I make a difference in somebody else's life? How can I make somebody smile? And how can I make a difference in my community and in my country?"

My father, Samuel, who emigrated from Enora, Sicily, as a child, was the one who compelled me to *make a difference* in some way in my life in order to make a difference in the world. He told me to rise above the ordinary and "to be known near and far for what you are." He said, "If you're going to have a hot dog stand, have the biggest and best hot dog stand in the world. If you're going sell shoes, sell the best. Even if you're a bum, be the world's most famous bum—one they're going to write about. Be known near and far for what you are."

That advice stuck and became a permanent part of my operating program in my life, plus a driving force behind my businesses. To this day, I'd rather fail at something exciting and different than succeed at something ordinary. I credit my father's advice for the passion that I have to make a difference in so many peoples' lives.

I have already created 30 restaurant concepts, producing $1.5 billion in annual sales and tens of thousands of jobs. But I am not done. Late at night as I settle down to sleep, I still ask myself what I did that was MAD that day and what I could do to be MAD tomorrow. I sleep much better that way.

So, here I am, at age 79, still creating and investing in the future. I spend all day in my MAD mode thinking about inventing, improving, and giving back. It's been 13 years now since my first book came out, the sold-out *Food for Thought: How the Creator of Fuddrucker's, Romano's Macaroni Grill, and Eatzi's Built a $10 Billion Empire One Concept at a Time.*

With so much going on in my life and in the restaurant business, including the creation of the world's first restaurant incubator, Trinity Groves, and all the reflection I've been doing on such things as creativity, ethics, success, and giving back, I realized it was time to write another book about the things that I've done in my life to make a difference in this world.

1

WHY I DONT WEAR SOCKS AND OTHER PRESSING QUESTIONS

Over the years, I have come to think of all my restaurants as stages.
The customers and the staff are the cast, the food is both the theme
and the star of the show. All those elements have to act in concert
down to the smallest detail.

Let's start with some questions and answers so that you can get to know me a little better.

Question: You've often said that your father is your number one role model. Why is this so?

Phil: My father, Samuel, was not only my top role model but also my hero. In my first restaurant, the Gladiator, he helped me buy out my partner by mortgaging his home. That's how much he believed in me. I was proud to pay him back double even though he didn't expect it.

He raised me with a great respect for family. But he was much more than that to me. When he was in the navy during World War II, at first I felt like he had abandoned me and didn't like me. I didn't know where he was. But then he'd write and send me pictures that I would show to everyone and brag that he was a war hero. When he returned, I clung to him and went just about everywhere with him, even to work. We talked constantly. He helped give me a perspective on life that I still have today. He'd do things like point to a man leaning on a wall and say, "He can't stand on his own two feet," or at a coffee shop, he'd say, "Watch that guy. He's never going to pay the bill or even help to pay it. There are just some guys with fishhooks in their pockets." It was like getting a lesson in thinking.

Question: Tell us about your grandfather.

Phil: Well, I was named after him—my grandfather, Philip Romano. He was born in Sicily and came to Ellis Island in 1907 looking for a better life. But he broke out in a rash during the voyage so the U.S. Immigration and Naturalization Service (INS) turned him back. He never gave up, though. From there he traveled to South America, where he worked as a carpenter in Argentina and saved nearly everything he made. Two years later, he went back to Italy to get my grandmother, Rosalie, and their son, who would later become my dad, as well as two of his brothers and one sister. They all boarded a ship to New York and were allowed in. They soon relocated to Auburn in upstate New York. There, my grandfather built a carpentry business from the ground up.

Grandpa Philip helped raise me for three years while my father served in the navy during World War II. He didn't speak much English, and I think that helped me develop ways to communicate nonverbally. It's funny that I never learned to speak Italian. It was the same with my Italian friends. Our parents told us that when we went to school, we were going to be American-Italians, not Italian-Americans.

Question: And your mother?

Phil: My mother's name was Rose, short for Rose Immaculate. She was a loving, patient woman with a great sense of humor. And could she cook! She would just light up a room when she entered. She'd say things like, "Talk of the devil, and he will appear; talk about failure, and it will happen; talk about success, and you'll have it." She was a little thing, weighing only 89 pounds. I weighed 12 pounds when I was born! That's why I tell people that I'm Caesarian, not Italian. "The problem I have when I leave the house," I'd say, "is that I don't know whether to go out the door…or the window." I was born on Columbus Day in 1939, so I asked my mother why she didn't name me Christopher. She replied, "I couldn't because the milkman's name was Christopher."

I was a constant daydreamer in school. When my lessons were being taught, I was miles away in my mind. I felt like my mother and I were in grade school together because the principal would ask her to come to school and the teachers would all come into the office and tell her how poorly I was doing. Once, when the teachers told her that they couldn't teach me and that I might never amount to anything, my mother shot back, "Well, ma'am, I'm not worried about my son. And you say you 'can't teach him'? You're the teacher. Teach him!" I could do no wrong in her eyes. When the cardiac stent I would eventually go on to bankroll landed me on the cover of *Inc.* magazine in 1989, alongside H. Ross Perot in an article called "Who's Really Financing America's Start-ups?," my mother asked, "Who is this Ross Perot fellow on the cover with you?" I said, "No, mom, I'm on the cover with Ross Perot."

Question: How did your parents meet?

Phil: They were working at the old Dunn & McCarthy shoe factory together in Auburn, New York. He was a machinist, and he'd fix all the belts on the machines. So he'd have to get under the machines to work on them, so he saw all the girls' legs. One day he spied my mother's legs, and he really liked them. So he asked a coworker to introduce him to her, and they hit it off. My father said they both saw fireworks when they first met. In fact, they got married on Independence Day! My dad often said, "We started out with a bang." That was 1934, and they moved into a small apartment and worked mostly 12-hour days. When I came along, my father started repairing small appliances for people in the neighborhood as a second job. He could do anything with his hands, even build a house from the ground up. He built the bars in many of my new concepts. He eventually settled in as an electrician, but behind the scenes, supporting him and the rest of our family in every way you could imagine, was my mother.

Question: So, your mother obviously had a huge influence on you as well.

Phil: Yes, she was everything a son could ever want in a mother. To give people an idea of what she meant to me, let me read a letter I wrote for her eulogy. I will pass this onto my son, Sam, so he will know how I felt about his grandmother.

Dear Mom,

With your permission and without embarrassing you, I am going to read this letter I wrote to you aloud and tell the world what a great mother you are and you were. You always told me how proud of me you were. Now I want to tell you how proud I am of you and of what you did with your life. I remember you telling me that you came over from Italy when you were four years old and the first thing you saw when you came here to America was the beautiful lady. Every time I see the Statue of Liberty, I think of that very moment. I remember you telling me about my father when you both were working at the Dunn & McCarthy shoe factory. You two got married, and five years later I was born. Four years after that my sister Rosalie was born.

You often said you raised three children: me, my sister, and my father. You always had a great sense of humor. You told me you were 85 pounds when you became pregnant with me and when I was born I weighed 12 pounds. You told me I wasn't Italian; I was Caesarean. I remember a phone call you got not long after my father died from a man at the insurance company. He asked to speak to my father. You said that he wasn't there. Then he asked if you knew when he would be home, and you said "no." Then he asked if you knew where he was, and you said, "I've got a pretty good idea where he is."

I also remember the little tree you had in the corner of your bedroom. You got all upset one morning and called me to come and look at it because it fell over. As I looked at it, I started laughing because you said the tree had looked so green and healthy, so you couldn't understand what happened—it just fell. I couldn't believe you were watering an artificial tree for two years and it got "dry rot." Sometimes I felt like we went to grade school together. You were always asked to come to school and talk to the teachers, and they would tell you how bad I was and how I would never amount to anything. I remember how upset you were, not with me, but with the teachers. You'd tell them that they did not know what to do or how to teach and that they didn't like Italians. Well, ma, I think the teachers were right: I was bad. I want to thank you for the confidence you had in me.

There is a special bond between mother and son, and there comes a time when a son must say a final goodbye to his mother, but only in body. You will always live in my mind and my prayers and my thoughts; those same thoughts have given you life, just as they have given me life, and you have given me love, hope, joy, happiness, and the ability to enjoy the life you've given me. Thank you for everything.

Your son,

Philip

Question: If you could do anything else with your life or be anyone else, what or who would that be?

Phil: I've thought about that before, and I've always concluded that I am happy with who I am and what I do. I wouldn't want to be anyone else. In fact, I sit back and wonder, "Why me? Why was I gifted with all this success?" I've always felt purposeful and knew that I needed to get the most out of my gifts. I tell people that creativity is a gift from God, and using that creativity is a gift back to God. To me it's a sin to waste that gift.

Question: How do you come up with that signature "point of difference" when you start a business?

Phil: When I first have a vision of a new business, I try to determine what sort of a need there is for it. This usually includes seeing a problem in the market and then coming up with a solution. Then I start working backward from the end goal, I ask myself how I will go about accomplishing this and what I need to make it happen. I basically break it into five questions that I need to answer: What do people really need? Is it going to solve a problem? Is it really unique and different? Is anybody else doing it? If so, are they doing it the right way?

I'll go into a restaurant and look around and think to myself, "This ought to go there, and that should be different, and so on." Then I'll wrestle with myself about whether I should make the owner aware of these observations or if I should take the basic concept and do it differently and better—the way it should have been done in the first place.

Question: You've hired thousands in your career. What do you look for in a prospective employee?

Phil: I like to see what a person has done with his or her own life. Whether the person has gone to college, has a family, takes care of a family, is married, and has stayed married. If the person can't do these things, how can he or she possibly do them for me in my business or care about my business or anybody else? I've had a lot of people come to me and say they want to work for me and make me rich. I tell them that I am already rich and say, "So what's the matter with you? You don't care about yourself or making yourself rich or successful?" I don't look for people who are overly intelligent. I look for staff who have people skills, are smart, and who have emotional intelligence.

It's a little like a casting call. I also look for a person's passion and desire to fill a role with creativity. People's physical appearance says a lot about how they care for themselves and how they might care for customers and for my restaurant. I also look for people who want to carve out a niche for themselves in the business and who are excited about being on the ground floor of a new concept and feel like the sky is the limit. I hire people in different age groups, but the younger ones typically have the most energy and willingness to learn, along with the basic smarts. I can always apply the wisdom.

Question: What kind of advice do you give new hires, and how do you prepare them for the realities of the job?

Phil: I tell them they should work hard because they're working for themselves and not for me. People don't really work for me; they work *with* me. If they work hard and go the extra mile, they will succeed with me or with someone else. I want decision makers, not "yes" people. I tell them I will try to put them in niches that fit their personalities and natural abilities and let them excel there. I also tell them I will give them leeway to be creative within their specialties and that I will always respect their opinions if they have an idea that can improve the restaurant. I tell them I expect them to treat others with human dignity, the way they would like to be treated and that I will treat them the way I would like to be treated.

One common mistake restaurateurs make is assuming that people they hire already know their jobs. I am not going to be upset with employees if they do something wrong but weren't told the right way to do it. So I tell them what's right and what's wrong, and then they know. I want to empower them and give them the opportunity to do a good job. I emphasize that they must treat customers with human dignity, that they must make decisions on the floor that make customers happy, and that they must treat customers the way they want to be treated. I tell them to put themselves in the customers' place and ask themselves what they would like to have done to correct a mistake if they were the customer.

When I'm opening a new restaurant, I send people to our own operations classes once or twice a week. I make sure they understand business basics such as profit and loss. I can't assume they'll just get it, so I test our people on their knowledge. A concept is only as good as its weakest and strongest parts. You can put together a strong kitchen team, a strong floor team, a strong front-door presence, a strong office team, a strong accounting department, and strong management team, but if you have just one weak link, it can all fall apart. I tell my people that they are very powerful and have the whole organization at their disposal—the chefs, the managers, the other servers and so on—to make the customers happy, to make things more convenient to the customer and allow them to enjoy themselves and have a story to tell about their experience that they will take home and tell others. That's our job.

Question: How important is the physical real estate aspect in the success of a concept?

Phil: People says it's location, location, location, and in the beginning it is, because no matter what you have, you've got to put it where there's a market for it. But what's really important, ultimately, is authenticity, authenticity, authenticity. Each day your restaurant has got to be as good as the day you started it. You've got to keep your core intact. A great piece of real estate won't compensate for a poor idea or a lack of execution.

Question: How important is the financing?

Phil: Well, that's what gets your doors to open. But the concept is always more important than the money. If you've got a good concept and present it properly to the right people, you should be able to raise the money, all things being equal. One reason we started Trinity Groves, my Dallas restaurant incubator, was because economic conditions have made it harder for young people with good ideas to advance them, especially in the restaurant world. So we are helping finance some of the idea people who otherwise might not have a chance to showcase their talents. Insufficient financing is actually the biggest killer of new restaurant concepts.

Question: The restaurant business is obviously a tough one. Is it really true that 90 percent of new restaurants close within a year?

Phil: Fortunately, no. But it is true that about 25 percent of new restaurants either close or change ownership in the first year, and that jumps up to 60 percent after three years. That's why you have to have a point of difference coming out of the gate, although even that's no guarantee. If you have the wrong demographic, especially in fine dining, a great concept may not rescue you.

Question: You often talk about small-business start-ups being down. Why is this, in your opinion?

Phil: Even though entrepreneurs are the backbone of our country, more businesses are being closed than opened. More and more regulations and higher business taxes make it extremely hard to go forward with a good restaurant idea or other good business idea. I call it regulation without representation. Why doesn't the government understand this? It has preyed on businesses like they are its personal ATM machine. The most important elements to the economic health of our country are our entrepreneurs and businesspeople. One solution is to get businesspeople, not more lawyers and professional politicians, more politically involved with our country, and we are starting to see this. What really scares me is who's supposedly educating the future generation of entrepreneurs. Teachers and professors seem more interested in forming unions and fighting for tenure than in educating our young people. Professors who've never had a real job are teaching people how to start a business, and their theories aren't grounded in experience or reality. It is a self-perpetuating trend.

Question: What do you look for when you are evaluating potential restaurant tenants and their concepts for your Trinity Groves incubator?

Phil: As I do with all my own restaurant creations, I look for distinct points of difference. I ask myself certain questions: What would make me want to eat this person's food instead of someone else's food? Is the concept unique? Does the food stand out? Is it presented better than someone else's food? Does it compete with anything else? Does it offer a different take on an existing idea, or is it more of a hybrid of different ideas and cuisines?

Question: What advice would you give to a budding restaurateur besides creating a point of difference?

Phil: Don't get ahead of yourself. So many new restaurateurs overspend and overbuild and run out of capital. They try to operate like a major restaurant. Instead, they should operate by going to school and learn how a major restaurant or chain of restaurants became a major restaurant or chain. Study how that restaurant or chain and other successful businesses grew to be so large, especially how they started and operated in the early days, and then run their restaurant in a similar way. Seek advice from successful independent restaurant owners, too. Take them to lunch to pick their brain. Also, be smart, passionate, and committed, and have a great deal of energy and be good with people.

I ask prospective restaurant owners the following questions: What's going to make people come to your restaurant rather than the one down the street? Once you're successful, how will you stay that way? It's one thing to create a successful concept, but how will you give it longevity?

My solution is to give every restaurant that I open a "Bill of Rights." I ask myself what is sacred to the concept. What gives it a constitution and a personality? People are attracted to a personality. But if that personality changes somewhere along the line, it won't be the same, act the same, be perceived the same, or taste the same. You've got to create your Bill of Rights and stay true to it.

Question: Do you have any advice for young entrepreneurs in general?

Phil: Don't wait to follow your dreams. The world is full of so many gifted people who are afraid to take a chance. I call them "shoulda-doneits." There are still businesspeople in San Antonio today who are kicking themselves about the one that got away: Fuddruckers. When I was looking for 10 people to invest $15,000 each, a lot of good businesspeople refused to invest. And some of those who didn't refuse, like Herb Kelleher of Southwest Airlines, jumped out early. The few who stuck with it made $3.4 million each in under two years. The ones who refused said, "I shouldadoneit." To this day, when I'm looking for investors, I point to my track record and tell these potential investors, "Don't be a shouldadoneit."

Question: You seem to have a joke for every subject. Do you have any about entrepreneurs?

Phil: Sure. Entrepreneurs have to think on their feet because things change all the time. If they don't, they're dead. It's like the story of the guy who was robbing the bank and his mask fell off while he was standing at the teller window. He put the mask back on and asked the teller, "Did you see my face when the mask fell off?" The teller said "yes," so the robber shot her. He turned to the guy standing next to her and asked, "Did you see my face when the mask fell off?" The guy said "yes," so the robber shot him. Then he turned to the lady standing next to him and asked her, "Did you see my face when my mask fell off?" She said, "No, I didn't, but my husband did."

Question: You've said that the restaurant world is your stage, to borrow from Shakespeare. You've been called "the Steven Spielberg of the restaurant industry." How do you add theatrical elements to your designs and decor?

Phil: Very few of my restaurants have windows. I want the dining experience to be a one- to two-hour vacation for our customers from the outside world. You can't just tell people what you're going to do; you've got to show them how it's done. In the 1990s, someone finally coined the term, "experiential," for exhibition kitchens. I've been doing these experiential kitchens a lot longer. At Fuddruckers, I had my bakers yell "hot buns coming through" as they balanced trays of fresh hamburger buns through the main eating area. At Macaroni Grill, I created an Italian courtyard and had opera singers on staff. I put a grand piano in the middle of the kitchen of Nick & Sam's. I like to say that my restaurants are high energy and what I do is high energy.

Question: How do you handle customer complaints if things don't go quite right for them?

Phil: One of my jobs is to protect customers from the results of a manager's potentially bad decisions. If there is a legitimate complaint, I make sure that what happened never happens again. From the consumers' standpoint, people are willing to spend money on consistent quality. It all goes back to human dignity and customer dignity, which I've talked about—treating people like you want to be treated. Put yourself in the customer's place and ask yourself, "What would I like to have done if that happened to me?" Turn the problem around. People are more apt to tell stories about how you turned a problem around than about the problem itself.

Question: What's your opinion of food critics?

Phil: Not very high. Most have been fair to me, but some of them don't know what the hell they're talking about. Also, I just don't like the way they operate or the process they use in reviewing a restaurant. I even had to sue the *Dallas Morning News* over some unfounded comments that their critic, Dotty Griffith, made about my Il Mulino restaurant that hurt the place. She admitted she had done some unethical things.

Reviewers can be lethal, and their observations can be random and subjective, especially if they don't have a discerning palate about certain spices and certain specialty foods. They may make assumptions without asking the restaurant about food preparation, seasoning, and other important details. Food critics should help, not hurt, a restaurant. If I were a food critic and had a bad experience in a restaurant, I'd write to the restaurant manager and say, "Here's what I think was done wrong, and this is where I think you could improve. We're not going to publish a review this time, but I'll return later." That's a lot better than writing something that will hurt a person's business. Newspapers and websites often send out people who have no culinary knowledge, and they offer very little insight and get things wrong. The food editors and critics at most of the major newspapers and magazines have worked as chefs and have owned restaurants, so their observations are a little easier to swallow.

But there has been one good development. In this age, every customer can be a reviewer with Yelp, Facebook, blogs, and other forums. So, we really don't need traditional reviewers any more. The general public can express themselves without having to rely on one local critic. We don't just get one person's opinion, we can get everybody's. The majority rules.

Question: You spent years driving the Hunger Busters' van to deliver food to homeless encampments, and that's a pretty sobering undertaking. Dare I ask if you have any jokes related to that?

Phil: Yeah. You know, I am not a P.C. kind of guy. So here's one: I'm driving down the street one day, and I see a homeless guy panhandling on the corner. I call him over and I say, "Look, I'd give you $25, but I know you're just going to spend it on booze." He says, "No, no, no. I don't drink. I haven't had a drink in 10 years." I say, "Well, I suppose you're going to blow it on gambling then." He says, "No, I don't gamble, I can't afford it. It never turned me on." I say, "Then what about women? You're going to spend it all on women, I bet." He says, "No. I'm done with women—all done. I don't mess with women anymore." So I say, "I tell you what. You stay here, and I'll be back in 20 minutes. I'm going to give you twice the money, $50 bucks." He asks, "Where are you going?" I say. "I'm going to go home and get my wife and bring her back and tell her, "See what happens when you don't drink, gamble, or play around."

Question: In your speeches at colleges and organizations, you mention a phenomenon called the "absence of sales". Can you elaborate on this?

Phil: In any business, it boils down to sales and what you've got to do to create sales. The absence of sales is nothing but pain. I tell entrepreneurs to not think about making a profit; think about serving people's needs instead and you'll get your sales and make twice as much profit that way. When I start a concept, I first try to build up as much in sales as I can—put the pedal to the metal and see what I've got, and put everything in that first unit that is important to the concept. I don't worry about going national with it and projecting those sales out to multiples. I think about doing one unit and putting everything I want in that unit. Only after I hit a certain threshold do I figure out how to make money on those sales.

A good example was butchering my own beef at my first Fuddruckers. People said I couldn't do that at all, much less throughout the country. I said I wasn't worried about that. I didn't want to put myself in a box like that. When things are going well because I'm doing the things that I wanted to do at my concept, only then do I have to become smart enough to do the multiples.

You have to sell something that's needed, something that the general public wants to have. In some cases, like with the stent, people really do have to have that to live. In the restaurant business, you have to have the kind of food that people want and that meets their tastes and desires so that they'll feel like they have to have it and will come back for it. You always have to create new and different ways of promoting sales. Anyone in direct sales needs to offer something a little different from what everybody else is offering, to create a point of difference. It's okay to go against the grain a little. When you have that point of difference, people will come to you because you have something that they can't get anywhere else.

When I say that most restaurant start-ups are underfinanced, I'm saying that they're not prepared to NOT make money for a while. That is, they aren't in a position to invest back into their business. The first three years after I opened the first Macaroni Grill, I put $100,000 back into the restaurant each year. All my life, my modus operandi has been to create an idea, get it going real well, and only then turn it over to professional management to take it the rest of the way. They can do that better than I can do it.

Question: In the pages to come, you will discuss at length your restaurant concepts, your medical investing successes, and a few other non-restaurant operations that you started, such as karate schools and even a dance hall. Were there other businesses you dabbled in also?

Phil: Yes. After getting squared away with Fuddruckers, I decided I would fulfill a lifelong dream of opening a men's fine clothing store. As a kid, I would press my face against the window of a men's clothing store in Auburn and dream of the day I would be successful and dress up like that. In 1986, after several successful ventures, I partnered with an investor named Philip Marky, who knew the clothing business very well, and we opened Baroni's Italian Clothiers together in San Antonio. We had a fantastic clothing line, with gorgeous suits made out of imported fabrics, silk ties, and other fine men's clothing. You name it. Our tailor created a display window, and we had a beautiful lady barber who gave free haircuts and manicures to customers. We catered to an affluent clientele and started out strong. We then opened stores in Houston, Austin, and San Antonio. Customer satisfaction was off the charts, but the chain only lasted less than two years. Like with my Stix Eating Spa, the upscale demographic in the San Antonio area was too narrow to win enough repeat business, and the other locations couldn't carry us. I lost $700,000. I told people that I got a $500,000 suit and a couple of $100,000 ties out of the deal, but no socks because I don't wear them.

Then in 1987, I formed a more successful enterprise in San Antonio, an image-processing company called Docucon, which converted documents to optical disks. It's old technology now, but at the time, it was cutting edge, and it filled a huge need because people were being overwhelmed trying to find storage space for decades worth of documents. The company went public in mid-1989, I raised a $3.2 million IPO (initial public offering) and did well. I stepped aside as chair in late 1989 but remained a director of the company for a while. It was a good business for its time.

Question: You've created dozens of distinctly different concepts over the years. Are there any common threads that connect them?

Phil: Whatever I do must have a distinct brand — a clear-cut point of difference from anything else existing out there. That point of difference is my brand. In everything I do, I also ask myself, "What is sacred to this concept?" Then I give the restaurant its Bill of Rights and write down my founding principles. Each restaurant must be responsible to the public and to itself about what makes it unique in the first place, like the meat being ground and the fresh buns being baked in front of you at Fuddruckers, or walking into Eatzi's and seeing the food being manufactured right in front of you. I call it "Truth in Feeding." Don't just tell them; show them.

To me, a restaurant isn't just a place for eating. It's also a place for entertainment and escapism; it's always had a strong show-business element to it. At each of my restaurant openings, everything has to be perfect. It's like a big Broadway show—there's no room for error, the expectations are high, and everyone knows their roles.

Question: What do you think about chefs taking on a rock star status in the last decade or so?

Phil: It's good to see. A chef can be famous and create a brand, just like his restaurant is a brand, and have all kinds of opportunities for TV appearances, personal appearances, products, and so forth. For better credibility, it's usually better if the celebrity chef becomes the owner or part owner of the restaurant with which he or she is associated. A chef-owned restaurant is the fastest road to fame, although a great chef at a famous restaurant can also make it big, too.

Question: What's your definition of a great chef?

Phil: The greatest chefs not only have a talent to cook but also know what to cook. A good chef who can come up with all kinds of great new concoctions also has a place in this business because it is a business in need of new ideas. But a chef who can figure out what the people want to eat and then get creative with that food, works better with my concepts. People want choices, but they also want their comfort food.

I was on a seminar panel with three chefs not long ago, and the question of "What is real food?" came up. The chefs' answers were all over the board: organic, fresh, home grown, locally grown, gluten-free, and so on. When it was my turn to answer, I said, "You know, real food to me is food you like, comfort food, ethnic food, foods that have a connection to you." The chefs went on to talk about all the new innovations in the food business, such as the various machines that cook all kinds of different foods in different ways. I chimed in and said, "Then you're mechanics and not chefs. If I brought in all this equipment you're talking about into my kitchens and people saw it, they would stop eating there. People want to see food being cooked. It's the flames, the buzz, the action, the theatrics, not the machines doing it that are important."

Everything that really works today in the business has a personality. People like a restaurant because of its specific personality. Take Nick & Sam's. What do we sell there? We sell atmosphere, we sell energy, we sell a place where everyone wants to be, we sell sexiness with all the beautiful people coming there, and all of that in addition to great food, of course. The place and the plate of food each have to have distinct personalities.

Question: What's different about the restaurant industry today as opposed to 13 years ago when you wrote your last book?

Phil: The industry is seeing growth these days with a lot of independents who are being recruited to fill new or vacant restaurant spaces with something original or something authentic. Casual dining chains have gotten a little stale and blurry; there is not much personality to them anymore. People want something different, especially millennials, who like hybrids of different types of foods. They also want to be entertained. You can buy just about anything online today, but you can't have a great restaurant experience online. That's one reason I launched Trinity Groves: to create unique concepts by people who otherwise wouldn't have a chance to get their ideas and new concepts out to the public. We are an industry in need of new blood and new ideas.

Question: The restaurant concepts you created now serve more than 250,000 customers a day in some 45 states and more than a dozen countries, accounting for between $12 billion and $13 billion in sales over the past 52-plus years. You're 79. What's left to prove?

Phil: Nothing. But I am not retiring as long as I am mobile and lucid. There's no off switch in my brain. I keep thinking of new ideas. Ever since I had a cancer scare at the age of 50, I realized that life is short, and like all those foodstuffs in my restaurant kitchens, we all have an expiration date. I tell myself what I told myself then: "A thought just went through my head, so I have to do it now; I can't do it when I'm dead."

There are still problems to solve, life-saving medical devices to be bankrolled, paintings to paint, and investments to make. There's a lot to do yet, and I can't waste any time. I'll be 80 years old in October of 2019, and life starts to be like a roll of toilet paper when you get to be that age. The closer you get to the end, the faster it goes.

Question: Why don't you wear socks, by the way?

Phil: When I was young, I wanted to have a point a difference. I didn't want to be like everyone else, so I didn't wear them. Plus, I came from sunny Florida, so a lot of people didn't wear socks there. Once, I attended a meeting with about 100 investment bankers in New York, and I was wearing a nice shirt and tie but nothing between my shoes and feet. Finally, someone said, "Nice socks!" I replied, "Thanks, they match the gloves." These days, I don't wear socks because they're so goddamned hard to put on since I've gotten old, plus I hate bending over. Before, not wearing socks was a personal statement. Now it's a physical necessity!

Chapter

2

PHIL-OSOPHIES: INSIDE THE ROMANO BRAIN

When I first have a vision of a new business, I try to determine what sort of a need there is for it. This usually includes seeing a problem in the market and then coming up with a solution. Then I start working backward from the end goal.

The Brains of the Outfit

When it comes down to it, we are all brains, my father used to tell me. He would say, "In every head there is a different world, and in every head there's a brain that controls that world." It took a while for this to sink into my own brain. It was his way of telling me that we don't all think or perceive things in the same way, and as our brains go, we go. I can relate to that now more than ever.

Our brains have all these different compartments, or lobes, that fulfill certain functions ranging from reasoning to emotion to perception to speech, and even how we respond to stimuli. For my own brain to do its job well, I realized that I have to give these lobes information and proper nourishment in order for them to do what they're supposed to do, when they're supposed to do it. Every one of these parts is like a different department in a company, with a different person in charge of each department. I have to give each of them a purpose and then direct that person to work in concert with the other departments. In effect, I lead myself to my brain. When I control my brain, I control my personal "corporation."

I think about each business as a brain, too, with its various components working together to accomplish goals. A good leader keeps all of the parts together by giving them what they need to work well. In a company, you can't have one part of the brain thinking in one direction and another part thinking in another direction. You'd be disjointed or bipolar in a sense.

As I get older, I see everybody now as a brain. I don't care about people's color, gender, sexual preference, looks, body type, and so forth. Based on the way their brains process life—and you have to know people a while to understand how their brains work—I either like them or I don't. Of course, every person's brain has a different perception of the world. So, to have success and the right personal and business relationships, I need to surround myself with brains that are compatible with my views on life, entrepreneurship, companionship, unity, friendship, and so on. Even as I get older, I continue feeding my brain new information and harvesting that information in the form of new concepts, new ideas, and new paintings.

I stay active and fit, and I have hired a nutritionist in hopes of staying clear-headed and lively as long as possible to extend those abilities. I think that's what religion accomplishes: it gives unity to thought and gets all the brains in the "congregation" thinking in the right direction, providing strength in unity.

In order for us to live on after we're gone, we have to live on in people's brains. That's one reason I've tried to touch asmany people's lives as I can in my lifetime, not only with my restaurant concepts and innovations, but also with medical advances such as the heart stent that I supported and brought to market. A lot of people wouldn't be here without the stent; nor would their children and even their grand-children. I am pleased that I am able to touch lives generation after generation, and I want to continue to do that. I am MAD, Making a Difference, and doing that for a lot of people, so much so that I won't even need a tombstone when I die.

I speak frequently at college commencements, businesses, think tanks, real estate conventions, and the like. The larger the positive impact I make is, the longer I will live on once my expiration date arrives. The same theory holds true for people who leave behind a neg-ative impact. I feel that we all create a heaven or a hell here on earth for ourselves and, to some degree, for those we leave behind.

Thoughts are powerful and long lasting. Jesus Christ wouldn't be around in our lives if what he did didn't live on in people's minds. When I tell someone about an idea I've thought of, the idea becomes twice as strong. When I pass it along to 1,000 people, it gets 1,000 times as strong. If I can get an idea out to 1 million people, as I've done with my restaurants and medical devices, it becomes 1 million times as strong. That's a lot of staying power.

Diagnosing problems

I typically mind my own business when I am in someone else's restau-rant. But I'm always critiquing it in my mind—it doesn't matter where I am or who I am with. I don't say anything to a restaurant operator or manager about my observations unless I am asked. But if the situation were reversed, I certainly would want somebody to tell me where there was a problem or a choke point or if there was something important missing. One lone observer is not always right, of course, just like the trite but true saying about how opinions are like assholes and everybody's got one.

If I am asked to resolve a problem occurring in a restaurant, want to know the details of how the problem came to be. To do that, I would have to go back to the core—the founding principles akin to my restaurant Bill of Rights—of the business to find out how things have deteriorated badly, but it basically boils down to this: you are either doing something that the customers don't like or you're *not* doing something the customers do like.

I am constantly looking for better ways to do things: better ways for my customers to enjoy food, better tasting food, and better ways for servers to serve or to talk with the customers. Also, I am always looking for a point of difference or a way to solve a problem or to fill a void.

By their nature, people stop paying attention to the same old things. I guess that's why marriages typically don't last long. People want the excitement of experiencing something different in life, something new, something provocative, or something they've never experienced before. That's why I've always been drawn to positive points of difference in other restaurants and have been motivated to create my own. Forget the norm. It's like antibiotics: if you use the same one too long, it stops working. You need something new to make you feel alive.

Eatzi's was my response to the humdrum. Entire families are working at full-time jobs and either don't feel like cooking at day's end or don't know how to cook anymore. So I offered them good, fresh, "restaurant replacement" food for them to eat on the way home from work. I consider Eatzi's a lifestyle concept. About 80 percent of what we serve at Eatzi's is food our customers have eaten before—comfort food—and I wanted it to be the best comfort food they've ever tasted: high-quality restaurant food. The other 20 percent is food they've never tasted before. It's the solution to "Let's eat something new and different for a change." We try to be the epicenter for food in any community we enter.

Fleshing out a concept

Everybody has ideas. What makes a difference is doing something to bring them to fruition. In the restaurant world, you basically have to live the idea, think about it constantly, and brainstorm—,talk with people about it to get their input and ideas about your vision and determine if they like it when they see it. When I get it to a point where it works in my head, then I look at its role in the marketplace. I ask, "Is it really needed? Is there a large enough marketplace for it? Is everybody going to want this? Is it something that somebody else is already doing? If so, then I look at it to see how well the operator is doing it and whether I can make it appreciably better. A good example of that is Fuddruckers. There were already many hamburger places around when I started Fuddruckers and a lot more that served burgers as a sideline. But I was resolved to do hamburgers better than anybody else. That's why it was successful. And the burgers sell for twice the price of competitors!

If a restaurant idea passes all of my tests, I put the numbers together and get everything down on paper. What am I going to have to charge for the food to make it work? Can I offer a reasonably competitive price point? What are competitors charging for it? Is it where my customers are? That is, what kind of customers will like the food, and are there enough potential customers around the location where I want to open the restaurant? In other words, will the market support it? How big a place will I need? Should I build the restaurant or search for a space to rent? Will local zoning constrict it where I want to put it in any way? How many tables will I need? What will it look like and feel like? It's got to look authentic; everything will have to be consistent, too. Will it serve both lunch and dinner? How much will it cost? Does that number exceed my usual limit of $1 million to $2 million, depending on the complexity and category of the concept? Can I make any money based on that investment against all my costs? Next, I settle on the location after making sure that the location has all the physical attributes I need. Then I figure out whether I need to raise or borrow money for it or if it's something I want to put my own money into.

Then the vision and all my ideas for the restaurant sort of materializes in my mind. Some people can't understand how I can "start at the end" like I do. But it's really just a natural progression, although in reverse. And, of course, I will be thinking about the concept and refining it in my brain well after I have that early vision of it. After three or four months, that vision becomes a reality.

Once I open the restaurant, I ask myself more questions: Is it doing what I want it to do? Is it appealing to the right market? Do I like the natural direction it is going in? And is that a good direction? If it is, I push it in that direction, adding momentum. But if the restaurant is not going down the path I thought it would but sales are still going through the roof, will I change it? Heck, no. The people have spoken. And how do I know when a concept is successful? When it's time to build another one.

However, if I see that the concept is obviously not working, I know I've got no one else to blame other than myself. I'll close it down before the public closes it down. You can't beat a dead horse. My fear of failure is a motivating force, so I will close a restaurant before it fails on its own. It's like someone who is attached to a respirator when it's a hopeless case and the person is slowly dying. So I just pull the plug. But I will store that knowledge and rejoin the restaurant world by creating a different, better concept. From my mistakes I have learned what not to do again.

Here's some more food for thought for concept creators out there:

- Write down your dreams. They will become your goals. With no goals, you have no purpose. Make a list of the things you need to do in order to achieve your goals and a list of the things you must be careful *not to do*.

- We all know what we know, but do you know what you don't know? Don't try to do it all yourself. You can get so swept up in all the little details and lose touch with your customers and your founding principles in the process. You need to be visible and in the middle of the action, not buried in paperwork out of sight. Don't be afraid to hire specialists who can save you time, money, and anxiety.

- Stay open to change. A closed mind is like a closed fist. Your competition will make changes and pass you by if you're averse to changing with the times.

- Stay upbeat, even when things are going wrong. Wallow in happiness, not misery. You will project poorly if you are chronically unhappy. This can ruin your company's culture.

- Don't rest on success. The successful entrepreneur is a perpetual-motion machine, fortified by new ideas.

- Have an ethical purpose. That will help you stay successful. Having an ethical purpose means doing the right thing in the right way and doing things that are good for people. It's not how much money you make that counts but, rather, how you make that money that allows you to really enjoy what you've done and to sleep well at night. By doing this, your employees will feel good about what they are doing and that will shine through in their performance.

- Get M.A.D. (Make a Difference). Make the world a better place. Get involved. Give back.

- This one is worth repeating: Service is primary, and profit is secondary. Don't focus on making money; instead, focus on servicing a need, and you will make twice as much money.

- In the absence of sales, there's nothing but pain. Focus on sales. Make as many sales as you can possibly make. Don't worry about making a profit. After you are peaking on sales, then figure out how to make a profit on the sales you're making because in the absence of sales, there is no profit.

Be your brand

When I was young, my ambition was to change the world. When I was older and wiser, I saw that that would be a pretty tough job, even after I did help change the dining, entrepreneurial, and medical worlds with my innovations. But, instead of trying to change the world, I decided I was going to change myself—to adapt to what's out there. If

I couldn't change the world, I thought, I was going to change the way I felt about it.

I am often asked what it takes to be successful. For me, it was the privilege of being American, "choosing" the right parents, and growing up poor. I had parents who gave me the right value system and had me educated. Growing up poor, I appreciate what I have become because I remember what it was like to be poor and had nowhere to go but up. Here's one measure of success: if you're better off than when you were poor, you're successful. But why stop there?

If you can run and manage a successful business for someone else, you can do it for yourself. I have given big opportunities to promising young businesspeople on the condition that they go into business for themselves. With the right drive, confidence, and thorough research, you can be your own boss. And you will have more freedom to create. More people are choosing this option as corporate structures are changing. New generations aren't going to be working for 30 years in one job and retiring with a pension, a gold watch, and a pat on the back. They have to take care of themselves.

Put your creativity to optimal use. In my experience, corporations cannot create. They are too busy operating, replicating, and being profligate—they tend to waste resources. Creating is not one of their core competencies. They create by committee. If you want a horse, they produce a camel. And as a rule, they just can't shake free from their bureaucratic culture. A lot of the new blood and new ideas introduced into corporations are often smothered because of their hierarchies. Sometimes I wonder how many great talents and great minds are relegated to the back burners of these organizations. I've been known to say that being an entrepreneur is survival of the un-fittest, not the fittest because nonconformity is the best way to bring something new and exciting to the world. Doing things "by the book" is for stagnant companies and for those who aren't creative enough or free enough to figure out a better way.

For a concept to be successful, the concept has to become a brand—your brand. Most importantly, a brand must have distinct points of difference, and you should make those points of difference the basis of your brand. Brands are born by word of mouth and publicity, not by advertising. Once a brand is born, however, it usually needs advertising and marketing for it to stay healthy. A brand should own a word or phrase, even if it is a cliché,—to create both a feeling and a meaning in the minds of customers and the means to reinforce the brand. The brand must create excitement, serve a need, and provide value—or at least perceived value—to set it apart from the rest of the competition. and give the concept a secondary meaning in the eyes of the people. That secondary meaning is a big part of your brand, if not *the* brand.

You also need to distance yourself from the competition with your point of difference. People or the media don't talk about a product or service that is the same as everyone else's. Sometimes, you have to kill a sacred cow to get attention because those standards are the accepted way things have been done for a very long time.

Restaurant chains often claim they are doing things the best way or the only way because it's always been done that way. I can't tell you how many times I've heard people say, "Well, you can't reinvent the wheel." I always reply, "If the wheel was never invented, maybe we'd be getting around faster with something better; maybe we'd all be floating."

I was well into my 70s when someone finally showed me the easiest way to peel a banana. How I could be in the food business for more than half a century without knowing this is hard to imagine. Like most of us, I always opened the banana from the stem, which requires force, especially if the banana isn't ripe. Then came this revelation a few years ago: just flip the banana over and simply pinch the bottom tip, and then it will easily split so you can effortlessly strip back both sides of the peel. No fuss, no muss, as the TV marketers say. It's so simple that a monkey can do it. In fact, monkeys actually do it that way. That's how humanity learned that little trick. I'm never going to forget that guy who showed me. Now, every time you open a banana the "right" way, you're going to think about me, right?

When people ask me about my successes, I answer, "It was the fear of failure, not the sweet smell of success, that drove me." There is a difference between fear of failure and being scared. The former is good because it drives you. But being scared paralyzes you. The fear of failure has never stopped me from doing things differently. I would rather fail doing something different than succeed doing something mundane.

People also ask what drives me. To them, I say, "What motivates me is not having the solution—or the answer—to a problem." For every problem, there is a solution. People also tell me I have had more than my share of luck. If I'm lucky, it's because I've chased luck down, grabbed it, and held on for dear life. "Luck" doesn't happen by sitting around and waiting for the next big idea to strike. You need practical knowledge and a desire to learn in order to "get lucky" and execute a good idea. If you don't have that knowledge, you need to go to work for someone who does. The real secret to success in this business is being on the cutting edge and finding out what people need before they even know they need it. That includes making sure your concept is keeping ahead of trends and then servicing those trends. It's got to be a big trend, like riding a tidal wave; you need to be out in front of it to make sure you are getting swept along by it.

It took me and my brain 60 years of this kind of "luck" to become an overnight success.

3

ROMANO CONCEPTS (1965–1979): From The Gladiator to Barclay's

I realized at a young age that business wasn't just about profit. It was about serving the customer.

The story of the 30 restaurant concepts I've created over the past 50-plus years follows, but I will first provide a little background on how my entrepreneurial mindset evolved. As a kid, I wasn't forced to work but I did anyway. I couldn't bring myself to ask my parents for an allowance because they were of modest means. If I wanted something, I realized that I would have to earn it. So I mowed lawns and did other small odd jobs around my Auburn, New York, neighborhood and started saving money while I was still in elementary school.

In sixth grade, when other kids were fighting pretend army battles and still playing with toys, I was out in the elements delivering Auburn's daily newspaper, *The Citizen*. With my savings from the odd jobs, I had bought an after-school afternoon paper route from a kid named Marshall Bingham for the bargain price of $9 and I was making about $10 a week delivering the paper to 96 customers. I also "stuck pins" on the weekends at the local bowling alley. (This was 1951, and automatic pinsetters didn't come along until the late 1950s).

But I saw a lot more on the paper route than at my job in the bowling alley. While I was only obliged to toss papers onto subscribers' front porches, I got a brainstorm when the first big snowstorm hit. I knocked on all the subscribers' doors to ask the subscribers what they'd be willing to pay if, instead of just tossing the paper on the porch when it was snowing or raining, I put them inside their storm door. "That way you don't have to put on your coat or boots and your paper will always be dry," I'd say. Offers ranged from a nickel to a dime, up to 50 cents in one case, or free hot chocolate and cookies, which were very appealing to a kid. Only a few grouches offered nothing, and that was fine. I basically let each customer attach a value to what I was doing.

In doing so, I crossed over the line from paperboy to entrepreneur. I realized then that if I gave people something extra—a value-added product—I could parlay that into extra goodwill and, eventually, extra cash. In the process, I would also be offering these folks that "point of difference" that my father always spoke about. So I realized at a young age that business wasn't just about profit. It was about serving the customer. It was then that I first learned that when you go out of your way to give people added value, you can make twice the profit in the end. And I did; I doubled my income as a paperboy!

I spent some of that money on cool clothes, candy, and other kid stuff, of course. At the time, though, you could buy a $25 savings bond for $15, so I slowly started buying them with my added earnings. In high school, I eventually was able to buy my first car—a blue 1948 Mercury Coupe—with those bonds and other savings I stashed away.

My creative moneymaking ventures would lead to my mother calling me "Fabulous Phil."

I was a pretty decent football player in middle school and high school—a linebacker—and I played baseball and basketball, too. When my father, an electrician, had finally tired of the Northeast's cold winters, we moved from Auburn to Palm Beach, Florida, so I had to prove myself all over again as an athlete, which was another valuable life lesson. I started to realize that with a little hard work, I could reinvent myself anywhere and be stronger for it. This would come in very handy later on.

In my senior year in high school, the draft was still in effect, and I wanted to get ahead of that. The Army Reserve had a program in which you did six months of active duty and spent the rest of the time in the reserves when you were in college. So, the day after I graduated from high school, ten of my classmates and I joined the army! We would spend six months at Fort Jackson in Columbia, South Carolina, and be back in time for the second semester of college. While at Fort Jackson, I got on the base boxing team and had six fights and won four of them. When I got out, I was a boxer and trained killer, full of youthful energy and testosterone.

I attended Palm Beach Junior College that first year when I was still in the U.S. Army Reserve. I started one ill-fated business that year, cleaning carpets with a pal, Buddy Blount, using rented equipment and an old Volkswagen van. We did okay with carpets but went bust when we agreed to clean a set of expensive drapes for a wealthy woman just before an important party she was throwing. We ruined them, and she was rightfully furious. We quickly realized that we were out of our league.

I might add I had been offered a scholarship to play college football at St. Joseph's in Rensselaer, Indiana, but I didn't accept the scholarship. However, my former coaches had set up a walk-on tryout for me with UCLA after my army stint, and it went well, but UCLA wanted to redshirt me my first year and let me develop. But I wanted to play right away, so I joined a semipro football team in Los Angeles. The team couldn't pay players, but it gave them jobs, so I got a job delivering ice to restaurants. (This was in the late 1950s when restaurant ice machines were still pretty rare.) So, for the first time, I saw different restaurants' designs, interiors, and décor, and talked with the owners and managers, gave me real exposure to restaurant operations. It fascinated me and, it also planted a seed that would one day germinate—and in a big way.

I was also taking karate lessons. A Japanese girl I knew had a brother who was a karate expert, and she got him to let me in his dojo, where I was the only Occidental. At the time, I already had a black belt in judo, and I went on to earn my black belt in karate at that dojo.

I had put college aside for about a year before I finally decided I didn't want to go to UCLA or stay in the Los Angeles area, so I returned to Palm Beach to attend Florida Atlantic University.

In 1960, I was attending Florida Atlantic University, and I opened two successful karate schools in Palm Beach at a time when martial arts were starting to catch fire in America. Pretty soon, I was earning more than my professors, with each school making about $20,000 a year. Because I was putting myself through school, I had the freedom to take whatever classes I wanted, so I studied subjects that intrigued me in addition to taking the required courses for my major in general business administration and some physical education classes. (I had thought about becoming a teacher and head coach.)

But nothing prepared me for the dangers I faced when I went to work for a local private eye during college. The investigator's name was Jack Harwood, and he was seeking an "assistant" who could also provide a little muscle if things got out of hand on a job. I was hired mostly to help with insurance work and divorce cases. Jack would track down cheating spouses at motels or insurance fraudsters who claimed to have bad backs or other injuries but were actually out swinging away on the golf course.

Sometimes we'd do what was called a "crash job," which involved rushing through a motel door to take photos of a cheating husband in a compromising position. Jack would take a photo with one of those old flash cameras, and I was there to protect both him and the camera. If a guy got up, I'd just push him back down until we were done with our photo session.

One time, we burst into a room, and there was a big naked guy—a Miami Dolphins football player, it turned out—sprawled on the bed. As usual, Jack was behind me with the camera, but there was a short delay and I turned around to see what was taking him so long when his flash went off. It blinded me. Meanwhile, this huge guy got up and tackled me around the waist. Down I went, and there we were, wrestling around on the floor. There was a big glass ashtray that had fallen, and I picked it up and hit him on the side of the head with it. Jack had already fled with the evidence, so I needed to get out of there quickly and ran out the door. I turned around and saw the big naked guy running after me, hard-swinging dick and all. (To be honest, I was more scared of his dick than I was of him.) So there I was, running down the hall, and there was one of those old fire-escape doors with wired glass in front of me. He pinned me there, but I hit him with a left hook so hard that he went down. When that happened, I followed with my right, but he wasn't there anymore and my hand went through the glass door. I pulled it out and saw that I had really ripped it open. I still have the scars from that incident. Another time, a startled guy jumped out of a second-story window trying to escape from us.

It was a rough business, needless to say. Sometimes we followed mobsters around town at high speed. We'd puncture their taillights with an ice pick to make the cars easier to follow at night. It was a profession that I was glad to exit, though it did pay us as much as $5,000 a job, which Jack and I split. I was lucky I didn't get my head split open. As I approached my mid-twenties, I began to think that I would be better suited for a more gentle profession, in which dealings with people would be a little more positive, so I began my restaurant career.

Following is a list of the nearly 30 restaurants I've opened in my 50-plus years in the business:

1965 The Gladiator, Lake Park, Florida

A karate student of mine introduced me to his father, who was in the restaurant business. The father said he was looking for a partner to help open and run an Italian restaurant that he was naming The Gladiator, located in nearby Lake Park. I guess he thought I would be a hard worker based on my dedication to karate.

To be honest, I had never worked in a restaurant other than delivering ice to those eateries and bars in southern California in the late 1950s. While I helped cook some of the great meals that came out of the Romano family kitchen and could cook better than most male college students, this was a whole new world for me. If I was going to risk my savings, I'd better be a quick study, I thought. I looked at this as an opportunity to learn the industry from the ground up, but I also knew it would be a baptism by fire.

So I left Florida Atlantic University in 1965, sold my karate schools, hung up my black belts, and took the plunge. I had amassed $6,000 in savings, and my partner was able to put up another $6,000 to open the new Italian eatery on State Road A1A. I had earned 168 college credit hours over the years, well past the 120 that most students need to graduate. But I still lacked six hours of foreign language credits to graduate. That shortfall really didn't matter then, and it doesn't today. (I now lecture at universities!)

So, at age 24, I was co-owner of a restaurant. We opened the place using my mother's old recipes, serving a heaping meatball and pepper sandwich for 99 cents, a spaghetti dinner for $1.49, a full steak dinner for under $3, and lobster tail or shrimp scampi for $3.65, in addition to really good pizza.

People quickly found us. The Gladiator concept went over well and drew good reviews, and we built up a steady following, although I thought we should be doing better. My partner had poor people skills, very little personality, and an inflated idea of his abilities. He came across as a jerk to customers, and he embarrassed me. His main interest was wringing out a maximum profit and cutting corners, while mine was taking care of the customers. I recalled something one of my business professors had hammered home in college: "Service is primary. Profit is secondary. Don't focus on making money. Focus on servicing a need, and you'll make twice as much money." I tried to convince my partner we should be more concerned with giving patrons great service and value, and that profit would then follow. He disagreed. In fact, we disagreed on just about everything.

Six months after opening the Gladiator, I was really getting fed up with him. One night I hit a breaking point and said, "Okay, either buy me out or let me buy you out. This isn't going to work." I was determined that I was going to do the buying. The problem was, I didn't have the capital to back it up after using all of my savings to open the place.

As I fretted about what to do, my father came to me and said, "Son, I'll get you the money." I said, "No, dad, don't worry about it." I was concerned about where my father was going to get the money and on what terms. "Never mind, dad, I'll figure something out," I told him. About a week later, he came back and said, "Okay, I got the money for you." Startled, I asked him where he had gotten it. He said, "I mortgaged our home. Here's the money. Go buy out your partner." That's how much confidence he had in me. He literally bet the family house on his son.

The pressure was really on now. It wasn't the sweet smell of success that was driving me; it was the fear of failure, I realized then (and I still say that to this day). If I blew this, my parents were going to lose their home. I resolved I wasn't going to let that happen and would do whatever it took to make the place a success and pay my father back.

Meanwhile, my mother came aboard to operate the cash register, my father helped me close the place at night, and I tended to the less glamorous jobs myself. One busy Friday evening, I had to fire the head cook and take over his duties before finally elevating the dishwasher to the job. I handed him a bunch of my mom's recipes and then took off to tend to an emergency: unplugging a stubborn commode. By hand!

The plunger wasn't going to do the trick. "You've really arrived now, Romano," I told myself.

I pressed on and made the place work. Though it took about a year, I paid my father back—double the amount he had given me. The Gladiator grossed nearly $100,000 the first year, and we outdid that each year before I finally sold it in 1968. While I didn't make much on the sale, I sold it for twice what I had paid for it. The place was a catalyst—both a launching point for my restaurant career and a turning point in my life. There's no telling in which direction my life would have headed without my father, Sam Romano.

I also began to understand what it meant to be an entrepreneur. An entrepreneur is always taking a chance, I realized, and half the time he is betting the ranch. He has to work his butt off to make his idea work. Everything is on the line. He has to believe in himself.

That fear of failing that drove me then still drives me today. However, unlike many other people who fear failure, it motivates me to try harder. You can't move forward by being scared. It paralyzes you. I've never let fear of failure stop me from trying something new and different and exciting.

Points of Difference: The restaurant served large food portions. Spaghetti dinners cost $1.49. I introduced my lifelong philosophy that "service is primary, and profit is secondary.

Customer Bill of Rights: The customers will be taken care of above all else.

1968 Nag's Head Pub, West Palm Beach, Florida

My second restaurant concept, Nag's Head Pub on Palm Beach Lakes Boulevard, was considered to be highly innovative. It was an English-style pub and restaurant that set the stage for what would become a cornerstone of my future concepts: the demonstration kitchen, or what I call "Truth in Feeding." Henceforth, there would be no secrets kept from customers about their meal preparation. The kitchen and our open grill would be visible to patrons; there was nothing to hide here. There's trust building and excitement when your customers witness the food-manufacturing process, I've always felt. No longer would they wonder what was going on back in the kitchen and who was preparing their food. I put the char-broiler in the middle of the dining-room floor so that customers could see their food cooking and a little showmanship as well, with flames lighting up the dining room. Nag's Head Pub also had one of the first salad bars in the country.

I had two partners in Nag's Head Pub who each contributed an equal share of $2,000. To raise more start-up capital, I came up with the idea of selling engraved giant pewter beer mugs to patrons through our "Pewter Mug of the Pub Society" at $15 apiece. Before opening, we had sold 500 of them. That's $7,500! People would have their names and business phone numbers engraved on their mugs, we'd hang them up in the pub above the bar, and they'd drink from them when they came in. If they called ahead, we'd cool the mug for them. It gave people a sense of ownership, which would become a recurring theme at my restaurants through the years. This preopening promotion also gave us a built-in customer base before we even opened the doors.

We were the first to charge $1.25 for a hamburger at a time when a McDonald's hamburger was 15 cents and a Quarter Pounder was 35 cents. While it was hard to satisfy a hunger with either of those burgers, we gave people a giant 10-ounce, higher-quality burger using better meat, and served scalloped potatoes instead of fries. These quickly became customer favorites. We also sold martinis by the pound, if you can imagine doing that today. Our ornate matchbooks featured a horse's head and the slogan, "Meet—Eat—Drink." People did, and we became very busy.

One night, I was closing The Gladiator, while my father, being the helpful guy that he was, was closing Nag's Head Pub. We would rotate like that. A very attractive server whom I was, to use today's terms, "hooking up with" in The Gladiator kitchen from time to time—on the giant pizza table no less—had lingered behind to help me. We started going at it, and suddenly she began giggling, and then laughing. So I asked her, "What the hell is so funny?" She looked up at me and said, "You do it just like your father does." Oh?! It was one of those moments when you just don't know how to react. So, as a man of priorities, I continued what I was doing. Later on, instead of being disturbed by the whole thing, I also started laughing about this paternal revelation. I never said a word about it to my dad, though, or to any other family members, especially my mom! How many people can say that they had that kind of close relationship with their father? I'd like to see someone in the restaurant business top that.

Nag's Head Pub grossed $130,000 in its first five months of operation, which was very good considering that was half a century ago. Sadly, my partners were only content to rake in the profits and were against improving the place with other new ideas. As the late Yogi Berra said, "It was déjà vu all over again." This became another one of those push-pull scenarios: either they would have to buy me out, or I would have to buy them out.

One of my regulars, real estate developer, Vance Brittle, got wind of the dissent within the management, offered to buy out the partners on my behalf, and suggested that we build them all over the country. He thought Nag's Head Pub was the hottest concept of the time. He asked me how much I would expect for my one-third share. I paused and answered, "I'd probably have to get $50,000." He didn't bat an eye: "Okay, then we'll offer them $100,000 for their two-thirds, and if they accept that, then we'll build more pubs throughout the country, which you will operate. You will hold one-third equity in each store, and I'll put up the money If they don't accept the offer, then you're going to have $50,000 in your pocket from them." I agreed.

That $50,000 sum in my pocket sounded pretty good to a 27-year-old in 1968, although I still wanted to take the reins of the Nag's Head Pub. Vance gave me a check for $100,000, and I presented it to the other two partners. I told them that if they wanted to buy my share of the place, they'd have to come up with $50,000 for me. One of partner's parents apparently loaned them money, so they bought me out. Honestly, I thought that was a great deal for me, especially since I retained the right to build other Nag's Head Pubs.

Vance said I should throw my $50,000 back into the restaurant and we could start building another Nag's Head Pub. But then I realized that if I could create these concepts for someone else, I could create some far better things for myself. So I pocketed the money and gave Vance the rollout option. Not much came of the Nag's Head rollout. My former partners opened only one more location. What was missing? Phil Romano.

I didn't get rich on The Nag's Head Pub, but I learned a valuable lesson: other people will pay good money for my ideas.

Point of Difference: The demonstration (open) kitchen, a Romano cornerstone, was introduced.

Customer Bill of Rights: There will be truth in feeding and we have nothing to hide. The kitchen and grill will be visible to all customers.

1969 The Key Hole, Palm Beach, Florida

It's hard for me to do nothing. I'm just not cut out for it. I'm always at the office, which is in my mind, and I'm always tossing around new ideas from the time I get up in the morning to the time I go to sleep. It's a habit I've had for a long time, even as far back as 1969, when I was brewing up two new concepts.

With the $50,000 I pocketed in the Nag's Head Pub sale, I was busy planning my first fine-dining concept, Romano's 300, which would occupy the lower floor of a new six-story office building being built on Royal Palm Way in Palm Beach. I had worked out a build-to-suit deal with the landlord, who was more than happy to have a top-flight, lower-floor food anchor for his building. Because Florida had a limited number of liquor licenses at the time, I had to buy one from an existing license holder, and I paid the exorbitant sum of $30,000 to the owner of a place called the Red Lion, who was exiting the business.

I was glad to get the liquor license but wasn't too thrilled with a crummy building across the street from the building site, a bar called the Royal Pub, known all too well for its seedy clientele. I thought I'd just buy the place and knock it down to get it out of the neighborhood.

I bought it and just padlocked it. But it would be at least a year before the restaurant space would be ready for occupancy, I came to find out, and I wondered what I could do in the meantime. So, rather than tear down the old building, I decided to remodel it, rename it, and use it as my own bar, and more importantly, as a place to promote my eatery before it opened. But I really didn't want the seedy old customers to return to the new bar once it opened. How would I keep them out? One day, I was looking at the padlocked entrance, and a solution struck me: why not just put a lock on the door and be choosy about who gets a key to enter? At first, I'd give out some keys to friends, business associates, and preferred customers, and then I thought about selling them. I had an appropriate name for the place: the Key Hole. So, I started contacting old former customers of The Gladiator and Nag's Head Pub, customers, my fraternity brothers, friends, professional associates, and so on, and mailed each of them a key for the bar entrances, which, I decided, would have a gold lock. If these folks wanted keys for their wives, girlfriends, secretaries, or friends, they could jot down the addresses and I'd send them a key, too.

After we opened, I sold the keys for $25 each. I sold hundreds of them. I received so many requests that I had to have a "key waiting list." People would beg to use another member's key for a night out. By restricting entry, I created value and we also got talked about in the press and by word-of-mouth.

Drinks were a $1 each. We had a TV camera at the front door and a monitor on top of the bar so that patrons could see who was coming—and escape, if necessary, out the back. That came in quite handy for certain customers. We charged women only 25 cents for drinks from 4 P.M. to 6 P.M. so that the place would be packed with women and the men would follow in droves. As a value-added item, I had an artist come in who drew little charcoal caricatures of the customers. I offered him a corner booth and told him to charge $50 if the subject took the portrait home and only $25 if the subject consented to have it hung in the bar. The artist kept all the money from his work.

Patrons could have their names engraved on the bar for a $15 donation that went to charity. Customers would realize, "I have my name on the bar and my portrait on the wall. I belong here." The Key Hole quickly became one of the top watering holes in the city. Opening the Key Hole was an even better idea than I first thought because the building across the street was taking longer than expected to be completed, as commercial construction so often does. In the meantime, of course, I was heavily promoting my soon-to-open new restaurant, and the anticipation for it was building. After a year and a half, I had made $50,000 at the Key Hole but then had to close the place in order to transfer the liquor license to Romano's 300. By this time, the anticipation of the restaurant's opening was hitting a peak.

Points of Difference: The entrance was key-activated, patrons' names were engraved on the bar, and customers' portraits hung on the wall, creating a sense of ownership and exclusivity for members.

Customer Bill of Rights: This will be a private club. Customers will be insulated from undesirable clientele. They will know who is entering the bar at all times. They will feel like this is their bar, their home away from home.

1970 Romano's 300, Palm Beach, Florida

Using a Small Business Administration (SBA) loan, I opened Romano's 300, a medieval English-themed, fine-dining restaurant that would be like nothing the city of Palm Beach had ever seen. Even before opening the Key Hole across the street, I had decided to make Romano's 300 a private club at lunchtime and a restaurant/bar that that would be open to the general public at night. I sold 300 club memberships (hence the

"300" in the name) for $100 apiece just for day-time privileges, raising about $30,000 per year.

The 4,700-square-foot restaurant, which was about three times the size of the average eatery, was my personal medieval castle. It had a dozen dining areas and a basement wine cellar with an amazing selection of wines. A lot of members were young businessmen who couldn't get into the exclusive Everglades Club and other Palm Beach clubs, and they were happy to be welcomed at Romano's 300 and have a classy and comfortable place to impress their guests and conduct daytime business. I installed phones in the small dining rooms and provided pens, tablets, and other work accessories to accommodate them.

When the Key Hole was being remodeled, I traveled extensively throughout France, Spain, Portugal, and Morocco to gather outstanding recipes for Romano's 300 and get a better feel for European cuisine. Romano's 300 offered American, Italian, and French cuisine with prices listed in dollars, lire, and francs, respectively. For customers who were waiting for tables (the place seated 200 people), we offered complimentary champagne and hors d' oeuvres. Regulars got their usual drinks delivered to their tables without having to order them, and women would all receive a complimentary rose and some extra attention. We had two menus: one with prices for members and the other with prices for guests.

We also did some educational and sometimes quirky things for our members, such as arranging for unusual and compelling people to give presentations. These weren't your typical Kiwanis or Toastmasters speeches. A couple of cigar experts came and talked about (illegal) Cuban cigars, wine people discussed the merits of fine vintages, and a couple of high-priced call girls came in to talk about how to treat an escort, how to know when you're getting hustled, and how to avoid entrapment. Not surprisingly, the place was jam-packed that day. Word leaked to press, however, and I got blasted in the local paper for it. The resulting free publicity created even more of a buzz.

I thought my staff of 30 could benefit from a little enlightenment. So I brought in a strange and insightful woman whom I had met at a dinner party, who was a remarkable mystic, given her stunningly accurate observations about my life. I asked her to apply her philosophies about positive thinking, visualization, and the so-called third eye to my employees' various jobs. This was well before such ideas went mainstream.

She spoke to staffers in groups: managers, chefs, servers, wine stewards, busboys, office staff, and the like, and she instructed them to start each workday with a three-minute visualization exercise to imagine what they wanted to accomplish: large crowds, smiling customers, incredible meals, full reservation lists, jam-packed cash registers, awards, front-page newspaper articles, big tips, and so on. Almost immediately, the place got busier and the average bill increased. The food drew rave reviews, and gratuities grew. Staffers who had scoffed at the mystic's visualization exercise were now running full speed with it.

I went along with it as well. It was about this time, with the mystic's lectures in mind, that I started fine-tuning my self-promotional abilities. I was a regular reader of *Holiday Magazine* and wondered what it would take for us to win its prestigious, exclusive *Holiday Magazine* award for restaurants. I realized that an abundance of flattering customer letters held a lot of sway in their decision-making process. Instead of prompting a bunch of different locals to write in, I got my old fraternity brothers from Florida Atlantic University, who were scattered across the country, busy on it, asking each of them to send a letter to the food editor at *Holiday Magazine*, a Mr. Brazier, mentioning the service, the atmosphere, the vast wine selection, the steak, the seafood, the scampi sauce, or anything else on the menu. I told them to make it informal and write it in their own words so that it was believable.

It worked even better than I visualized. One day I got a call from Brazier. He asked me, "What are you doing there, Romano? I'm getting twice as many calls and letters about you than about anyone else. I've never received as many letters about any single restaurant in my life." It was all I could do not to laugh. I said, "Why don't you come down, have dinner, and I'll show you?" He visited and apparently had a great time because we came away with that year's *Holiday Magazine* award and won it in every successive year that I owned the place.

That distinction played heavily in our promotions and was prominently displayed in the restaurant. Brazier's input also helped us be named one of North America's top 175 restaurants. The awards continued to roll in after that, including the Florida Trends Award, the Silver Spoon Award, and more. I truly believed we deserved those honors.

The letter-writing campaign was just one illustration of how independent restaurant owners can make great things happen as long as they have the concept to support their claims. It's not always enough to have great food and service and an inviting setting. A good imagination and a little media savvy can go a long way in putting your best foot forward.

There was a chef at Romano's 300 named Pierre who really didn't get along with anyone, including me. He was a talented but arrogant, combative, American-bashing, pain-in-the-ass Frenchman who had a tendency to burn more than his share of meals at peak times. I had brought him in for the tourist season against my better judgment, and he was being paid very well—too well, in fact. I called him into the office one day and asked him, "How much am I paying you?" He answered, "About $25,000 for the season, Monsieur Romano. You're very generous!" To this replied, "Well, I'll tell you what, Pierre, I'm giving you a raise to $40,000 for the season." He said, "Oh, thank you, thank you, Monsieur Romano! Très généreux." Then I warned him not to tell anyone. I knew this jerk would go back to the kitchen and brag about his raise to everyone within earshot. And, sure enough, he did. The staff thought I'd gone crazy until a few days later when I called Pierre in again. I said, "Pierre, I'm really not very fond of your work or your attitude, and I asked you not to tell anyone about the raise but you did. So take your knives and get the hell out of my kitchen. You're fired." He jumped up and yelled, "You are firing me? But Monsieur Romano, you just gave me a raise!" I said, "I really don't like you, Pierre, but if you're going to lose a job, I want you to lose a good one. See ya' later." I probably couldn't get away with that today.

The lesson here is, if you make a mistake hiring someone, don't compound it by keeping the person on, because the problem will only get bigger and will affect morale. Too many restaurant managers feel that firing a bad hire will call their judgment into question. The opposite is true, because that person will hang around and do even more damage and make the customers angry. (Even if you make 90 percent of the customers happy, you'll have only 10 percent of customers who aren't happy, and they may never return.)

As it is now, the Miami–Palm Beach area is a huge tourist destination for international visitors and Romano's 300 has hosted many international dignitaries. One was King Hussein of Jordan, whose front men arrived days ahead of time with a list of exotic Lebanese food items that were needed to properly feed him and his royal entourage of 10. I told them it would be very time consuming to track down and prepare all of the exotic foodstuffs they wanted and it certainly would be very expensive. "Listen kid, we don't care what it costs, as long as it's good and everything's perfect," said one of the men, a reputed international arms dealer. "I think you just said the magic words," I said. I left the room and called my barber, a Lebanese man, and told him the items we needed, including stuffed lamb, stuffed grape leaves, a raw minced meat pureed with crushed wheat called kibbeh, and some things I had never heard of. He said he'd look into it and called me back: "Phil, I got the ladies from my church to prepare the whole meal for you," he said. We even found some of the rare wines they wanted. So I called the guy and told him that we were on. Now we had three days to organize and prepare a feast fit for a king. King Hussein had apparently bragged to an associate that he could go anywhere in the world and be served the finest Lebanese cuisine, and he was bent on testing his theory at Romano's 300.

My promotional mind was buzzing. Hussein's men were clear that photos wouldn't be allowed, but I still wanted to capitalize on this potentially king-size public relations (PR) bonanza. They hadn't, after all, said anything about photographing the meal or the food-preparation process. So I called the food editor of *The Palm Beach Post*, Rosa Tusa, and asked if she'd ever seen a feast prepared for a king. I told her the story about King Hussein, the barber, and the church ladies, and she ate it up. She agreed to hold off on filing the story until the morning after the dinner, and she and a photographer spent two days hanging around the kitchen and photographing the food and the Lebanese women cooking it, all for a big spread in the paper.

Right before the big dinner, a couple of U.S. Secret Service men arrived and they were angry with me because the wine was sitting out in the open. (It was breathing.) They said it was an open invitation for someone to tamper with it. I reassured them that I would sample each bottle personally before it was served, which I did as they watched. Hussein's security detail and I also sampled the food before it was served. After dinner, one of the king's men came to me and discretely asked if we could provide Hussein some "bubbly-bubbly," which we figured out was marijuana or hashish. I asked one of the Secret Service men about this unusual request. He shrugged his shoulders and said sure. One of our waiters was happy to oblige and hurried home to retrieve a bag of "bubbly" so that the king could have his after-dinner herbal cocktail.

When it was time to settle up, I went to one of the members of the king's detail with two different bills in my pocket, one for $4,000 and another for $7,000, both quite fair for a meal truly fit for a king. I asked how everything was, and he said, "Perfect, just perfect. It couldn't have been better! The king loved it." So, I took out the bill for $7,000, including tax but not the tip, and left the other in my pocket. They happily paid the bill and kicked in well over $1,000 more as a tip for the staff. I also made sure the barber and the Lebanese cooks were taken care of. We got our huge write-up in the paper, and Romano's 300 became known as "The Restaurant of Kings." Obviously pleased, the king came back to visit us again a couple of times over the years.

During the supposed 1973 meat shortage, I staged a meat "boycott," writing a letter to the paper saying that if other restaurants would join Romano's 300 in taking meat off the menu, it would leave more meat in the marketplace for American families. I sent a copy to

President Nixon and to Congress. The story not only made local and regional papers and the Associate Press and United Press International wires but also got picked up as far away as Japan and China, with the media referring to my place as the "Eatery of the King." One legislator even gave a speech before the U.S. House of Representatives mentioning my efforts. The truth is, I really took meat off the menu for only a few weeks. The free PR impact was winding down and so was the meat shortage at Romano's 300. During the energy crisis a couple of years later, I offered a 10 percent discount to any customers who ordered their meat rare and got even more free publicity. Anything I could do to help the cause I did.

The mystic helped me believe that the restaurant world was mine for the taking. I've been visualizing about my projects and investments ever since. Restaurateurs don't need a mystic to believe in themselves and their success, however. They do need an imaginative concept, positive people working for them, consistently great food and great service, a promotional mindset, and a willingness to serve the community, not to mention and the all-important point of difference.

Points of Difference: This was a private club by day and a public fine-dining restaurant at night. We offered complimentary champagne and hors d' oeuvres to waiting customers. We arranged interesting and sometimes controversial speakers for daytime presentations. I organized a letter-writing campaign to help win the *Holiday Magazine* best-restaurant honors for several years straight.

Customer Bill of Rights: Private-club members will be able to freely conduct business with clients. Employees will start the day visualizing the chef making the best meals possible and offering the best customer service possible. We will make those visualizations a reality.

1974 Friends of Edinburgh Eating and Drinking Society, Vero Beach, Florida

While Romano's 300 was still going great and winning awards, I opened a restaurant/bar in Vero Beach, Florida, about 40 miles north of Palm Beach, called Friends of Edinburgh Eating & Drinking Society, named after the capital of Scotland. There were Irish pubs everywhere but very few Scottish pubs, and I had gathered some ideas on how to run an American version of one during my travels to Scotland. A lot of the pubs in Scotland serve foods from England, Ireland, and other parts of Europe. So we did the same, in addition to serving Scotch eggs, meat pies, and other Scottish favorites.

My partner in Friends of Edinburg was Walter "Judd" Kassuba. At the time, he was the largest developer of apartments and condominiums in the United States. Judd's office was just across from The Key Hole in Palm Beach, and he had been a regular there. We became good friends.

I put together beautiful and elaborate booklets that served as a combination menu and history of Scottish pubs, and then I sent them to a friend in Scotland who then mailed them back to me. That way, the booklets would have a Scottish address and postmark on them for that authentic touch. I set up a deal with American Express using their choice demographics and zip codes—this was well before the days of customer-analytics firms—and I mailed the menus to prospective customers, inviting them to attend one of several grand-opening parties. The place took off.

The menus were a little too enticing. In fact, they became a local collectible and disappeared quickly: half of the original 10,000 vanished. What could I do? I wasn't about to frisk people as they left the premises.

When meat costs pushed up most of my prices by 30 percent, I had new menus printed, although I gave away a bunch of the old ones to regular customers and then allowed them to pay the old prices if they brought the old menus in. So people kept them in their glove compartments. That deal made them feel like insiders. This strategy also worked when we raised prices seasonally for tourists who descended on Vero Beach in the spring: Regulars received the old menu with the old prices; tourists received the new menu with the higher prices.

Judd and I did joint ventures on two more Florida Friends of Edinburgh locations, and they did well, despite the economic pinch that was starting to hit the state hard then. At the time, Judd had brought in an industrial psychologist to do some expensive testing on high-level people in his real estate firm. He said, "Phil, it's costing me about $2,000 a shot to test these people, and I've got one extra slot. Would you take it? It might even be fun, and you could learn something about yourself." I didn't hesitate. "Sure Judd," I said. So the psychologist spent a week with me and saw how I ran the company. Toward the end of the week, he said he wanted me to take a test the next day. He came in and put the test on my desk and lingered a few minutes, apparently to see my reaction. I never looked up at him. Later, he came back and asked if I was done. I said, "Yep, I've been done a while." He picked up the test and disappeared.

Two months later, he returned to tell me all about myself. The results were broken up into five parts. The first was "intellect." He said, "You know, this is the first time this has happened to me. I gave you the test, and you didn't ask me any questions, like what kind of test it was or how long it was going to take." He added, "And when I looked at the test, you did maybe half of it. The other stuff you left alone." I nodded and asked him, "How did I do on the ones I answered?" He said, "You didn't miss one. I responded, "Well, I didn't know the answers to those others, so I didn't do them." "That's what I thought," he said. He graded me as "high superior" in intelligence in that part of the test, based on my selectivity. "This is always how I operate: solve only the problems that you have an aptitude for," I said. "If I need something done that is out of my area of expertise, then I just find an expert to do it. I don't practice law, and I don't practice accounting, and so on. I don't try to self-medicate myself." The psychologist said my handling of that part of the test was rare.

The second part of the test was about motivation. "And what motivates you is problems," he said. "Yes, I like problem solving," I told him. "That's what stimulates me when I'm creating." He said I had "abundant" creativity. The third part of the test was on self-perception and how others perceived me. I was right on track with both, he said. A true jerk, I've always said, is a guy who perceives himself as the greatest guy in the world while everybody else perceives him as a jerk. The psychologist said I knew what I was and who I was, and everybody perceived me the same way. I had a lot of respect for other people and other people had a lot of respect for me, he said.

The fourth part of the test was how I applied myself in my organization and if my organization was structured properly. I don't do things by the pyramid organizational chart; I use a modified wheel chart with me in the middle.

Just as Judd had thought, I did get a lot out of the testing. In fact, I used it as base to reconstruct my thinking and as a guide on how I would approach the rest of my life. It was a turning point, a catalyst. In fact, I got more out of that test than I did out of college!

Meanwhile, our three restaurants were doing well, but Judd had rolled his Friends of Edinburg financial interests into a company that was quickly getting into trouble with a mounting number of high-leverage real estate loans, and the real estate market was cratering in Florida. So we agreed to liquidate the restaurants in bankruptcy and just move on.

Points of Difference: This was a rare Scottish pub in Florida. I had beautiful booklets printed that described the history of Scottish pubs and also served as menus , and sent them to Scotland for authentic postmarking. I gave old menus to regular customers who could use them to pay the old prices when the new ones were printed.

Customer Bill of Rights: We will serve great authentic Scottish and European dishes and drinks in a festive Scottish atmosphere.

1974 Shuckers—A Real Seafood Place, Lake Park, Florida

I couldn't sit on the sidelines for long. For reasons I couldn't understand, there wasn't a really noteworthy seafood place in the Palm Beach area in the early 1970s, despite its proximity to the Atlantic Ocean and the Gulf of Mexico. Just like nature, I abhor a vacuum. In the restaurant trade, I always look at such a vacuum as an opportunity.

While I was still operating Romano's 300, I bought an old barbecue joint on North Military Trail in Lake Park with a one-of-a-kind seafood place in mind. I had a catchy name in mind, "Mother Shuckers," but I caved in to political correctness and shortened it to Old Shuckers and then to just Shuckers. But I still needed a tag line. A cab driver who picked me up one night was the source of inspiration for that. "Just about everybody who gets in my cab asks me where they can find a really good seafood place around here," he told me. So there it was, with a slight modification: "Shuckers —A Real Seafood Place."

We used a New England-style seafood eatery theme and built a "raw bar" (oyster bar) in the back as a supplement to my trademark demonstration (open) kitchen. We charged $15 for a "Clam Bake" for two and were the first seafood place, to my knowledge, to serve red-jacket potatoes and corn on the cob with the meal. Other places followed my cue, and that's the way a lot of seafood houses still serve their dinners today. Imitation is the first sign of success, I often say. We were also the first seafood restaurant in the area to serve giant lobsters. It was at Shuckers that I first bought fish by the truckload. One of my cousins who was working for me cut a deal with some fishermen to buy fish directly from them.

We staged large clambakes and advertised lobsters "by the netful." The place was popular with a cross section of people, ranging from well-to-do folks arriving in limos to families walking in after spending a day at the beach. We sold humorous shirts with such sayings as "Keep on Shuckin'," "We Kiss Your Bass," and "Not Tonight, I Got a Haddock." I can think of at least one national seafood chain that started doing this sort of thing in the 1990s.

At the time, Shuckers was way out in the sticks, and the basic infrastructure around it wasn't very good. We had to have our own septic tank and drainage system, which was always backing up so the bathrooms were constantly clogged. I had to put a sign up on the restroom doors: "I know the bathrooms are not the greatest in the world, but you didn't come out here to use the bathrooms, did you?" Still, it was extremely frustrating.

The place was a hit, but it was too big and sort of clunky. It would be hard to roll out elsewhere, I thought, although I would go on to open one more in Texas in the coming years. I operated Shuckers profitably for two years before selling it to a foreign company that paid for it in Swiss francs.

For the most part, I have preferred to build restaurants, sell them, and move on to a new concept, instead of living with them forever, with a few exceptions. About the same time I sold off Shuckers, I sold Romano's 300 to a gentleman named Guido Gerosa who would go on to rename it Chez Guido. By the time I sold it, selling was the right thing to do. Also, I had other concepts up my sleeve.

Points of Difference: We bought fish by the truckload. It was the first seafood place in the area to offer giant lobsters and to serve red-jacket potatoes and corn on the cob with meals, which are staples at seafood houses today.

Customer Bill of Rights: We will serve the freshest seafood available, including the biggest lobsters in Florida, in a fun and informal setting.

1974 First National Bar & Grill/First National Productions, West Palm Beach, Florida

Like Romano's 300, my next venture took up the lower floor of an office building. But in the case of the First National Bar & Grill, there were far more office workers on site (about 1,500) spread out over the three towers that comprised Forum III. It was an ideal situation for us.

The workers all walked past my ground-floor restaurant and bar when they arrived for work and when they left for home each day.

I realized it would be a huge challenge to feed lunch to all of these workers within the time span of a few hours, and I knew it would be like a madhouse every day. So I decided to create a huge buffet with a twist: I would charge by the minute. It didn't matter what or how much the people ate; what mattered was how long they stayed. I needed to get people in an out quickly. I charged $5 for a half-hour and $2 for every ten minutes after that. It was very efficient set-up, and it worked out well. People would punch in using a ticket and punch out when they were done, and then present the ticket to the cashier. If they went over only a few minutes, we didn't charge them extra. The buffet featured chicken, beef, meat loaf, salads, and desserts, among other dishes. We changed the dishes a little every day to avoid being monotonous.

Most diners made it a point to finish in a half-hour. They were aware of our seating constraints, and most were happy to cooperate with my off-the-wall approach. It was a one-of-a-kind solution to a unique problem. At night, we charged a bit more for dinner and did so by the hour instead of by the half-hour, offering entrée items such as prime rib.

On the other side of First National was a huge nightclub that seated 300 people, which I operated separately, and it was quite a challenge as I soon discovered. We offered Las Vegas-style acts, including singers and dancers on a huge sound stage equipped with an elaborate lighting system.

Famed actor Burt Reynolds, an old high school chum of mine from Palm Beach High School, formed a talent and production company with me at the facility called First National Productions. Although Burt was three years older than me, we were both in the same high school fraternity, which helped keep us both off the streets, and we were also both ex-jocks there. (I went to school with actor George Hamilton, too.)

With our talent company, Burt and I planned to take local singers and other talent, help develop them, and possibly open similar clubs around the United States. Burt would bring his famous girlfriend, actress and entertainer Dinah Shore, home for the holidays, and we became friends. Burt and I taped one young singer, and we brought it to Dinah for her professional opinion. "Boys," she said, "she's good. But she's not going to make it. She sounds like every other singer out there. She has no point of difference in her voice." I repeated that term, "point of difference." Dinah was right on key as always. In a few short words, she had articulated what my father meant when he said that you had to stand out from the crowd. That's what I told my son, Sam, as he grew to be a man. Have a point of difference.

Nothing significant was coming out of First National Productions, so we shut it down. What did I know about picking out that kind of talent anyway? But now I had a vacant 300-seat nightclub space to fill, and the Florida economy was in a downturn. My solution was to organize a woman's club—yes, a woman's club.

I got five women together who were in their mid-20s and mid-30s for a free dinner—a hairdresser, an accountant, a travel agent, an architect, and a phone company executive—and made a little speech. "Men have been networking, organizing, and doing business with each other in the Rotary or Kiwanis or the like for a long time, and they network and help each other out. Women don't do much of this because there are fewer opportunities. Just think what you could accomplish if you got 100 or more women together. You'd always have a job with that kind of networking, and in this economy, that's important. We could form an organization here, and I could help you get perks like free checking, discounts at different stores and restaurants, and other things."

I suggested they get as many professional women together as they could, start a mailing list, and have a daily social hour with discounted drinks at First National, plus a party once a week, with the food on me. I asked that each of them to bring at least 5 more women to the next meeting, but most of them brought 10 or so. I bought them all dinner again, gave my speech, and they were excited that they had strength in numbers.

They called themselves, "The Lovers, the Fighters, and the Wild Horse Riders—a Ladies Club," with me as their social chairman. They had bylaws, custom shirts, a club fee of $25, and every day there'd be a cocktail hour with 75 to 80 ladies at the bar, and they all got discounts. At the parties, we'd charge $5 for the guys (they had to be members) to get in, and they were lining up. The club was packed almost every day. We orchestrated a First National/Ladies Club 4th of July beach party at a Holiday Inn in nearby Jupiter, Florida, and 3,000 people came at $15 a head for all the roasted pig and booze they could consume. The event stopped traffic on the main highway, and the state police had to come and unclog things.

I learned that if restaurants and nightclubs have empty space and use a little imagination, the ways they can fill them are unlimited. There are always organizations and business groups looking for a free place to meet.

Point of Difference: We charged by the minute due to the large daytime population in the adjoining office building. I formed a talent company with actor Burt Reynolds in the nightclub space next door that I later turned into a bar, which would become home to woman's business and networking club—a rarity at the time—that I helped organized.

Customer Bill of Rights: On the restaurant side, customers will have access to a regularly changing lunch and dinner buffet and will be charged by the minute in order to keep tables available for the large office population. In the nightclub, women will have a unique place to network with other professional women.

1974 Pasta Palace, Lake Worth, Florida

First National was still going strong when I decided to open an Italian restaurant in the old Lake Theatre, a classic Art Deco, box-style movie house that was originally called the Lake Avenue Theatre when it opened in February of 1940.

I decided to show silent movies and old serials on the theater's screen using the old-fashioned projector that we inherited when we took over the place. Our menu would be shown on the side wall with the projector flickering on and off with photos of our food and prices, with the entire menu shown every few minutes. The movie screen curtain was highlighted by neon lights.

I bought a $7,000 pasta-making machine—very expensive for that era—from Italy that could yield 65 pounds of pasta per hour, and we put it in the lobby as part of my "truth in feeding" restaurant principle. My father, Samuel, and my aunt, Florence Colella, churned out the pasta and helped out elsewhere. Our pasta, made of semolina (from hard durum wheat), eggs, salt, and oil, became an instant hit. After we mastered the making pasta, we held a "sauce-off" among family members to select the Pasta Palace's meat sauce, with my family and some of my old fraternity brothers and other friends as tasters. Tasters were blindfolded.

My sister, Rosalie, edged out my aunt and my mother in the final tasting, although it was a close competition. After that, my mother retired from her sauce-making duties with some sense of relief, I'm sure. She was a diabetic, and her eyes were starting to fail, plus she had done more than her fair share of cooking over the decades. The baton was passed to Rosalie.

It was at Pasta Palace that I unwisely got away from my habit of never investing my own cash in anything. Banks considered me a good bet and kept trying to lend me money for new concepts, and investors and partners were still asking to get into deals. But I thought this concept couldn't fail. Unfortunately, about the time I opened the place, the Florida economy was faltering and the real estate industry was going into the tank. Still, I was sure it was going to rebound. People still needed to eat and have fun in those times—and especially drink. Why not at my place? If the economy turned around, I reasoned, I would be way ahead of everybody, and if it didn't, there would be no shame because I would be in the same boat as everybody else.

I spent a lot of money on Pasta Palace, and food critics and my customers alike enjoyed it, but the market just wasn't strong or large enough to support it. It was a bit ahead of its time, like a few other projects of mine that didn't work. Movie diners are now the norm, and Art Deco buildings are rare and highly sought after.

I decided to close the place within a year of its opening. It would later become a disco and then a museum. By then, I had also closed First National. I knew I wasn't going to remain in the area, so I liquidated everything, paid my bills, and came out of it with about $100,000. Things did get better in the Sunshine State, it turned out. Timing— good and bad—can be everything in the restaurant business. It was time to pick up stakes—and steaks.

Points of Difference: It was located in an old Art Deco movie theater, so we showed the menu, as well as silent movies and old serials, on the screen with an old-fashioned projector. We had a state-of-the-art pasta machine from Italy in the lobby that could yield 65 pounds of pasta per hour.

Customer Bill of Rights: Customers will see the pasta being made fresh in our lobby and eat in an historic movie theater. The sauce will be freshly made daily using a Romano family recipe.

1977 Shuckers—A Real Seafood Place II, San Antonio, Texas

With the Florida economy still soft, my developer friend, Judd Kassuba, had exited Palm Beach and moved to a more favorable real estate climate at the time—Houston. He told me I should come there also to check out all the new opportunities. So my first wife, Libby, and I got into our Corvette and drove to Texas, visiting Judd, who showed us around. I was impressed by all the rapid growth.

Judd did a lot of business with insurance companies at the time, and one of them owned a large financial share of a country club in San Antonio. So Judd made a deal with the insurer, allowing me first rights to take over the place and turn it around. I would own 30 percent of it—real estate and everything.

I liked San Antonio even more than Houston. But at the country club, it was obvious the guy running it was well liked by all the members, and I figured that if I bought him out, I'd come off as a carpetbagger, and that might jeopardize my chances of succeeding locally.

This was also about the time that San Antonio and other parts of Texas were finally allowing liquor to be served in restaurants—no more "BYOB" stuff. My eyes got big. I said, "Oh, wow, I know that business." I also knew it was going to be a huge opportunity. If I'm going to do that, I thought, I am going to get involved in Texas because the restaurant business is going to boom. So we settled in the Alamo City.

I realized I could get back into the mainstream eating business in Texas, an act that would have been perceived as a step down for me in Florida after my fine-dining restaurants in Florida. But nobody had any expectations of me whatsoever in San Antonio; I had freedom to maneuver. San Antonio didn't really have a wealth of fish places, and I immediately thought of "Shuckers." A couple of my Florida partners went in on one with me, and it was well received. The partners wanted to build more, but I declined, in part because I would only own 25 percent of the deal, and I wasn't going to work my ass off for that. I just didn't think it was a very mobile concept anyway, and I was right. I quickly sold my interest to the partners, and Shuckers only lasted another year or so.

Points of Difference: This was among the first seafood restaurants in the area to serve alcohol—and large lobsters.

Customer Bill of Rights: Customers will be served the freshest seafood available, including the biggest lobsters in Texas, in an informal setting.

1978 Enoch's, San Antonio, Texas

A small, intimate, private steak-and-fish house, Enoch's was my tenth concept. Named after the biblical character, Enoch's would incorporate elements of my earlier concepts, including the required key entry that I had initiated at the Key Hole in Palm Beach. At the time, San Francisco Steak House was the hottest restaurant in town and was churning out 300 or more dinners every night. I wanted something more exclusive—about 125 perfect meals per night in a 75-seat restaurant with a limited menu.

But there was one stumbling block. Texas was still in the process of loosening up its liquor laws, and you had to be a resident for at least a year before you could get a liquor license. I was still short of that. My San Antonio Shuckers partner had been a local resident for a while and got us one there. But getting Enoch's a liquor license posed a problem.

I complained to the Texas Alcoholic Beverage Commission and told them I had served my country and had no records of arrest or alcohol violations at my previous restaurants. "Sorry, a liquor license is a privilege, not an entitlement," I was told. Fortunately, I had become good friends with a popular city councilman, insurance salesman, and realtor, Gene Canavan, and he came in as a silent partner and got us the liquor license.

Gene and I pulled together the names of 25 couples who were upright citizens, and I sent them invitations for a free steak dinner at our exclusive new restaurant. They feasted on free prime rib, T-bone steak, shrimp, and fettuccini Alfredo, and loved it all as well as our New York-bistro-style atmosphere. "My friend and your friend, Gene Canavan, has brought the 50 of you in here tonight for a complimentary meal," I told the gathering. "And what I'd like to do is put you on our members' Rolodex because I want it to be a nice place where we have the right kind of people. So, we're locking the front door, but your names are going to gain you access. If you want to make reservations, you can come in and eat any time you want and with anyone you want. But we won't let a group in unless one of them is on that Rolodex."

We asked those couples to supply us with the names of another 10 couples, and we sent letters to all of them, telling them that they were invited to be founding members of Enoch's. All of a sudden, we had started a little society of people who all knew one another. They felt like they were part of something exciting and exclusive and could pass along their good fortune to friends, relatives, and colleagues.

Like at the Key Hole, this created a mystique and that all-important feeling of ownership. I quickly built up a core group of 250 Enoch's patrons, and I asked each of them to add another 10 people to the list. We eventually wound up with a customer base of about 10,000, charging $100 for a membership to those who hadn't been invited.

Enoch's was a classy steak house with an ornate bar that ran along one full side, with a long brass rail, all handmade by my father. (He and my mother moved to Texas to be near me after he retired.) He was always a craftsman, and like me, he had to stay busy. So he set up a woodworking shop and did artisan-quality finish-out work for Enoch's and other restaurants. Enoch's had terra-cotta floors and all-mahogany ceilings and walls. My sister, who also moved to San Antonio, came in to help, along with my first wife and my mother.

There was no printed menu. The main attractions were displayed on a tray brought by waiters to the table with no prices attached. If people asked, we'd tell them. A decade later, the famous Morton's Steak House chain did the same thing. Everybody got a Caesar salad made fresh at the table. The place was always packed, and our patrons loved the intimate atmosphere. At the time, there were many large restaurants serving 400 or more meals a night, and that kind of volume always increases the chances of serving bad meals. My answer to those big cattle calls was to have a beautiful little place that served only 125 meals nightly and did every one of them to perfection.

As a point of difference, I wanted my young and enthusiastic bartender, Dave, to do magic tricks behind the bar between drink orders. I saw an ad for a place called the "House of Magic" in the newspaper, and I informed Dave that I was taking him there for training. We walked into the place, which was nice, and into a reception area. An extremely nice lady, who was somewhat provocatively dressed, greeted us warmly from behind the desk. I said, "I want my friend here to take a course in magic." She said, "Oh? What kind of tricks would you like to learn?" I said, "Magic tricks." She was amused and said, "Well, we do a lot of magic tricks here."

It was then that we finally realized we were in a house of ill repute and the only "learning" Dave was going to get was from a different sort of trick. I said, "I don't think we need that kind of magic. We already know it." We laughed our heads off. "Now that's one hell of a training program," I told him on the way back to the restaurant. "I ought to be a magician myself." Dave finally bought some books on magic and learned on his own, and the patrons really liked the novelty of it. Our House of Magic visit was a running gag for a long time.

It was at Enoch's that I finally solved the mystery of the disappearing restaurant silverware. People just assumed that the employees or even customers were pilfering the missing knives and forks. While there may have been some of that, I discovered that a surprising number of utensils were getting wrapped up with the table cloths in haste and tossed in the laundry.

We made the employees aware of that, and they were more watchful. And I soon cut deals with restaurant laundry services to buy their stray silverware to use at my less-formal eateries where mix-and-match forks, knives, and spoons were acceptable. Another tactic: If my kitchen was suffering excess dish breakage, I posted a sign indicating the replacement cost of each glass and plate. If we had $500 in breakage per month, I put a sign up offering a $150 or $200 bonus, split between the busboys at the end of each month, minus everything they broke. So, now they were taking ownership of the situation, losing what was, in effect, their own money on breakage, and I was saving $300 or more a month.

Points of Difference: This was a small 75-seat restaurant. Membership entry maintained an upscale clientele of hand-picked members. Limited-menu entrees were displayed by tray with no prices. There were no printed menus.

Customer Bill of Rights: Customers will be served a perfect meal every visit because we only prepare a limited number of them each night. This will be a private restaurant, but with a reservation, customers will be allowed to come in and eat any time they want and with anyone they want.

1979 Barclay's, San Antonio, Texas

A couple of doors down from Enoch's was a time-worn little bar that was starting to attract an undesirable clientele. I worried that the unsavory clientele would drag the restaurant down. The owner said he wasn't about to turn any of his patrons away, so I realized the only way to clean it up was to buy him out.

I bought out the owner's lease and fixed the place up so that it would complement Enoch's. I also created a backgammon club there at a time when board games were at the height of their popularity and sold memberships in it for $100 apiece. All told, I sold about 1,500 of them for $150,000 without pouring a drink. We were entertaining a more upscale clientele than the old place and drawing a healthy after-dinner crowd from Enoch's. I sold drinks for a higher price, of course, and we hosted events like a midsummer New Year's Eve party with women in gowns and men in black tie and tails, and we got the newspaper and TV stations to do a feature on it.

It was at Barclays that I first experimented with the concept of eye-level seating. The bar, another of my dad's creations, was in the center of the place, and the tables along the walls were set at the same height as the barstools. That way, everyone was at eye level and patrons could meet the glances of more people. Customers could approach tables to talk with someone without bending down awkwardly. We had bands, a piano bar, and backgammon lessons and tournaments. I put a small library in the place to make it feel a little less like a bar and more like a social club.

Barclay's and Enoch's were both doing well as the 1970s came to a close, and I had a number of other profitable concepts behind me, but the real heyday of my restaurant creation career was just around the corner.

Points of Difference: There was a bar in the center of the pub created by my wood-working father. Tables along the walls were the same height as the barstools, creating eye-level seating. I created a popular backgammon club with a $100 membership fee.

Customer Bill of Rights: This will be a safe, upscale club with a desirable clientele and we will have music, backgammon tournaments, and other games that will create a fun social scene.

4

ROMANO CONCEPTS (1979–1995): From Fuddruckers to Rosalie's Cucina

I have learned through both practice and observation that ideas considered "unfit" because of their nonconformity have gone on to change the world.

Fuddruckers, San Antonio, Texas

It was late 1979, and I was itching to create something new. I had positioned Barclay's and Enoch's well and didn't need to be there. Plus, I wanted to get away from the fine-dining business for a while and work on a food concept that I really loved—something that was authentic but simple. While I always loved my mother's authentic Italian home cooking, some of my fondest food memories as a kid were the simple pleasures of biting into a juicy hamburger or a hot dog. Despite all the pasta, steaks, seafood, barbecue meat, and other entrees I've served, my last meal would be a burger or a hot dog.

While I was out on business one afternoon, I was lamenting the lack of decent hamburger choices out in the market. There were fast-food places and there were conventional restaurants that made ho-hum burgers as sort of an afterthought. Still daydreaming about burgers, I found myself pulling into a McDonald's, as if by conditioning. Eating a Quarter Pounder in that atmosphere was not conducive to relaxation, I thought. The burger I ordered was pretty good, but it was no different than the Quarter Pounders I ate in college, except that it was almost three times the price. Charging a lot more without improving a product is a cardinal sin in my book, and neither McDonald's nor its competitors catered to adults who might like to linger over a meal with a friend or relax with a cold brew or two. The décor seemed to say, "Don't get too comfortable, and when you're, done, get out of here, and fast."

I realized I could do burgers much better than that, as I watched a bunch of screeching toddlers bounce around the McDonald's playground. I could create a better and more upscale burger place and make it more of a playground for adults. While the hamburger wasn't a new concept, I could add a few imaginative twists that would take the concept to next level.

I always dive into a new challenge, and this challenge was no exception: make the world's greatest hamburger. In a short time, I laid out what I called my restaurant's "Bill of Rights," or those things that I would hold sacred to the concept: (1) the meat would be the best, (2) the buns would be the best, (3) the burgers would be cooked exactly the way the customers wanted them cooked, (4) customers would be able to put whatever condiments they liked on their burgers and as much as they liked on their burgers, including cheese, all for free, (5) The atmosphere would be exactly what customers expected of the home of the "World's Greatest Hamburger," and the employees would do things better than any burger house in the industry.

After some spirited brainstorming with friends, which I must admit involved a few intoxicants, I came up with a fun and funky name, Freddie Fuddruckers, based in part as a riff on the fictitious Fudpucker Airlines that aviation nerds joked about at the time and was also as a semi-suggestive name that wasn't really offensive in itself. Based on the amused reactions of people, the name stuck, although I later decided to shorten it to Fuddruckers. It wasn't long before I refined each of the five points of Fuddruckers's Bill of Rights:

1. Meat: Fuddruckers would grind its own beef, buy its beef in four quarters, debone the beef in-house, and use no additives. The day it was grilled was the day it was ground. It would never be frozen. We would do this behind glass so that customers could see how it was done.

2. Buns: We would make the buns fresh on the premises all day long, and customers would be able to smell them being baked. They would be served hot to the touch to customers.

3. Cooking: The cooks would prepare the burgers on cast-iron griddles to customer specifications, searing the meat first and then cooking it to perfection. Cooking the meat would be one cook's sole focus and baking the buns would be another cook's sole focus.

4. Condiments: We would deliver a perfect burger to the customer, who would then take it to a fully stocked condiment bar just a few feet away. The condiment bar would be so big that it would resemble a supermarket produce stand, and it would be full of fresh condiments and feature a pot full of melted cheese.

We would offer customers everything they could want on their burger and as much of it as they liked.

5. Atmosphere: We would put customers in the middle of the space where the world's greatest hamburgers were made and they would experience truth in feeding; the food would be prepared and cooked openly. There would be a glassed-in butcher shop where the meat was visibly ground. The restaurant floor would be lined with premium products and supplies, including bins of produce and cases of ketchup, mustard, and beer. There would be a separate visible bakery where the buns would be baked fresh from scratch. Customers would smell the baking bread and watch as bakers carried trays of hot buns across the dining floor to the serving area, yelling, "Hot buns, coming through." All the preparation areas would be clean and well organized because they would be seen by the customers.

Next it was financing time. I went to see my trusty old San Antonio banker, Charles Cooney, thinking he'd love the idea. After all, he had arranged funding for Shuckers, Enoch's, and Barclay's, and he had made out well on those deals. But he wasn't at all warm to the idea of Fuddruckers.

I showed him my planning materials, explained my bill of rights, and said I needed $150,000 to launch this ground-breaking hamburger restaurant, which I would call Freddie Fuddruckers. He listened carefully but shocked me when he said he'd have to pass. "I'm going to play the Dutch uncle here and do you the favor of a little tough advice," he said. "I just don't like the idea, plus you've done very well at fine dining. Why lose your focus? Forget about burgers and beer, and stick to what you know." Further, he said that I would be jeopardizing my other restaurant deals with the new venture.

"But, Charles, I don't have any other bankers here in town," I said. "You're the only one I've dealt with since I got here, and you've never let me down before. Where am I going to get the money?" He said, "Trust me, I don't think anybody will give it to you for this Fuddruckers thing. And I'm not so sure about that name either."

I said, "Charles, I'm still going to do it. It's a great idea, and the timing is right for it." He said, "Fine, but you're not going get the money from me." On my way out, I thought of the old definition of a bank: a place where they'll lend you money if you don't need it.

Other people too, including bankers and restaurant people, said the idea was beneath me or unworkable or frivolous. I heard it all. "Poor yield." "Pain in the ass." "People aren't going to want to see you butcher your meat." "Freddie Fuck-ruckers?!" It was not a fitting idea, they said.

But I had learned through both practice and observation that ideas that have been considered "unfit" because of their nonconformity have gone on to change the world. How else can things change for the better? Someone has to take risks. And it's often the case in my industry that the so-called unfit are really the ones who blaze the trail. I call it survival of the un-fittest. Unfit? Guilty as charged.

So I turned to "angel investors," in the form of friends, associates, customers from Enoch's, and private investors. If I could find 10 of them to put in $15,000 apiece, I'd be on my way. I'd give these loyal folks a cumulative 48 percent share of the company, and I'd keep the controlling 52 percent. I threw my net out, gave away a lot of drinks and dinners, and made my pitch to anyone who would listen.

Richard Signorelli, president of the local Friedrich Air Conditioning Co., was first to take a shot. When I explained to him my truth-in-feeding concept, my bill of rights, and my plans to make the world's best burger, he jumped right in. "When these are opening up from coast to coast, you're gonna look pretty damn smart," I told him.

Finally, I managed to bring together a group of nine investors and was just one short, though I did have enough capital to start the project. I settled on a former print shop building near the San Antonio Airport on Botts Lane near San Antonio's I-410 loop.

As work began, it became apparent to my father, who was making it a habit to show up at the work site, that my contractors weren't working out. "These guys are as slow as shoemakers, and they're not doing a very good job, son," he said. "Get 'em out of here. I'll build you this place myself." He was in his mid- 60s, but he still knew what he was doing, so I fired them and worked side by side with my father for several weeks. Those were memorable weeks.

One day, before we opened, a dapper young businessman came by to check out this new Fuddruckers restaurant that he'd been hearing about. He stopped at the front door, looked around, and asked who the owner was. He said he was interested in investing in it and was told there was one investment unit left at $15,000. Three days later, I received his check. The guy was Herb Kelleher, who had cofounded Southwest Airlines in 1971. His confidence said a mouthful to me.

My goal all along for Fuddruckers was to take the mystery out of the hamburger. From my experiences with meat suppliers, I could never be sure how fresh the meat was or what fillers might be in the meat, and the system I was intending to use provided me with quality control. We were still going to do all our grinding of the meat, and not only that, we were going to do it in plain view of the customers behind glass.

By buying four quarters of beef, I figured out a way that my hamburger would, in effect, cost me only 35 cents per pound. Each quarter weighed about 110 pounds, at about 95 cents per pound. We'd deboned the quarter, took out the rib-eye, and cut it up to make 13 to 15 pieces, which we'd use for fresh rib-eye steak sandwiches, which would sell for about $5 each, I thought. That was a quick $70, which when I subtracted it from my original cost that left 90 pounds of hamburger, which came to roughly 35 cents per pound. People said there was no way my ground beef could be that cheap because they were paying $1.80 a pound. Ha!

My burgers weren't cheap for the era—about $3.50—but customers got a half-pounder-plus. My goal wasn't to move McDonald's patrons up to a pricier burger. It was more to move steakhouse and other table-service restaurant patrons down to my burger concept and offer them a sort of getaway. It's always easier to get people to spend less money than more.

Fuddruckers's menu would be simple: burgers, steak sandwiches, hot dogs, bratwurst, beans, fries, ice cream, and cookies. We designed the place so that when customers arrived, they'd see crates of top-quality fresh lettuce and tomatoes, cases of premium beer and ketchup, and sacks of potatoes, sweet onions, flour, and beans; functional décor, I called it.

We invited 50 friends for a test lunch. The "Wow Factor" was quickly evident. More "wows" followed when they came to the condiment bar and even more, of course, when they sank their teeth into their first Fuddruckers burger. Based on their smiles and reactions, I knew we had a hit.

My mother came in on our first day of business, saw all the dry goods on the floor, and exclaimed, "Oh my God, Philip, you're not ready to open yet! Is this the back or the front door?" I assured her the place was supposed to look like this.

We custom-cooked our burgers on a cast-iron griddle to taste—medium-rare to well-done—you name it. Even when we were busy, we would never mash the patty to speed up the cooking. People would see their food prepared every step of the way. It was truth in feeding personified. No one complained about the visible beef preparation. People got it: their burgers were fresh. If this was a sacred cow, then we killed it.

We stuck with just one burger size, the half-pounder, but it was actually nine ounces, though we didn't advertise that fact. We just wanted people to perceive it as the best product around in the hamburger business. My bakers would yell, "Careful, hot buns coming through; out of the way!" to reinforce their freshness. I made up a tongue-in-cheek tale about Sir Frederick Fuddruckers, our "founder," and sold prints, T-shirts, and "Mother Fuddruckers" mustard, too.

We were the first burger restaurant to offer unlimited toppings and as much free melted cheese as people wanted. This helped give patrons full ownership of the feeding process. We were also among the first restaurants to give out free drink refills and one of the first to offer buckets of beer. Remember, this was nearly 40 years ago.

We hit it big; so take that, Charles the banker! The place was enormously popular, and we packed them in, despite one local food reviewer calling the place a "poorly located, dime-store-decorated burger joint."

And what's more, Fuddruckers had legs. After we got the first one right, we opened a second one in Houston about a year later. Several franchise locations around the region and the country followed. We tried to locate them in areas with high apartment densities because those customers didn't have traditional backyards to cook out and we wanted to be their replacement backyard. In fact, our seating area, with tablecloths and a yellow-awning ceiling, suggested a backyard patio. We also had covered patios, and we quickly became a comfortable hangout for families and friends.

I'm a marketer and showman at heart, as well as a restaurateur and entrepreneur. I'm always looking for angles to market my creations. A restaurant may have great meals, but the best ones may be the products of the owner's or the manager's imagination. Remember the letter-writing campaign to *Holiday Magazine* for Romano's 300? This time, for Fuddruckers I concocted a national PR campaign as Fuddruckers expanded around the country.

Because there was no organization handing out awards for great hamburgers, I created one myself, the Hamburger Appreciation Society of North America (HASNA). I called up a good friend in Minneapolis to ask if he'd serve as its figurehead president. Each year, HASNA had a "Best Hamburger" contest. And guess who won? Why Fuddruckers, of course. After a while, my HASNA "president" was getting letters from people all over the country asking how they could join the society and telling him how great Fuddruckers's burgers were. Ha!

Every time we entered a city, I bought out lists of American Express cardholders there and sent them a booklet from HASNA headquarters, informing them that the award-winning Fuddruckers was coming to their town and that we accepted American Express. The six-page booklet included pictures of the five things that set Fuddruckers apart from other burger places: the freshly ground meat, the freshly baked buns, the well-stocked condiments area with free melted cheese, the burgers getting cooked to order, and the fun atmosphere. On the back of the booklet, I noted that we had won the coveted HASNA award and said that if customers brought this booklet in to Fuddruckers, they would get a free hamburger. The booklets poured in, and we reused most of them to send to people in the next town where we were opening another Fuddruckers.

Several imitators, such as Flaky Jake's and Purdy's, rose up, and we fought them in court one by one, over their use of our look, or "trade dress," which I'll talk about later. In the meantime, I had to sell off Barclay's and Enoch's to two different investors because of Fuddruckers's increasing demands on my time. Enoch's lasted about five years after that, but Barclay's continued to operate as a pub until the late 1990s.

A couple of years after its founding at that little "poorly located" Botts Lane location, my longtime friend and attorney, Cecil Schenker, and I were prepping Fuddruckers for an initial public offering (IPO). We opened at $7 a share and soared to $18 on the first day of trading. We had a great secondary offering eight months later, and by the end of 1984, we'd expanded to 25 company-owned stores and 30 franchise units.

Just when I was on top of the world, my father became ill. It was cancer, and it was spreading quickly. He was going downhill pretty fast. We still hung out together, though, and he even attended my board meetings. One time, he fell asleep next to me during a board member's monologue, but I couldn't blame him. Sometimes he'd just get up during long meetings and never return.

When he was on his last legs, I told my father, "I'm so sorry, dad. I'm just at a point now where everything in my life is going to pop." He said, "Don't worry about it, son. Think about me when you're doing this, and I'll be there." My father died at the age of 72 with me at his side holding his hand. Though he didn't live to see most of my successes, I felt at peace because of the length of time we spent with each other. Today, I feel his presence in whatever I do.

Life went on, and I continued to dream up unconventional promotions. We published the eight-page Fuddruckers's *Burgereater's Review* magazine every month for our restaurant with capsule "Movie Menu" reviews and ratings from one to three burgers. We gave out a total of about 1 million of them throughout the 1980s. Customers could voice their opinions and pass along jokes in a "Laughing Stock" session. We listed local events and had a record-review section and a "Pro and Con" page where politicians could debate the issues.

We also had a scholarship program in place: We would take a percentage of gross sales from each restaurant and apply it to college scholarships for workers. The better our workers treated the customers and their jobs, the more gross sales we'd have, so that was a motivator. The kids would vote to see who got the scholarships at each restaurant, and we'd spread out about $3,000 per unit to four workers per restaurant. The kids would wear buttons saying "Because of you, our customers, I'm going to college." I also ran promotions saying, "Not only are you getting a great burger; you're helping put a kid through college."

We had a Fuddruckers University (let the F.U. jokes begin), an exhaustive six-week program featuring a real butcher shop, bakery, and grill. "Students" had to come up with the correct yield for a quartered slab of beef before graduating.

Fuddruckers continued to grow, but I found myself getting claustrophobic because there were other things I wanted to do. I was making $500,000 a year plus perks, but I still felt like I was being held captive. I loved dealing with customers but had grown tired of dealing with real estate people, bankers, accountants, and lawyers. Besides, I had $30 million in the bank at age 40. So, I said, "Hey, the company is in good shape, so I want to step out of this thing. I'll sit on the board and still oversee things. If you don't want me doing these things while I'm sitting on the board, I'll get out." They kept me on the board.

In 1986, I sold my majority interest in Fuddruckers, which soon merged with Boston-based Daka Restaurants, so the headquarters were moved to Boston. I stayed on the board for another few years, and in 1988, I left Fuddruckers, which by then had 150 restaurants. I just felt like I'd done everything I could do for the concept. The world needed a better hamburger, and I gave them one. I can't complain; my creation has lasted 39 years so far. Also, I eventually made that $30 million from my Fuddruckers's stock, which made it a little easier to walk away.

Of those 10 people who had enough faith in my concept to invest their $15,000, only 4 of them remained until the end. They made $3.4 million each when we went public, which was an enormous windfall in less than two years' time. And they never had to put in more money or assume any liabilities. That's an 11,283 percent annual growth rate, to be specific. But Herb Kelleher wasn't one of those four. He got out early after I informed investors I was going to take the big chance of expanding Fuddruckers nationally. He made out okay but nothing like $3.4 million. For years, I chided Herb about this; he should have flown round-trip with me!

Today, Fuddruckers is headquartered in Houston and has about 200 total company-owned and franchise locations, with restaurants in the United States, Puerto Rico, Canada, Mexico, Panama, Italy, the United Arab Emirates, Bahrain, Saudi Arabia, Morocco, Chile, Colombia, the Dominican Republic, Lebanon, and Poland. While the chain had corporatized its presentation more than necessary and had pinched pennies where they shouldn't have, it was still a great burger. Fuddruckers was my twelfth restaurant concept, and, by industry standards, that's quite a few. But I would go on to nearly triple that number.

Points of Difference: It was the first upscale hamburger chain and the first to visibly butcher its meat in-house. It was the first to offer an all-you-can-eat condiment bar, including melted cheese, with buns baked fresh in the dining area; the first to openly display crates of top-quality fresh lettuce, tomatoes, beer, ketchup, sacks of potatoes, sweet onions, flour, and beans that were visible on the dining floor; and the first to offer a "half-pound burger" that was actually nine ounces.

Customer Bill of Rights: The meat and the buns will be the best; the burgers will be cooked exactly the way customers want them cooked; customers will be able to use all the condiments they like, including melted cheese, for free; the atmosphere will be exactly what customers expect from the home of the "World's Greatest Hamburger"; the employees will do their jobs better than any burger restaurant in the industry.

1986 Stix Eating Spa, San Antonio, Texas

Stix Eating Spa, a Pan-Asian concept featuring Yakitori cooking and named after the tasty beef and chicken kabobs (on sticks) that we sold, was a big deviation from anything I had ever done. Inspired in part by my travels through Japan, our fare was geared toward young urban professionals, or "yuppies" as they were known at the time, a group that was becoming more weight- and health-conscious and eating less volume per meal but eating more times a day. They had become concerned about such things as colon cancer, especially after Ronald Reagan's diagnosis, and were seeking "clean food."

A few years before it opened, I had visited Tokyo with my Fuddruckers senior vice president, Bill Baumhauer, to sign some deals with a company that was developing Fuddruckers in Japan. We walked into a restaurant, and I immediately saw food skewered on small wooden sticks, grilled next to the tables. In about 10 minutes, I envisioned the Stix concept, and I had to go back to my hotel room immediately and draw it out.

It felt great getting back into the restaurant business. At Fuddruckers, it seemed like all I did after we went public was talk with lawyers, accountants, and executives. Stix had a theater configuration, with high ceilings and tiered rows of stadium-style seats in booths overlooking the bustle of a central exhibition kitchen, all part of my "truth in feeding" ethic. People would order their stir-fry and kebob entrees from glass display cases.

By the time Stix opened 18 months later, on January 4, 1986, it was a somewhat different place from those sketches, although the main idea was intact. Our 3,300-square-foot restaurant had a medley of themes, with white walls, oversized hand fans, and handsome active-wear uniforms worn by a young, energetic staff—sneakers, chinos, and V-neck sweater-vests—reminiscent more of a health club than a restaurant.

Patrons ordered at the counter, where each dish was displayed, and we called out each customer's name over a loudspeaker when the dish was ready and it sent out to our "runners" with their food. All of the activity was designed to enhance the notion that customers were getting fresh and nutritious food.

We to do things in a healthy way, using gas broilers instead of char broilers and no microwaves, and it was a no-smoking restaurant some 20 years before it became mandatory. There was also no hard liquor, though we offered diverse selections of beer and wine. The entrees were served in Japanese bento boxes that were actually compartmentalized containers. In addition to the healthy entrees and such things as spinach salad and cold pasta with pesto, we offered chocolate-covered strawberries for dessert.

We opened with high expectations. A lot of people were watching this restaurant after Fuddruckers to see if I still had the golden touch. Patrons and reviewers told us our food was fantastic. But here's the bottom line: we were only doing about $60,000 in sales per month when we needed to do $100,000. So I started pouring in more advertising money, but I saw only small bumps in sales. In promotions, you're supposed to get a 10 percent return on your investment. I hired a marketing-research firm to get to the bottom of the problem. They found that I had 100 percent acceptance of the food and theme and that patrons were returning more frequently than they would to fast-food places, which was an amazing accomplishment.

The bad news was that while our prices weren't exclusive, we were still only attracting an upper-crust clientele, the $65,000-and-above annual income family, which was at the high end for the times. And there were just 6,000 of those families in all of San Antonio! Plus, the latest nutritional information hadn't filtered down to other potential customer groups. While more people were thinking thin, they were still eating fat.

The place was ahead of its time for this market, it turned out. It would have thrived in New York, Boston, Chicago, Los Angeles, or San Francisco, but not in the Alamo City. But I wasn't about to move it. We shot videos of the operation and closed it a year after I had opened it. I learned some important lessons with Stix: cutting-edge ideas work best in densely populated areas, and market research will henceforth become mandatory for all of my restaurant concepts. Those lessons cost me $1.2 million out of my pocket.

Points of Difference: It served health-conscious Asian fare, had tiered rows of stadium seats, gas broilers, and smoking was not allowed. Entrees were served in Japanese bento boxes. Customers ordered stir-fry and kebob entrees after looking at them in glass display cases.

Customer Bill of Rights: Customers will eat healthy food in a healthy environment. and be served quickly by a young, energetic staff. The central exhibition kitchen will serve as "truth in feeding" to diners.

1988 Romano's Macaroni Grill, Leon Springs (San Antonio), Texas

I shrugged off Stix soon after I closed it and focused on the home I was building in the Dominion neighborhood, which I would come to call the "The House That Hamburgers Built." I like to keep a keen eye on the progress of everything I create, and my custom house was no exception. Most days, I showed up at the work site and joined right in with the bricklaying, hammering, and landscaping, no doubt angering the crew and the foreman, who probably didn't see eye to eye with my idea of taking ownership in everything I do. I found myself missing my father more than usual. As work progressed, he would be telling me how well I was doing and more importantly, how well — or poorly — the construction crew was doing.

When the house was complete, my mind moved again to restaurant creation, even as friends and family were telling me I should just kick back and enjoy the fruits of my labors. Golf, painting, travel, investing, working on the new house: those would keep me busy, they said. But I wanted to keep creating.

In the fall of 1987, I pulled into an Olive Garden for lunch after hearing so much about the chain. It had gone national since its founding five years earlier and was getting a lot of buzz in the press.

But even my modest expectations went unmet. I grew up in an Italian community, and I didn't feel like I was in an Italian restaurant at Olive Garden. The place was serviceable alright, with decent entrees and service, and the unlimited salad and soup. But the food had no authenticity, and the décor was flat and generic. What's more, I looked around for the kitchen and couldn't see it. This always bothered me because I can't see how the food is prepared and who is preparing it. What's to hide, I always wonder?

Yet people were going there in droves, and there was a buzz, despite the obvious fact that this was a corporatized version of an Italian restaurant. I am an authentic Italian who already knows how to create restaurants, I thought. If Olive Garden can take this concept national, there's no limit to what I can do. It takes a real Italian to make a real Italian restaurant, and "Romano" is about as Italian as you can get.

I immediately got to thinking what my own Italian restaurant might look like and what kind of food I would serve. My mind drifted back to the kitchen table of my youth, growing up in upstate New

York. Most homes around us didn't have dining rooms, including ours, but the Romano kitchen table was extra-large and round, and often there full of family and friends sitting around it. It was a gathering place for us and a hub of animated conversation, off-color jokes, and loud arguments, with my mother's sauces and other culinary artworks being prepared just a few feet away. Everybody hung around for dinner!

My mother would drape the table with a white tablecloth and place fresh-cut flowers in the center next to a gallon jug of homemade wine that my grandfather made in the basement. We would munch on fresh-from-the-oven Italian bread and dip it in olive oil, and gorge ourselves on pasta. I fondly remember these as happy and animated gatherings with laughter and emotional outpourings, as the old family phonograph in the living room was playing Italian sonatas in the background.

If I could just project this authentic Italian experience into a restaurant and put people in the middle of a giant kitchen with a jug of wine and have them experience all those authentic tastes and smells, patrons would come back again and again.

I started putting the place together in my mind. At about the same time, I started getting curious about a little town off Interstate 10 called Leon Springs that I could see off in the distance from my picture window, set in the famous Texas Hill Country that surrounded it. One day, I exited from Interstate 10 onto Boerne Stage Road heading toward Leon Springs and then slowly drove past several little stone buildings that were sprawled out on about a half-dozen acres, with a few of them occupied. I made this drive regularly, and as time went on, I noticed that more and more traffic seemed to flow past this little town along I-10 as the area grew.

For a long time, I had a theory that a person could put a restaurant out in the middle of nowhere like this and serve outstanding food in a welcoming environment, and people would still find it (with the right amount of promotion of course). If I had to choose between a perfect location and a great concept, I'd take the great concept any day. Maybe this quiet little town, which was 10 miles northwest of San Antonio, was the right place to prove it, I thought.

There was an old dancehall there, which had been converted to a hardware store that had gone belly-up. Though it was larger than you would need for the average restaurant, I couldn't help but think what a nice building it might be for my authentic Italian restaurant. There was also a grocery store/gas station called Rudolph's. Through discrete inquiries, I found out that Rudolph's was doing about $400,000 in volume annually. There was also a vacant two-story former restaurant building that had once been a bordello. I wondered if I could get a different kind of bang for the buck out of that place. It was a quaint town, with nice buildings. Maybe I should buy one—Or two. What the hell, maybe I should buy the whole town, I thought, laughing at the idea.

I had been mulling over other ideas besides the Italian restaurant, come to think of it, including a Mexican and barbecue concept. This might just be the test lab for those, too. I got to thinking what the property was worth. It so happened that I knew the investor/realtor who owned all of the Leon Springs commercial property, and I went to him one day and asked how much he wanted—for the whole place. "The whole place?!" he asked. "The whole place," I said. He indicated it was all for sale but that he would have to think of a sales figure.

We batted some numbers back and forth for a couple weeks, and I got him down to about $600,000, though I know he had his heart set on a bigger sum. The economy was dragging in San Antonio, and a lot of businesses were going bankrupt there, so he took my offer. By buying the whole town, it would help insulate me from potential grief from inspectors, zoning snags, petty regulations, and other costly little headaches that could add up to delayed commercial projects. (But I still had to deal with accountants.)

That old fear of failure was rearing its head again. Would this same bad economy also keep people from driving way out to Leon Springs just for food? I tried to calm myself by thinking that all I really wanted out there was a decent place to dine. "If people come or don't come, then fine," I rationalized.

At the time, Olive Garden was the only national Italian chain; most Italian restaurants were still mom-and-pop restaurants. But I was determined to create a new hybrid Italian concept that the restaurant world had yet to experience, And I decided I would put it in the huge stone ex-dancehall building with the high ceilings.

I set out to create an environment where guests would feel they were eating in an Italian kitchen. Over the years, I had noticed that at most parties, people tended to congregate in the kitchen, close to the booze, watching the meal prepared. A visible kitchen would give patrons a homey feel for the place from the very start. It would also put staff on notice to keep the things clean and to look sharp. I decided to split the large, long kitchen I would build there in half so that it would be on both sides of the dining room entryway and, like in my childhood, people would be in the middle of my Italian kitchen.

The planning was nearly complete. Not including my $600,000 purchase of the town, I put another $150,000 into the place, including

$100,000 into the renovation of the aging 5,000-square-foot building, which featured massive stone walls, a huge fireplace, and exposed rafters.

Just like in my family's New York home, we put fresh flowers and a jug of wine on each table and let people drink the wine in tumblers. I also decided to do something that was unheard of in the industry. I let customers pay for the table wine on the honor system. That's right, they would tell us how much they drank. Colleagues, accountants, and others scoffed at my idea. Alan Dreeben, who headed my local liquor distributor, Block Distributing, said, "The idea is crazy—the jug is too heavy. People won't want to drink jug wine, Phil. And the honor system? You'll lose money on it."

I was not deterred. In fact, I looked back at all the things people told me not to do, as with Fuddruckers, that have turned out to be landmark ideas. Besides, I felt using the honor system for paying for the wine would make people feel more at home and maybe think they were getting one over on the system if they fudged on their estimates. It would be part of the shtick: "You trusted us to cook your food, so we trust you to tell us how many glasses of wine you drank," I would put that on the menu. Besides, with our bulk buying, we would make out very well on the table wine concept by any measure. We always knew how much wine each diner drank. And our wholesale wine costs, by the way, were only about 15 percent, I figured.

I would call my masterpiece restaurant Romano's Macaroni Grill because everybody in our Italian enclave when I was growing up used the term "macaroni" for all types of pasta. Vermicelli, penne, fettuccine—it was all macaroni to us. The Macaroni Grill format and the wine were not only a nod to my upbringing as a first-generation American Italian but also a homage to my grandparents' Sicilian home, where family and friends also shared wine, song, and spectacular Romano food.

We were trying to slowly build up to a full house, but we got slammed when we "soft opened" in April of 1988, serving 1,500 meals our first full week, which was 30 percent over our initial projections. Business was so brisk on Saturday that we ran out of food and had to close early on Sunday for the same reason. Fortunately, my mother and sister were on hand to help us with this controlled chaos, as were other relatives.

Soon after opening, I went to San Antonio's Italian-American Club to ask all of the ladies to come out for a free lunch at Romano's Macaroni Grill and to dress up a bit to celebrate. There must have been 50 of them, all dressed in their Sunday best. When they finished, we asked them to come outside for a group picture, and we used that shot in one of our very effective ads, identifying them as Italian-American Club members, saying, "Now that's Italian! They can't be wrong."

Romano's Macaroni Grill featured huge portions at medium prices; grilled meats, fresh vegetables, gourmet pizzas made with fresh tomato sauce, and other northern Italian fare, plus such appetizers as New Zealand mussels with saffron and meaty portabella mushrooms with polenta. Ironically, my mother didn't really like the cuisine at Macaroni Grill when we first opened, but we added some of her recipes and she changed her tune.

There was an elevated entrance, so when people came into the restaurant, they stood above everything and looked down on all the activity. They could see everyone enjoying themselves and all the cooking activity going on in our split giant kitchen. They also saw a long glass case displaying the day's fish, meat, and entrees on their way in.

We employed chefs, not cooks, and the wait staff wore aprons and ties. Tables came equipped with crayons, and we encouraged patrons to doodle on our butcher block paper. Servers were taught to write their names upside down to amuse guests—more shtick!

Romano's Macaroni Grill, you see, was as much a theater as it was a great eatery. Over the years, I have come to think of all my restaurants as stages: the customers and the staff are the cast, and the food is both the theme and the star of the show. All those elements have to act in concert down to the smallest detail. I intentionally had no windows at Romano's Macaroni Grill because I wanted people to have a mini-vacation from the outside world in there. If it was cold and ugly outside, it was warm and inviting inside. I created my own environments so that people could get away from their cares. Romano's Macaroni Grill was like a stage. There was action, dramatic entries, an interplay between the cast and the audience, bright colors, music, the din of happy conversation, surprises, entrances, exits, and emotion. The smiling faces were my applause.

We thrived on creativity and contrast. Our guests loved our informal elements like the bare light bulbs that we strung along the entire ceiling for an Italian courtyard effect. Walking in, customers would see these and presume the place was inexpensive. Then they'd see the tablecloths and think, "Oh, it's going to be a nice place after all." But when they realized they were walking on concrete floors, they'd think, "Well, inexpensive then." Then they'd see the flowers on the tables, and they'd think the opposite. When they got to their tables and saw the jugs of table wine and crayons on the tables, they'd think, "Or maybe not." All of this put people on a roller-coaster ride, and it served to remove any intimidation they might be feeling. We were anything but pretentious.

Because I don't like to break the mood, even when customers are using the bathroom, I had tapes of Italian conversations and Italian music playing in the men's and ladies' rooms.

Centrally located counters in the dining area displayed our specials and salads, and others were loaded with appetizers, desserts, and condiments. Just like in the Romano family kitchen, diners munched on bread that they dipped in olive oil and freshly ground pepper as they waited for their food.

It took Fuddruckers almost a year to earn the recognition and foot traffic it deserved, but it took just a few weeks for Romano's Macaroni Grill "trattoria." People came in waves. We could seat over 200 diners in our 5,000-square-foot space, but on weekends, we still had consistent hour-and-a-half waits. We didn't take reservations, but people could call ahead to get on the waiting list. Once they had driven out to Leon Springs and smelled the food, they weren't about to be put off by a long wait. To ease the wait time, I greeted them with glasses of free wine I poured from a jug, saying, "I am grateful you are here."

For most restaurants, Monday and Tuesday nights are slow, and after the initial onslaught, Romano's Macaroni Grill was no exception. However, I knew that if I advertised more, it would only create even longer waits on weekends, so I devised a scheme that would fill the place on those nights. Dinner would be free on one Monday or Tuesday night each month. That's right—free! The trick was, customers didn't know which day it would be. We rigged the telephones for most of those evenings so that nobody could call out to tip off other parties. That sort of promotion would be impossible today, of course, with everyone carrying cell phones. When you think about it, diners only had a one-in-eight chance of getting a free meal.

On the first night we did it, people had absolutely no idea it was going to happen. When they asked for the check, I gave them a letter instead. It said, "I am in the restaurant business. I really love the restaurant business. And the only thing I don't like about it is having to give you the bill. So one night of the month, either on a Monday or a Tuesday, I'm going to really enjoy myself and I won't charge anybody anything."

I said if they really liked the place, the atmosphere, and the food, would they please tell other people about it, because I think a restaurant should be talked about, not advertised. "I'd rather make you fat than the newspapers," I said. And I reminded them to be extra generous with the servers. People went nuts over this. One guy who came in with a party of 13 literally danced a jig when he found out. Some even cried. Others said they just couldn't accept what we were doing and insisted on paying. We wouldn't let them, so they left huge tips. The guy with the party of 13 came back to me several weeks later and said, "If you think your idea didn't work, you're wrong. Every one of those people from my party has come back with their families and has brought other customers in, too. We all thought that was one of the greatest things that ever happened to us at a restaurant."

Never one to waste a promotional opportunity, I had someone take my letter to the newspaper and tell one of the editors that he had dined at the restaurant and that this amazing thing had happened. The newspaper printed the entire letter, so the whole city knew about our Monday and Tuesday promotion. Customers would wonder, "Am I here on the lucky night?"

I calculated the promotion cost of this strategy to be about $1,500 the first night based upon the $5,000 in business I didn't bill. A cross-media promotional campaign would have cost me upwards of $25,000 a month, but I spent only $1,500, which won us far more business at far less cost. For our efforts, American Express awarded us for the best "Promotion of the Year," and the place was swarming on Mondays and Tuesdays. Other restaurants adopted the tactic. We did it for about six months and then just stopped it cold. No one complained. People still loved our food and the way we treated customers, so they still came. We also won the Silver Spoon award for the best restaurant in the San Antonio area in 1988 and a wall full of other awards.

We sold over $1 million in wine our first year—about a quarter of our $4 million in annual sales—and that meant that we made more than $850,000 on it. I would tell people that I didn't care if I made money on the food, because I was in the wine business. Again, if I didn't do what people had told me not to do, I wouldn't be where I am today.

Once, I hired a high school band to march into Romano's Macaroni Grill playing "The Star-Spangled Banner" and then to march out. It was quite a sight. Everybody stood up and looked surprised. We had a music student named Gina from the University of Texas at San Antonio working as a server. One night, she exercised her amazing vocal chords by singing happy birthday in operatic fashion to a customer. The whole restaurant erupted. She did the same a couple of nights later and got the same response. Wow, what a perfect complement to our theme, I thought. People love surprises. "Are there more like you at the University of Texas at San Antonio?" I asked her. "Oh yes," she said. "Well, bring them in here, and we'll make them hostesses and waitresses," I said. The resident opera singer would go on to be a staple at Romano's Macaroni Grills everywhere.

We did a promotion based on changing the menu twice a year, and it really challenged our chefs to come up with unique items. My grandpa always said that Mother Nature made certain foods and wines taste better seasonally, which makes sense since we eat heartier in the winter than in the summer, for example. He liked to compare winter wines to the robust, large-busted Sophia Loren and the summer wines to the more streamlined Audrey Hepburn, so we offered more stick-to-your-ribs fare in the winter, such as roasted meats, fowl, and spicy stews, as well as robust wines, and chicken and fish, with lighter sauces and lots of vegetables, in the summer.

How did Romano's Macaroni Grill expand nationally? That's where Norman Brinker entered the picture, or more accurately, reentered it. My sister Rosalie was working at the original Fuddruckers when the influential Mr. Norman of Chili's Inc. (which became Brinker International) came in, gave her his business card, and said, "Will you tell Philip to give me a call?" She told him that was very busy and rarely had time to return phone calls, so he angrily yanked his business card back. Rosalie didn't tell me about the visit from Norman, who had also launched Steak & Ale, for quite a while. When she did, I still didn't call him.

With Romano's Macaroni Grill putting out great numbers, I finally picked up the phone to call Norman and said in a matter-of-fact voice, "This is Phil Romano, and I'm returning your call." There was a very long pause, and then Norman said, "Damn it, Phil, that was 10 years ago!" We both had a big laugh. I went on to tell Norman that I really didn't want to call him until I had something unique to share. Then we talked about Romano's Macaroni Grill.

Norman was about ready to leave on a business trip, but he arranged to send a team down to San Antonio immediately, including Lane Cardwell, who headed strategic development, and Doug Bates, vice president of food and beverage. I sat down to dinner with them, and they tried everything on the menu. They raved about the food, the atmosphere, and the presentation. They were also intrigued to discover that our average check was $15.50 compared to $7 at their flagship Chili's at the time. They said that they'd better get Norman and another Brinker higher-up, Ron McDougall, down to Leon Springs as quickly as possible.

Norman called from the road and said that Lane was just beside himself about the concept and the sales I was posting. After his trip, Norman flew down to San Antonio with Ron. To show you how perceptive he was, after about 20 minutes, Norman asked me how we could do a deal, how much I wanted for it, and "Could you come aboard to do this with us?"

I was very much my own man. I don't wear socks, and I had a ponytail at the time. I didn't want to build a huge corporation like I did with Fuddruckers. I didn't have the stomach to go through that again. I said, "Norman, I'd come in and ruin your culture. I've never worked for anyone since I got out of college, and I and won't be able to work for you." He then asked me, "Well, why don't you come in and help us out as a consultant? We'll pay you $500,000 a year for 30 percent of your time to help make sure that Romano's Macaroni Grill is run right." I thought about it awhile and said. "Okay, I'll do it under one condition: that I can quit in 30 days or you can let me go in 30 days. Because if you're not going to listen to me, you're wasting my time and yours." So we finally agreed. We shook hands, and in 26 days, we closed the deal.

For the sake of disclosure, I did offer Romano's Macaroni Grill first to Fuddruckers, which was fair since I was still on their board when I created it. But Bill Baumhauer, their CEO, said they weren't interested.

So I sold Romano's Macaroni Grill in 1989 to Brinker for stock, valued at $15 a share at the time. Within two years, and after several stock splits, it was worth $125 a share. I made almost $30 million on the deal when I sold it off on an initial investment of $150,000. Of course, I took care of some of the people who helped me make the concept so successful.

I thought I'd just stay on with Brinker on a month-to-month basis. After the first full year I was there, I told Norman and Ron McDougal, "Okay, you understand Romano's Macaroni Grill now. I am going to go off now and do other things." They asked me what I wanted to do, and I said I wanted to create more restaurants. I told them about a different Italian concept I was working on, which would later be called Spageddies. They said they'd do it with me. I asked, "How? I am an entrepreneur. You are a big corporation."

Here's how the arrangement was going to work, we agreed: I would come up with an idea, and then Brinker would do the research to make sure it was going to fit the marketplace. We'd be 50/50 partners. Brinker would put all the money in it, but it would still be a joint venture. I had full creative and operational authority, but I also had all of their resources at my disposal: marketing, advertising, financing, and accounting. They gave me full authority, and I could hire all my own managers and other key staff and create my own culture. If I used all of their people, I told them, it would be operating like a corporation. "I will set up three Spageddies," I said. "If the first one works out, we'll open a second, and if the second one works out, we'll open a third.

After the third one, you can buy me out for stock against the earnings—a multiple. So, if the venture we do together makes $1 million and your stock is 25 times earnings, I get $25 million in stock but you own half of it, so I really get $12.5 million in stock.

After I built each concept, and they did extremely well, they said, "We want to buy it now." They did the projections this way: I would get $10 million to $15 million in stock for each concept. If the concept really worked, the stock would rise and I could sell it later on. Worried about all the stock I owned, Norman came to me one day and said, "Phil, how much stock do you have?" I said, "Norman, don't worry about it. I don't want to control a public company; I don't want your company. All I want to do is keep on doing what I am doing." He was relieved.

The stock market can be a trap for restaurant companies. I explored this topic with a long-time friend of mine, Rich Melman, who is a sharp guy and an entrepreneur in Chicago. He's the founder and chairman of Lettuce Entertain You Enterprises, which now owns about 100 restaurants nationwide, including gems like Wildfire, Mon Ami Gabi, and Cafe Ba-Ba-Reeba! We were having dinner one night in Chicago in the mid-1990s, and though Rich is very smart and creative, I remembered that he had told me that the money he was making wasn't commensurate with the effort he was putting in. At the time, he owned about 15 restaurants, all in the Chicago area. This time, Rich said he was planning on doing an IPO with his red-hot new concept, Maggiano's Little Italy. I had been through the IPO process and said, "Rich, why do you want to do that?" He said, "Well, all my guys want to grow and go public, and I told them okay." I asked him how much he was going to raise on the IPO. He said about $30 million. I responded, "Rich, you are going to blow that on your first restaurant, and then what are you going to do?"

I went on to tell him that stock analysts would enter the picture and give him high valuations. "Then you won't be able to meet those evaluations, the company stock is going to go down, and you won't be able to sell it. So, you'll have to hold it, and you're going to take a bath and you'll never make any goddamn money on it." I went on: "Rich, the only way you can really make money in the restaurant business is you have to make it in multiples and roll them out around the country. Do the same thing I do. Sell your concept to a public company, get their stock, and arrange it so that you can sell it anytime you want to." I told him my stories about Fuddruckers and Romano's Macaroni Grill. "What you ought to do is take your Maggiano's concept and sell it to Brinker. When that happens, all he will do is give you paper—it really doesn't cost the company anything, and the value of the paper is exactly what people will pay for the stock," I advised. "And you will have the ability to sell when you want. But you should stay on because your concept is good; it's going to make the stock go up, and you are going to make more money. In other words, instead of going public, jump in with a public company."

He said that he was about to go into the pre-IPO quiet time with the backers, so he was a little reluctant. But I helped set up a "clandestine" meeting with Rich and some of his people to meet Norman Brinker, Lane Cardwell, and Ron McDougal, with Brinker in a private room in the famous Water Tower Place restaurant in Chicago. They hammered out a deal that closed in August 1995, and Rich got $75 million in Brinker stock for his piece of the pie. In about six months, the stock split, and it was worth $150 million and just kept going up. I now call him "Rich Rich." Brinker made a bunch of money off Maggiano's. It's one of their best producers.

Anyway, that month-to-month relationship I entered into with Brinker, despite my own skepticism, spanned 13 years because they stayed true to their promises and let me do my thing. Today, Romano's Macaroni Grill has gotten away from some of its founding principles for the sake of cost savings and convention. The kitchen is in the back, taking some of the energy out of the place. They've added booths, and if you've been to Italy, you know that Italians don't eat Italian food in booths. The wine-display area is gone. Operatic singers are a rare sight. But patrons still walk down an elevated ramp into a bustling scene and get the feeling of instant excitement. The displays of fish and the cabinets of pasta and other foods remain. Waiters continue to write their names on the tablecloths with crayons. Those jugs of wine have been replaced by smaller bottles. And other little touches remain. But the company paid me well to forget it. And it's still a damn good meal.

Brinker sold a majority share in the chain in 2008 during the recession and sadly, its latest owners filed for Chapter 11 bankruptcy protection in late 2017, with plans to restructure its approximately 100 remaining locations. They blamed a downturn in casual dining. Before its recent troubles, Romano's Macaroni Grill's owners asked me to give a speech to a group of managers, vendors, and others affiliated with the company who were gathering for a big meeting in Denver. As I looked around, there were about 500 people in the audience who were thriving and making a good living, all because of that little place that I opened in Leon Springs. I got more satisfaction out of that than the money I had made. Of course, I can't complain about the money.

Between Romano's Macaroni Grill and my other Leon Springs concepts, I made $60 million.

Points of Difference: It was created to make guests feel like they are eating in an Italian kitchen, and customers were charged for wine consumed in jugs that were placed on each table using the honor system. Huge portions were served at medium prices, there was open seating rather than booths. A promotion offered a free dinner on one unspecified Monday or Tuesday night each month. Customers dipped the bread dipped in olive oil, menus were changed from lighter fare in the summer to heartier fare in the winter. Opera singers entertained guests.

Customer Bill or Rights: Meals will be created by chefs, not cooks. The atmosphere and presentation will be perfect. Food will be authentic Italian. Customers' visits will be mini-vacations with lots of action, bright colors, surprises, emotion, and imaginative dishes.

1989 Texas Tortilla Bakery, New York City, New York

On trips to New York City, it was a continuing source of frustration for me and other visitors, especially transplants from Southwestern states, not to be able to find quality Mexican food. One of the reasons for this was that Manhattan lacked large numbers of Mexican-born residents who might be inclined to open such businesses.

My deal with Brinker freed me up to do outside things, so I joined with one of my old high school pals, Arthur "Christy" Powers, to help address that problem and open a chain of taco restaurants in the Big Apple. This gave me the chance to do something else I'd always wanted to do: create a restaurant chain funded entirely by penny stocks. We got a New York company to do an initial public penny-stock offering (IPO) to launch a local restaurant chain that we would name Texas

Tortilla Bakery, including an option to raise an additional $3 million for expansion if we exercised our warrants.

We'd sell New Yorkers soft tacos, singly and in buckets that were similar to theater popcorn containers. Our Tex-Mex fare would be new to many New Yorkers and would be priced well below the fancier, less-savory Mexican fare that Manhattan restaurants offered. Our first restaurant was in the Wall Street area and featured visible cast-iron rotating grills and flour tortillas made from scratch. The freshly made soft tacos came in several "Texas-style" varieties, including beef fajita, chicken fajita, bean-and-cheese and sausage-and-egg. Each item cost less than $1, and the tacos could be eaten on the go or at tables just outside.

There was a struggling small chain of Mexican restaurants in town called Peso's Mexican Food. I offered its owner stock to merge his locations with mine, which would save me capital since I wouldn't have to build each restaurant from scratch in pricey Manhattan. My plan was to give away "scrip," or certificates entitling the holder to stock certificates, to my regular customers during the first six months of business, instead of free tacos. This would give them literal ownership in the taco stands and an incentive to return to them to support their investment. If they accumulated 100 certificates in that time period, they would be able to trade them in for 100 shares of Texas Tortilla Bakery penny stock.

The idea got squashed before it really got going. My underwriters told me I couldn't do that because of Securities and Exchange Commission (SEC) regulatory concerns, including the requirement that I'd have to hand out prospectuses to every one of those customers who were trying to amass certificates. *Inc.* magazine picked up the story and posed me on a Times Square street corner handing out shares. I told *Inc.* that I didn't understand the furor because I was trying to give the average guy something back at a time when so many big-time stock players were being indicted for stealing from them. It was a no-go, though.

My Wall Street stand was doing a brisk trade, so we started planning our second location and the conversion of the Peso's sites. Christy and I went back to the same underwriters to exercise our option. There was a much bigger problem than the taco-stand share issuance to customers: the underwriters were going belly up, and our second round of financing disappeared from under us. Even though the concept was working, we closed the business. It just didn't make sense to put a pile of my money into a public company.

Points of Difference: We offered stock certificates to customers. Tacos cost under $1. It featured visible cast-iron rotating grills and made-from-scratch flour tortillas. Tacos came in several varieties, including beef fajita, chicken fajita, bean-and-cheese fajita, and sausage-and-egg fajita.

Customer Bill of Rights: Customers will find our Tex-Mex fare to be cheaper and tastier than the mostly bland and expensive Mexican food that Manhattan restaurants offer. Customers will also be served quickly and efficiently to accommodate the constraints of New York lunch and rush hours.

1992 Nachomama's (Cozymel's), Leon Springs, Texas

Back in Leon Springs, a town that some of my friends (and the press) would come to call "Philville," I was devising strategic plans for some of those other small buildings. I'd thought about opening a Mexican restaurant there, although we were right in the middle of a heavily Hispanic area where there was no shortage of Tex-Mex joints.

There was, however, growth potential for authentic Mexican cuisine. While there were some of those restaurants around, most were small one-offs lacking presentation. So I started working on that "authentic" premise.

My creation would serve coastal-Mexican seafood and other authentic dishes, with some of the Tex-Mex favorites thrown in, plus a few of those zany Romano twists to give the format that "Wow Factor." I had the perfect space for the place: the sturdy old brothel building on Old Fredericksburg Road. I brought in a talented young chef named Beto Rodarte who would go on to thrive with Brinker corporate before rejoining me in a different deal 25 years later.

I had a great, funny un-P.C. name, Nachomama's. I would make the place a feast for the eyes as well as the stomach. To achieve a madcap look, we put burlap bags and billboards on the ceilings and strung empty tomato cans to serve as light covers, plus we used vibrant colors for an exotic touch. Sandbags pulled the restaurant's front door shut behind entering patrons. There were bushels of peppers and bins of onions and other produce displayed near the entryway. Rotating rotisserie chickens lined the wall of the visible kitchen. Instead of stainless steel, we used galvanized steel to give the place more of a Mexican flair.

We served our tortilla chips in hubcaps (we made our own tortillas) and offered eight kinds of nachos as well as such authentic dishes as red snapper with a sweet-chili crust, shrimp with garlic-lime butter sauce, and Mexican-style lamb shank, plus enchiladas and other mainstream Mexican favorites. Entrees came with black beans and corn instead of the standard refried beans. We also served a delicious Mexican cinnamon coffee. Another big focus was our line of frozen drinks made with real fresh fruit and mixed in colorful machines. Research showed that frozen alcoholic drinks with funny names are the most inoffensive alcoholic beverages people can order in front of their families.

Most of the staff was either of Mexican descent or took Spanish in high school, so I asked them all to approach the tables speaking Spanish, removing one potential barrier. If customers didn't understand them, they could just speak English.

We opened in April of 1992 with fun-loving crowds and flattering reviews. The place had a humorous vibe, with off-color signs hanging over the bar, including "No Farting Allowed," and signs over the urinals that said, "Piss on Drugs." There was a dressed male mannequin in the ladies room that would often become unclad by the end of the night with plenty of strategic lipstick prints. At a time when designated drivers were coming into fashion, a crazy friend of mine approached two slightly inebriated women at the bar and asked, "Excuse me ladies, do you have a designated fucker?"

Brinker execs cast a keen eye on Nachomama's and liked what they saw. They bought it for stock and ended up building slightly toned-down versions of it in the Dallas area. We renamed it the more P.C. Cozymel's. We even manufactured a little folktale for it that read, "Once upon a time, two guys had a grocery store in Cozumel, Mexico. They sold a lot of groceries. Then they began to make meals, and soon they were in the restaurant business. They moved to the states and wanted to have the same kind of place they had in Cozumel, but they got the name wrong and now they call it Cozymel's Coastal Mex. "

Most of the original Nachomama's theme was kept intact in the rollout, including the splashes of color. The first Dallas-area Cozymel's had twenty-nine different hues of paint, and its walls and floors were covered with weather-aged planks from an old, second-hand lumberyard. The restaurants took off.

But at about the same time that Brinker was building Cozymel's restaurants in their various locations, he acquired the struggling On the Border chain. Suddenly, Brinker had 20 On the Border restaurants, plus a distinctly different Cozymel's Mexican concept. Oddly, he put the same guy, John Miller, in charge of both of them. Usually when a man has two mistresses, one is going to get more attention than the other. So Miller developed On the Border twice as fast. Brinker eventually decided to operate Cozymel's as the higher-end Mexican concept and gave it an even stronger seafood focus.

In early 2004, a firm called Food, Friends and Company, bought Cozymel's from Brinker. The chain, though small, lives on today. I would eventually get $7 million for the stock I received from Brinker for the concept, and that's not a bad pay day.

Points of Difference: There were touches of irreverent humor, frozen drinks made with fresh fruit and poured from colorful machines, an open kitchen, bushels of produce displayed near the entryway, and rotating rotisserie chickens lining the kitchen walls.

Customer Bill of Rights: Customers will be served authentic coastal-Mexican food in a colorful, fun environment. Servers will speak Spanish and English.

1992 Rudy's Country Store and Bar-B-Q, Leon Springs (San Antonio), Texas

Do you recall the Rudolph's gas station/country store in Leon Springs that was doing about $400,000 in annual sales I mentioned earlier?

The place also came with my package purchase of the town's commercial properties. With my other ventures rolling out, the gas station/country store became the next target of my active promotional mind.

Since Rudolph's, founded by Rudolph (Rudy) Aue, was literally next door to the Leon Springs Volunteer Fire Department, we posted signs noting that we were going to give a percentage of every sale to the fire department. It seemed as though everybody in the surrounding community responded, coming out to buy gas, snacks, and sundries, and they felt good to be pitching in. We ended up raising enough to buy a "jaws-of-life" tool for the fire station. We also bought a giant popcorn machine and displayed it in the front window, offering free popcorn to all our patrons. Awareness of the store was slowly increasing, as were sales. But I'm a restaurant guy at heart, so I started seeking a food solution for our fair-to-middling revenue at the place. What if we put a barbecue pit on the outside of the place, I wondered? Texas is known for its barbecue as much as for its Mexican food. I could sell barbecue at the store and maybe attach a barbecue joint to it without much of a problem, zoning or otherwise. But I'd have to serve barbecue with a point of difference to make the operation stand out above the rest.

So I hit the road in my quest for the best barbecue, driving the Texas highways and byways for weeks. The parts of central Texas that were settled by Germans seemed to have distinctive and consistently delicious ways of cooking meat, including barbecue joints around such towns as New Braunfels and San Marcos.

But the best I found was in Lockhart, Texas, about 25 miles south of Austin, operated by a humble local German family. Their meats, which were fall-apart tender, were cooked with oak instead of the industry-favored mesquite. Everything I tasted there was incredible, and that's not a word I throw around much. Impressed, I offered the owners a partnership if they'd like to come to Leon Springs to help us open a similar operation. They said no thanks; they were content where they were, but they'd be glad to show us how they cooked their barbecue. Not only did they do that, but they also gave me permission to copy their custom pit cooker, and they wouldn't accept a thing in return for it.

As we worked to accurately mimic that barbecue formula, we built an addition onto Rudolph's and shortened the name to Rudy's. In August of 1992, Rudy's Country Store and Bar-B-Q made its debut, ahead of the curve of all those cobranded restaurant-convenience store combos we see everywhere today.

In the Rudy's cooking system, the fire was built in an outside chamber and the heat slowly and evenly cooked the meat, which was placed on grills inside a giant walk-in cooker. Other cooking processes tend to dry out meat, but our meat was perfectly cooked and juicy, facilitated by the slow-burning oak wood. Instead of cooking the sauce into the meats, we treated ours with a dry seasoning rub and then slowly smoked it in the wood-stoked pit. We cooked brisket for 8 to 10 hours and the other meats for about 3 to 4 hours.

We offered a wide selection, including brisket, baby-back pork ribs, chicken, sausage, turkey, chopped beef, pork, and even prime rib. To my knowledge, there wasn't a place around where you could buy prime rib for $7.95 a pound, and it became a hot item. Patrons ranged from doctors to construction workers to truckers, vacationers, stay-at-home moms, and corporate executives who would drive all the way to Leon Springs from San Antonio to feast on our distinctive product.

People could buy the meats by the pound or in smaller increments. The place was self-service like a butcher shop, and all the meats were sliced to order and served atop butcher paper, accompanied by white bread, chips, fresh onions and tomatoes, with soda, ice tea, and cold beer available. We would later add creamed corn and other sides plus peach cobbler.

The place was operated by a passionate forty-ish African-American named Mack "Doc" Holiday Jr., who also ran the grocery portion of the store and was a friend to all. He honed his culinary skills by cooking meals en masse for hunting groups at a local ranch. Though we didn't want to make it a "sauce place" because the meat was our specialty, we sampled Doc's personal brand, patterned after his mother's zesty recipe, and decided we couldn't afford not to use it. The sauce, which we spelled "sause," quickly became legendary, and we shipped cases of it all over the world, though with a strong caution on the label: "Do not use during sex. Use before or after."

Texans can be a boastful bunch, and every barbecue joint in the state claim it has "the best barbecue in Texas." So we jokingly billed ours as "the worst barbecue in Texas." Customers got the joke, and they loved the product. The Rudy's environment had a nostalgic feel to it, with old road signs and ads and funny signs. One read, "You can't beat our meat."

The barbecue business not only fulfilled my goal of beefing up sales at the gas station property but also became a local staple, mostly by word of mouth. It also tripled our gas sales. Our team took the Rudy's concept to Houston, Dallas, Austin, and Albuquerque and a few other places, gas pumps included.

"Doc" ran the original Rudy's until his death at 58 in 2007. There's a plaque in the place that reads, "Doc put his own unique touch into an existing neighborhood general store and gas station called 'Rudolph's' and helped to create a true 'Barbecue Joint' like the roadside barbecue stands he used to frequent as a kid. He believed that good barbecue is a celebration, especially when it is shared with family and friends. Doc always had a smile for everyone, and his hospitality served as a role model for all of us. Doc will be missed but not forgotten by all those he touched through his words and barbecue."

Now, Doc's old haunt has to be doing at least $6 million in annual sales. We eventually sold Rudy's to Creed Ford, the former Brinker COO, and his wife, Lynn. It now has various franchise owners and is doing well with about 45 locations in Texas, Colorado, Oklahoma, Arizona, and New Mexico, with more planned.

Points of Difference: We added barbecue and seating to an old country store and gas station in order to beef up revenue. We used a slow-burning oak wood, treated meats with a dry seasoning rub, and then slowly smoked them in a wood-stoked pit. We offered prime rib by the pound in addition to brisket, baby-back pork ribs, chicken, sausage, turkey, chopped beef, and pork.

Customer Bill of Rights: The Texas-style barbecue will be made using the best recipes and cooking processes in Texas. Meat will retain its juiciness because it will be slow-cooked. The savory sauce, which comes from the founding manager's personal family recipe, is unlike any other.

1992 Spageddies Italian Italian Food, Plano, Texas

The success of Romano's Macaroni Grill concept prompted Brinker to try out a new Italian creation of mine, a family-oriented Italian eatery with a price point that was one rung above Spaghetti Warehouse and one rung below Olive Garden, the chain we hoped to flank with both of our Italian concepts. We settled on a test location in Plano, northeast of Dallas, and introduced Spageddies Italian Italian Food in July of 1992.

The prototype seated 216 people and featured an exhibition kitchen, bright décor, colorful miniature billboards, decorative canned goods, and a pair of bocce ball courts to keep customers and their kids amused while they waited for seats or their orders. We baked the bread in-house, and the first loaf was always free to customers; they could also take one home for 50 cents. Salads and soups were sold at our cost—about 25 cents each—when served with an entree.

We had huge wine casks on-site to fill the wine bottles that the wait staff took to the tables. There were checkered tablecloths, and kids were given fake mustaches that the waiters and waitresses wore. We were the first restaurants to "tag" our first-time guests, as churches do, singling them out for special treatment. A big yellow flag was placed at their tables. The manager would personally greet the new guests, and the wait staff would stand before the tables and introduce the new guests to the other diners and then spend a little extra time with them explaining the menu. New customers seemed to appreciate those added touches and efforts, and they made it a point to tell their friends.

I loved the concept, and the food was economically priced, but a couple of problems cropped up. Instead of the parents bringing their kids, the kids were, in effect, bringing their parents. That is, we had turned into a babysitter of sorts. Our clientele was almost all families, at the exclusion of solo couples and singles, and we were starting to compete with sales of Macaroni Grill. Upgrading would have made the problem even more acute, I thought. So I sold it outright to Brinker for about $6 million in stock, and Brinker rolled it out. I eventually sold that stock for about $15 million. Brinker franchised Spageddies and took it to the Pacific Rim, and then later sold it to the couple who bought my Rudy's concept, Creed and Lynn Ford.

Spageddies was the forerunner of Johnny Carino's Italian Kitchen, which has about 80 locations across the United States and Middle East. There are still a few Spageddies around, including a location in Lafayette, Indiana.

Points of Difference: This was a family-oriented restaurant with an exhibition kitchen and bocce ball courts to keep customers and their children amused while waiting for their seats and their food. The first loaf of fresh-baked bread was free to customers. Salads and soups were sold at cost when they served with an entree.

Customer Bill of Rights: Children will be welcomed and treated as valued customers. First-time guests will be flagged for special treatment. Our prices will be more affordable than most Italian chains.

1995 Rosalie's Cucina, Skaneateles, New York

My baby sister Rosalie, who was three years younger than me, helped me launch many of my restaurant creations, including Romano's Macaroni Grill and Fuddruckers, serving at the latter as a regional supervisor for years. She was a tough, hard-working woman who basically raised three kids by herself after a divorce.

Rosalie had semiretired to the Auburn, New York, area where we had grown up and where I still keep a summer house in neighboring Skaneateles. In 1994, Rosalie asked if I would build her a restaurant that she would run, and I was more than happy to oblige her. Besides, I wanted a nice Italian place to eat when I was in town. The site, on Genesee Street, was a former retail store that I wanted to convert to a quaint country-style Italian restaurant called Rosalie's Cucina. I would first need a zoning variance.

The building sat next door to a gift shop called Chestnut Cottage, a place I was sure would benefit from the added traffic, but its owner saw it differently and started a campaign against my pending restaurant. I had already bought the building and wanted to start work right away, but the gift shop's owner succeeded in bogging down the case. He wrote angry letters to the local paper and appeared before the zoning board, claiming Rosalie's Cucina would attract rats, noise, traffic, and other negative things. I tried to assure him and the zoning officials that the place would be nothing but a class act and that we'd go out of our way to respect everybody's space. But he persisted.

Meanwhile, I found a better location further down Genesee Street with clear zoning and no issues with the merchants. However, I still owned the other building and thought I might as well open my own little gift shop to compete directly with Chestnut Cottage, so I did. I even put up a sign that said, "Country Store and More. Cheaper than the guy next door." I first had to get the sign approved, but the zoning board chairman flat out told me that the board wasn't going to approve it. "But it meets architectural standards," I said. "It meets color standards. It meets size standards. My business meets all of your other city standards. What don't you like about it?" The board chairman replied,

"We just don't like what the sign says." Angry, I replied, "I thought I saw an American flag out front when I came in here today. I thought this was the United States of America and that we abide by the U.S. Constitution. You're abridging my First Amendment rights of free speech." One of the ladies on the board stood up at that point and blurted out, "The Constitution of America doesn't count in this town, Mr. Romano!" Flabbergasted, I pointed over at the city attorney and asked, "Is that on the record?" He said, "No, no, it's not on the record. Go ahead and put up your sign."

My sign went up, and the controversy resulting from it was the talk of the town. Residents thought it was hilarious, but not the owner of Chestnut Cottage. Instead of a top-flight restaurant as a neighbor, he suddenly had a hostile competitor. I kept my shop open about a year and took a lot of his business away before finally selling it. After that, it served as a competing gift shop to the guy for more than a decade.

I began retrofitting Rosalie's Cucina into the location, and all systems were go when disaster struck. Rosalie had taken ill and was diagnosed with lung cancer. We were devastated. I asked, "Rosalie, do you still want me to open the restaurant? I can just give you the money, and you can live happily ever after." She said, "No, please build the restaurant, Phil. It will give me something to do and keep my mind off things." So, with a heavy heart, I proceeded with Rosalie's Cucina, all the more determined to make it a thing of beauty, just like my sister.

Based on what I saw in my travels through Italy, I would build Rosalie's Cucina from the perspective of the patron. The same talented young architect who had worked on my home in Skaneateles, Andy Ramsgard, designed the place. I saw great things in Andy. He had a master's degree in architecture from the University of New York in

Buffalo and is exceptionally bright. I told him, "I'll make a deal with you. I'll give you your first solo job, and I'll even help you on the project. But there's time pressure. I need you to finish this in four months. Also, I'll give you twice as much money—that's $40,000—than you'd make in a year working for the architecture firm you are with. And I'll try to find you more business. (I did.) But you've also got to promise me that you're going to go into business for yourself." He agreed.

Andy finished on time, did a fantastic job, and fulfilled his promises. He's now a top-flight architect and a designer of buildings and high-end custom furniture. His work has been featured in movies and on the old "Queer Eye for the Straight Guy" TV show, among other programs. He's won numerous national and international awards for his imaginative work with hotels, nightclubs, casinos, and other businesses.

Rosalie's Cucina seats 120 people, has an open kitchen, an intimate downstairs wine cellar, an upstairs Romano Room for private parties, a bakery, an outdoor bocce court, a wood-burning fireplace, and a Mediterranean-style courtyard with a vineyard and vegetable and herb gardens.

Before its opening, we arranged for some prominent locals to throw dinner parties for 8 to 12 people at their homes, with our chef bringing the food in and doing all the cooking which was a twist on the old preview-party idea that I used with earlier concepts. We'd show up with servers, offer the attendees appetizers, and pour some of the wines we planned to serve at the restaurant. We did that three or four times a week with different people, and suddenly we had all of these folks taking ownership in Rosalie's Cucina who couldn't wait for it to open. Before we opened, we served about 400 meals. I liked to say they were pissing out of my tent instead of in it.

We opened around Thanksgiving of 1995 in our beautiful salmon-colored building, specializing in country-style Italian cuisine. Italian music played in the parking lot as patrons walked to the entrance. Chefs cooked in a framework of hanging garlic ropes and other bountiful ingredients as chickens roasted on the visible rotisserie. Our bakery, Crustellini's, produced the pastries and breads that we served as well as such confections as tiramisu, cannoli, and biscotti.

Several varieties of sensational goodies were also sold. It wasn't long before Rosalie's Cucina was packing in the diners, with our bocce court, wine cellar, and courtyard all serving as "holding areas." We served bread, cheese and olives to the customers to make their waiting for a table more tolerable. Rosalie came in most nights to serve as hostess, which helped her forget her discomfort for a while. The walls were filled with signatures of customers who had donated $25 in Rosalie's name to the Make a Wish Foundation. There's not an open space on the wall today.

There were a lot of professionals living in the area who took pride in their knowledge of wines. They loved us because I didn't mark up my wines the standard 300 percent when we opened. All I cared about was making about $10 for every bottle we sold. I'd buy an $80 bottle and sell it for $90, for example. People knew the prices were well under market and would often buy three bottles per table because of the bargain. The way I saw it, it was like getting a $30 cover charge per table. Early on, I knew the customers appreciated the wines because they were buying brand wines. But they didn't know my food yet. With the wine prices, patrons were more than glad to pay full market price for entrees, which we served in huge portions. After they became familiar with my food and loved it, then I increased the prices of my wines. First the wine was bringing them in, and then my food was.

Rosalie, who was three years younger than me, died of cancer less than a year after we opened the restaurant. Rosalie was cremated and we buried her under her favorite tree in the back of the restaurant property where there is a grave marker for her. To this day, the place is a homage to Rosalie. There's a plaque on the wall from me that says, "Built for my sister with love…and with way too much money." (About $1.5 million to be exact). But it was worth every penny.

In 1999, I structured a deal to allow a talented young entrepreneur, Gary Robinson, to buy out Rosalie's Cucina. Gary was a teacher at the local high school, and when I first came to town, I hired him to teach the restaurant's operations manual to employees. He did a great job. After Rosalie died, I needed someone to operate the place, and Gary told me he would gladly quit his job at the school and operate the restaurant for me, and he did. Gary did a great job, was very conscientious, and kept the place the same. After a while, I said, "Okay, Gary, go to the bank and get this thing financed, and it's yours. You can buy it from me. Just give me the money I've got in it." The bank loaned him the money. I had paid cash for everything, so there was no lingering debt. Now Gary runs it and is doing well with it. I couldn't do a better job myself. He remains true to the concept, and the restaurant remains a great attraction for the town of Skaneateles. I dine there when I'm in town, and I still feel Rosalie's presence.

Points of Difference: There was an Open kitchen, bakery, intimate downstairs wine cellar, outdoor bocce court, wood-burning fireplace, and Mediterranean-style courtyard, with a vineyard and vegetable and herb gardens. We sold wine well under the market price at a profit of just $10 a bottle. Waiting patrons were served bread, cheese, and olives to make their wait more tolerable.

Customer Bill of Rights: The restaurant will be built from the customer's perspective. Food will be authentic Italian, the service will be attentive, and the wine list will be extensive. The restaurant will be a consistent and enduring amenity for the community and a lasting legacy to my sister, who passed away soon after the restaurant opened.

Chapter

5

ROMANO CONCEPTS (1996–2018): From Eatzi's to Saint Rocco's New York Italian

I don't want employees to work for me; I want them to work with me. If you want everybody to be just like you, they'll limit themselves to thinking only like you.

1996 Eatzi's, Dallas, Texas

In 1994, Brinker came to me and told me that he wanted to get into the home-meal replacement segment of the food industry, which was really taking off at the time, so I got a team together for some fact-finding and creative input. There was a sharp Cornell graduate by the name of Tori Rogers, who I recruited for Brinker, plus a chef, a designer and a builder. We went to work.

I sensed the timing was right for this because, at about the same time, I noticed a growing number of customers who wanted to buy their meals to from full-service restaurants. The customers would have to stand at the bar waiting for their food, most of which really wasn't intended for takeout. This created distractions for the staff and a disruption in the work flow. It also meant that those customers would be getting less-than-perfect versions of their entrees, since the food usually had to be reheated by the time they got it home.

It struck me that there were really no eating places where people who were pressed for time could get a full line of quality food to take home. Delicatessens were limited in what they offered, and fast-food places didn't offer much in consistency, palatability, or nourishment. Yet, meal preparation was the last thing on the minds of exhausted and stressed-out people, who were cooking less but still desired quality meals. Dining out was time-consuming and wasn't always affordable, plus it could be too difficult for families with young children. Just as it was a big treat for me to go out to eat when I was a kid, it's now a treat to eat quality food at home. People are cooking less and less. So there was an obvious niche to be filled, and one of my favorite pastimes is matching a solution with a problem.

What was needed was a hybrid: the best of all dining, grocery, and take-out approaches, I thought. So, to get a cross-representation of ideas, the team and I traveled to 20 different places around the world that were addressing this segment of the market. On our tour, we visited the renowned Balducci's and Dean & DeLuca, both in New York City. We stopped in mom-and-pop bakeries, stand-alone delis, corner markets that served take-home food, and sandwich shops. We visited Harry's in a Hurry in Atlanta and Marty's gourmet shop and liquor store in Dallas, not far from Brinker corporate headquarters. We looked at everything, not to copy it, but as guideposts to make our concept different.

We also traveled to London to visit the famous Harrods food hall, which had been around for over a century. We gained a lot of knowledge—and a few pounds—in our quest. As good as these places were, however, none of them really pulled it all together. My fellow travelers and I returned to join a group of restaurant, marketing, operations, and grocery people to share our research and photos, and to brainstorm about how we could address this emerging market.

I wanted our creation to have the feel of a great European marketplace, with opera, classical music, and concrete floors. It should let people know we were thinking foremost about food, not décor, because the food itself was going to serve as the real décor. It would be the boldest creation yet in my career and would incorporate the combination of all of my talents, tastes, and experiences: a cross between a deli, a kitchen, a pantry, a home-meal-replacement restaurant, and an upscale gourmet grocer, with gourmet-quality restaurant food.

At a grocery store, people shop with a list and are usually just buying brands off the shelf. At a restaurant, people "shop" with a menu. At our new hybrid eatery , we wanted people to shop with emotion and impulse. A grocery store might have a couple of cooks, but we'd have real chefs—dozens of them. We'd make each shopping experience a fun-filled 15 to 30 minutes.

In a grocery store, 95 percent of what shoppers buy has been manufactured elsewhere, dampening quality control. We planned to manufacture 80 percent of our offerings. We'd put people in a world of food and beverage. The customer would walk through the kitchen, which would create confidence in our manufacturing process. Our shop would be a category of its own—a new brand. It would be the customers' personal chef for an endless variety of ready-to-heat meals that they could pick up on their way home; it would be the next generation of America's home-meal replacement industry. The term "home-meal replacement" is a misnomer. We were creating a category: restaurant-meal replacement.

We would have a wide variety of price points to appeal to a broad spectrum of groups, from budget-minded apartment dwellers to the affluent. About 80 percent of our dishes would be comfort food, and the other 20 percent would be food that most patrons had never had before: up to 1,500 different food items in total. Customers could see them, smell them, and sample them. Hundreds of items would be made fresh daily. Our prices would be cheaper than restaurants and more expensive than supermarkets. We wanted to be the epicenter of food in the community. But, unlike restaurants, we wouldn't be turning over seats; we'd be turning over parking spaces.

The naming of a new eatery at Brinker corporate headquarters is a drawn-out process. The concept creator and the creative team come up with a list of about 100 possible names that they'll splash on an office wall. During our first naming meeting, four of us would each pick five names of those suggested by staffers that didn't belong. We would do the same with the second and third meetings. Some of the rejected names for the concept included "Chef a Go Go" and "Yumbo."

The name we chose, Eatzi's seemed to say a lot and was a nearly unanimous choice. Our affinity for "eat" is self-explanatory, and we liked the "Zi's" on the end because of its Italian flair. We finalized that moniker to "Eatzi's Market & Bakery," with a slogan following the name, "Meals for the Taking."

Eatzi's started out as a 50–50 ownership, split between me and Brinker. As we were building our first Eatzi's, Norman Brinker would drive down on I-635 from his offices to check the progress. We were going to offer 1,500 fresh products per day, which was daunting. "I don't know about this, Phil," Norman would say, and I'd reply, "Me neither, Norman. If it works, it's going to go crazy, but if it doesn't, we'll have spent some serious R & D money on it." Whatever would happen, I did know the place was still going to look great. I thought of the saying, "If I'm gonna pull my pants down, at least I want my rear end to look good."

The first Eatzi's went into a relatively compact 8,500-square-foot building at 3403 Oak Lawn Avenue at Lemmon Avenue in Dallas. To the west is the upscale Highland Park, to the east is an affluent gay community, to the south is the downtown area, and to the north is more upscale housing.

We opened in January 1996 and hit the ground sprinting, doing twice the volume we had originally anticipated. We were relieved! The parking lot was jammed. People came into Eatzi's on their way home from work, and the first thing they saw was a lot of action and the food, and they were reenergized. The press was calling it "The Disneyland of Food" in a "Willy Wonka-like atmosphere for grownups." The *Dallas Observer* said it was "A farmer's market, a deli, and a football bowl game halftime show all rolled into one.…" Another journalist wrote, "What the Colonel is to fried chicken, Phil Romano is to Eatzi's." A *New York Times* writer described Eatzi's as "the food store that ate Dallas." The *Dallas Morning News* even wrote an editorial praising Eatzi's. Women were coming up to me at Eatzi's and saying, "Phil, I'd like to kiss you. I'll never have to cook again," while guys were coming up to me and saying, "Wow, Phil, I'll never have to get married again." It's funny. We had single young women coming in Eatzi's looking for single men buying single meals, and vice-versa.

An interesting side note: a friend of mine, then the CEO of the Texas-based HEB (Howard E. Butt) grocery chain, James "Fully" Clingman, called me up in 1994 and wanted me to come look at a new grocery concept, HEB Central Market, which he had just opened in Austin. He wanted a restaurateur's view of what was going on there. He had his own plane and met me in Dallas. We took a look at it. It had a European bakery, a deli with meats and cheeses from around the globe, juice and ice cream bars, lot of high-quality foodstuffs, and a huge selection of wine, as well as some of the more common commodity grocery items. I gave him my opinions and ideas about improving it, some of which he would go on to adopt.

When Eatzi's opened about a year later, I asked him to return the favor and come up to Dallas and critique my new concept. I explained that Eatzi's was not really a grocery store but more of a market, and I was wondering if I should have grocery store people or restaurant operators run it. When Fully got there, he stepped through the door and he exclaimed, "Son of a bitch, Phil. You did it! You created the thing my industry needed so badly. You took all of the bullshit out of it, all of the toilet paper and the canned goods and the like." As he walked around, he said, "You got it—you got it! This place is going to do fantastic." After a while I asked him, "How much business are we going to do here?" He guessed about $125,000 week. I said. "Oh, wow, that's good, because I figured we would do about $80,000 or $90,000 a week." He said, "No, no. A lot more than that."

About a month passed, and I called him back and said, "Fully, you've been sandbagging me; you're lyin' to me." Surprised, he asked what I meant by that. "We are doing $250,000 a week," I told him. He said, "Holy shit!" Fully said he would like to bring Howard Butt

Jr., one of the sons of the company founder, to see Eatzi's if I didn't mind. I said sure. Howard, a friendly, creative, and folksy kind of guy who liked to write poetry, came in and politely asked me if I minded if he hung around. I didn't mind one bit, I told him. Howard lingered quite a while. Afterwards, in his correspondence with me, he wrote poetically, especially about Eatzi's. After a while, the HEB folks asked me if I wanted to do a joint venture with them that incorporated some of Eatzi's elements, but I put them off because I didn't know exactly what we were yet.

To help determine our identity, we did several focus groups with Price Waterhouse. We learned that we were unique and convenient, that we had a food culture, not a shelf mentality, and that we were considered an epicenter of food. From these sessions and from experience in our early operations, we realized that we should hire restaurant operators instead of grocery people. The grocery industry had shelves, sold brands, and let those brands and labels sell their product. Our concept had people who were making and selling our products.

We also concluded from our research that if I put this concept in grocery stores, the perception would be that the stores were taking food that was going bad, cooking it, and selling it to the customer. That's not what we were about. It would be the kiss of death to put this in grocery stores.

The grocery industry was intrigued by what we were doing and asked me to sit on panels at industry conventions. At one convention, I noticed all the other panelists were dressed in fancy double-breasted suits, projecting a stiff, holier-than-thou attitude. There I was with my sports jacket, a wild-looking tie, and no socks. I got up, gestured to the panel, and cavalierly said, "Look what's happening. I am a fresh breath of air. Look at my tie, look at theirs. They wear suits and socks, I don't. I am new and different. Your business is tired; it's old. You've been doing the same thing in your business for years and years and years. Mine is unique and exciting. I am taking the best things you've got and selling them in a fresh new format, making meals more convenient. People in Eatzi's can see our products made as they walk in and through my kitchens. I am not just telling them about my food. I am showing them."

A little brash? Sure it was. They looked a little shocked, but I was just trying to wake up the industry. How did they respond? They started trying to copy me. They put up diluted versions of Eatzi's with exhibition kitchens inside their stores, but they also made it inconvenient in the process.

People don't want to go into a grocery store, buy a lot of good hot food, and then walk through the whole maze and pile up all of the groceries they need on top of it. It's like the mentality of putting the pharmacy in the back of the store so that people will have to go through and buy other things. What they should have done is put these outside their stores on the corners of their lots so that people could easily pull in and buy these products and not have to navigate the aisles. They didn't get it, and they still don't.

It took seven months to get Eatzi's into the black. The food costs and the complexity were almost overwhelming. We had been oblivious to our start-up expenses to get it running. That's how I operate, and that always makes my accountants shudder. We projected that our first Eatzi's would serve about 1,000 customers a day, but it averaged more than twice that, translating into $16 million in annual sales.

In the summer of 1997, we opened our second Eatzi's, at the intersection of San Felipe Street and Post Oak Boulevard in Houston. Each store cost between $4 million and $5 million to build, nearly three times the Brinker average for each Chili's restaurant. Labor costs were nearly 25 percent of total expenses. Each store had up to 140 workers, including 20 to 40 chefs and cooks, 10 pastry chefs, 10 bakers, a general manager, three managers, and 80 or so other support people.

Our overhead was high, and profit margins were only around 15 percent, several percentage points below Brinker restaurant averages. We did five times the volume of an average Chili's. We'd do more than $100,000 on weekend days in Dallas. We had tour buses full of awestricken French and Japanese tourists coming to our locations. A Japanese publisher even did a book on me (in Japanese), focusing on Eatzi's, called *The Eatzi's Way*. It consisted mostly of verbatim interviews. And I mean verbatim. Every time I cleared my throat, they printed "Huhhuhhuhhum. Huhhuhhuhhum."

Walking through the entrance of Eatzi's is like entering a quaint old grocery store, although that's where the similarities end. The first one-third of the restaurant is a full-display manufacturing area, populated by a sea of chefs in traditional white chef hats. Customers instantly smell freshly cooked meals and two dozen different freshly baked breads. The clanging of kettles and the cries of the chefs calling out "Hot bread, fresh out of the oven!" or "Soup's on!" add to the atmosphere. The centrally located Chefs' Case has 50 different platters of food that change throughout the day and a deluxe cold pasta station. Eatzi's menus can change up to 25 percent from day to day. A refrigerated case chills a variety of specialty beers, and signs encourage customers to mix-and-match their own six-pack. Sandwiches are elevated to an art form. People were actually telling me the food was "too cheap."

There's a lush produce stand, where our own chefs "shop" to gather ingredients. People see this and realize that everything that the chefs use is also available to them. There are made-to-order salads and a dozen other food stations that are jam-packed with visual appeal and unending assortments of top-of-the-line products. Chefs and assistants are at the customers' service to dish out fresh meats, poultry, and vegetables from their pans into the customers' take-home plates. There are plastic boats of sushi, bone-in rib-eye steaks, honey-soy flank satay, poached raspberry salmon, lemon-grilled shrimp, and hundreds of other items, including box lunches. It's the "Wow factor" multiplied by 1,000.

There are funny little signs throughout the display floor that are designed to help keep things light. One of the earlier ones read: "The only way to get a better piece of chicken is to be a rooster." We carry a huge assortment of international wines to go with the meals. The food sells the wine, and vice versa. It's a huge component. Connoisseurs shop Eatzi's for wines they can't find elsewhere in town. We averaged well over $1 million a year in wine sales alone at that first Dallas location.

One of the tricks we've perfected is cooking our food until it's only about 85 percent to 90 percent done. If it were fully cooked, then it would be overcooked after the customers heated it at home. Though we were selling mostly take-home restaurant meals, there was some outdoor and indoor seating, predominantly for lunch-hour crowds. Eatzi's is built with inner and outer "race-track" loops so that diners can make an easy sweep through the store if they've come only for the convenience of buying a take-home meal. At 9 P.M., a red light comes on, and all of the prepared food is sold at half the price.

We opened additional stores in Atlanta, Georgia; Rockville, Maryland; and in the basement of the famous Macy's Herald Square department store in Manhattan, plus on Long Island in Westbury, New York—all choices highly favored by Lane Cardwell, who was CEO of Eatzi's and one of those Brinker folks whom I first wowed with my Romano's Macaroni Grill concept.

But New York City is also where Lane, Eatzi's, and I got into some trouble. Stores in Dallas, Houston, and Atlanta were doing well. The problem with the New York City location was you that we couldn't sell wine and liquor in grocery stores, which was what New York City considered Eatzi's to be. Because food and wine sales drive each other, I told Lane when he was convincing the board to do the Macy's location that we would compromise our concept if we couldn't sell wine and liquor. I told him also that we would have limited visibility and be opening in someone else's core concept. But Lane signed the deal there anyway, and we basically had to open a second New York location, on Long Island, for market penetration.

The Macy's store opened to much fanfare and crowds, and while it did bring in a large volume of customers, the customers were trying to eat at a relatively limited number of tables. They weren't taking the food home. That was a disturbing development, because we wanted them to fill their baskets at Eatzi's, not their bellies. We weren't in a heavy residential area either, which was another negative. We did a great lunch business, but people weren't coming by to grab dinner to take home at night. We belatedly discovered that New Yorkers prefer to return home to their neighborhoods and then shop for dinner. They typically don't carry food with them on the subway or the bus, because it might get crushed and it might be tough to hold standing up, or it might weigh them down if they had a long walk home from their subway stop. It was a poor premarketing mistake and a lack of understanding of our customers' traits and indigenous habits.

As the months went by, Dallas, Houston, Rockville, and Atlanta Eatzi's were all averaging $250,000-plus a week, but we couldn't get our Long Island store in Westbury to top $100,000 a week. We weren't convenient to motorists, and they didn't want to fight the traffic to get there. Also, we weren't allowed to sell wine there either.

It was obvious that Eatzi's was going in the wrong direction; we made a $15-million mistake going to New York and had to close both stores there. In the summer of 1999, Brinker let Lane and both the Eatzi's COO and CFO go. Lane had done good things but had fallen in love with my concept and thought it could work anywhere. His confidence in it made it difficult for me to be upset with him. Lane left Brinker and went on to serve on corporate boards and enjoy life a little more. But we all had a loud wake-up call, and it forced us, as the saying goes, to put on our britches the right way.

I went on to buy 80 percent of Eatzi's common stock and took over as CEO, meaning Brinker would no longer be involved in the Eatzi's decision making. My job was to stabilize the brand and come up with a new strategy, which later would include creating smaller restaurants that would feed off a central locale.

In late 2002, I partnered with a venture capital group from Newton, Massachusetts, called Castanea Partners, to buy out Eatzi's from Brinker, effectively ending my 13-year association with his Dallas company. My Brinker relationship had been fruitful, but I knew going in that being part of a huge public company like Brinker would eventually go against my grain.

Castanea was a good company, it seemed. They came from a family that owned Neiman Marcus and Kate Spade, and they knew how to create brands. When I sold Eatzi's to them, they wanted me to stay on the board, which was a good sign, so I did, retaining a 20 percent ownership. I also put $2 million more into the concept because it was a good one.

The first thing Castanea did was to spend $6 million on a new system as part of a push to grow the company. But it was if the new system was more important than the customer. But if the employees didn't use that program properly, it would screw up everything. If customers wanted something special or different, workers told them the system wouldn't allow it. That's no good. The system was designed to do the ordering, payroll, accounting, and so on. But if the company and employees didn't operate it properly, it would screw up everything. The new system caused pandemonium. Castanea also placed less emphasis on our prepared foods, which had made up about 90 percent of Eatzi's sales when I ran it. They were treating the concept as a corporation, and I was hearing nothing but complaints from my old customers who found quality lacking in the product. Business fell off, the customers were unhappy, and the employees were unhappy. There I was, an empty suit, holding on to only 20 percent of the company despite my position on the board.

Castanea decided to put a store in Chicago in the Lincoln Park area in a high-rise building with a parking garage. That made the store inconvenient. Nobody was going to park in a garage to go to a market. An Eatzi's store was designed to be freestanding; Castanea was, in effect, hiding Eatzi's. The strategy didn't work at Macy's in New York, and it wasn't going to work in Chicago, I told them. But they did it anyway.

Castanea wasn't making what they thought it would make on Eatzi's, and they decided to sell the company, but nobody was buying because Eatzi's was far too leveraged. So they decided to break it up into pieces and parcel it off. I told Castanea that if they were going to do that, I was going to resign from the board and bid on the Dallas location. Because Eatzi's was a very complicated operation, there were no other takers. I was able to buy the Dallas store back from Castanea for $1.5 million. By then, sales there had dropped from nearly $300,000 a week at its peak to under $115,000 a week. With no buyers, Castanea closed the deal with me and liquidated the other Eatzi's stores.

Now I had everything I needed back: the Eatzi's brand, the copyright, and so forth. I paid cash and had no debt on it. Then I went off and got some of the key people I had under me when I first operated Eatzi's to come back, and this time I offered them a piece of the operation. I also hired Adam Romo, who was chief financial officer for Eatzi's at Brinker when I was there, to be CEO. Trinity Groves partner Stuart Fitts and investor Jerry Meyer came in, too.

The first step was to put the focus back on the customer and become profitable in Dallas again. We made about $1.9 million back the first year, and I had already made back my reinvestment of $1.5 million. By 2009, we felt it was finally time for a new "sister store" addition and began work on an Eatzi's Market & Bakery inside The Pavilion on Lovers Lane in Dallas, which opened in March of 2010. At 5,000 square feet, it was barely half the size of the flagship.

We've since opened larger suburban stores on Highway 114 in Grapevine, Texas, in mid-2012, and on the Dallas North Tollway in Plano, Texas, in 2013. We opened our first Tarrant County location in Fort Worth, Texas, at University Park Shopping Village off Interstate 30 in 2017 in a former Chili's location. We envision as many as 10 additional Eatzi's Market & Bakeries in the Dallas-Fort Worth Metroplex and possibly stores in other markets. Eatzi's celebrated its 20-year anniversary in 2016. It is one of my prized creations.

Points of difference: We created a new concept and brand, "restaurant-replacement meals." It is a cross between a deli, a kitchen, a pantry, a home-meal-replacement restaurant, and an upscale gourmet grocery store, serving gourmet-quality restaurant food. It employs dozens of chefs. Chefs and assistants dish out fresh meats, poultry, and vegetables from their pans into shoppers' take-home plates. Chefs "shop" the lush Eatzi's produce stand to gather the ingredients they need for their creations. A huge assortment of international wines is offered.

Customer Bills of Rights: We will be the personal chef for time-pressed people, offering them an endless variety of ready-to-heat meals that they can either pick up on their way home or eat on the premises. Customers will be able to walk through the kitchen on their way in and witness the food-manufacturing process firsthand. Food will be the freshest possible. We will sell mostly food products that we make personally. Menus will change up to 25 percent from day to day so that customers can experience new dishes and new food combinations.

1997 Johnny Angel's Heavenly Burgers, Skaneateles, New York

I often had a craving for a Fuddruckers-quality hamburger when I visited my summer home in Skaneateles, but the pickings were slim. After Rosalie's Cucina opened and my dear sister passed away, I played around with a few ideas in my head for a burger joint there, but nothing came of it for a while.

However, one day I ran into an old high school football teammate and pal of mine name Johnny Angyal, Hungarian for "angel." Johnny had been as a police officer and then had served as town supervisor for two terms but had recently lost a reelection bid. He was in his late 50s and confided in me that he was trying to figure out what to do with himself after he had lost the election. I thought about it for a while, got back to him, and said, "Johnny, what Skaneateles needs is a good hamburger place. How about if I build one and get it going, and then you can buy out my position and have a business for the rest of your life?" He loved the idea.

I bought a former Colonial Kitchen restaurant at 22 Jordan Street that ended up converting to a place called Johnny Angel's Heavenly Burgers. The concept would be a mini-Fuddruckers, with cast-iron iron grills and folding chairs that were banked along rows of long tables. Cooked-to-order, half-pound Black Angus burgers in fresh-baked buns and other items such as grilled chicken sandwiches would be served on metal trays, and the customers could top them with whatever they wanted from all-you-can-eat condiment bar. Paper towels were used in lieu of napkins.

We opened in 1997, and Johnny picked up the business pretty quickly. It's a well-received restaurant concept, with chicken dishes, hot dogs, shakes, soups, and salads in addition to the popular burgers. Johnny was able to buy me out in a fairly short time, and he operated the place well. The atmosphere remains warm, very clean, and child friendly, and the place serves a mean breakfast with huge omelets.

After I sold Johnny Angel's Heavenly Burgers to Johnny, it made the national news in 1999. Like me, he was not a big fan of Bill and Hillary Clinton, who were in Skaneateles for several days that year. Johnny caused quite a stir when, with the Clintons still in town, he added a tongue-in-cheek "Bill Clinton Sandwich" to the menu, which he described as "a little bread and a lot of baloney." But he raised even more eyebrows with his "Hillary Sandwich," which he described as "a little breast and a lot of thigh." He got harassed a little for it and made the wire services, getting mentions in the *Wall Street Journal*, the *New York Times*, and dozens of other newspapers, plus network TV. Most people got a kick out of the Clinton sandwiches.

Johnny passed away of cancer in 2010 at the age of 69 but I had gone to see him before he died. New owner Bill Lynn, who took it over before Johnny died, has been true to the concept. I couldn't attend Johnny's funeral, but I had the folks at the church announce at the funeral service that there would be free hamburgers at Johnny Angel's Heavenly Burgers and that Phil Romano was going to pick up the tab. The announcement got around the high school, and the place was apparently swarmed, because I got a bill for nearly $20,000!

To this day, the burgers at Johnny Angel's Heavenly Burgers are still big, tasty, and fresh and live up to the restaurant's name.

Points of Difference: It is a Fuddruckers-quality burger restaurant that uses cast-iron grills and serves cooked-to-order Black Angus burgers on fresh-made buns. It is located in a small town that had lacked a quality hamburger place.

Customer Bill of Rights: Much like Fuddruckers, the meat and buns will be the best available, the burgers will be cooked the way customers want them cooked, and customers can use all condiments they like for free, including melted cheese. It will employ high-quality, well-trained employees.

1999 Nick & Sam's, Dallas, Texas

It was the late 1990s, and Dallas had a bunch of pricey steakhouses with excellent food, but they all seemed to be such gloomy places. Did eating steak in a restaurant really have to be like going to a wake? It reminded me of the joke about the horse going into the bar and ordering a drink, with the bartender asking him, "Why the long face?"

A night out at a steakhouse should be a festive occasion. So, in my mind, I started designing a more cheerful place. For a while, I had my eye on the vacant Lawry's The Prime Rib building on Maple Avenue just north of downtown for a possible restaurant, and it soon became the focus of my new fine-dining steak concept.

Patrick Colombo, one of the cofounders of the Sfuzzi chain, had come to me earlier and had said that he would like to operate a restaurant in Dallas. I told him about my plans for an upbeat, upscale steakhouse, and he came in to run it as a 10-percent, sweat-equity partner.

We needed a distinguished name. Patrick and his wife had just had a baby boy, Nick. My son, Sam, was a toddler at the time. So, we ended up naming the place Nick & Sam's. Sam & Nick's, we both agreed with a laugh, sounded too much like an exterminator.

We carefully handpicked our entire team, from the chef and the general manager, to the wine steward, bartender, and wait staff. If we liked how we were treated at lunch or dinner by any restaurant staff members, we'd ask for their business card or give them one of ours. We hired our head waiters the same way and then let them put their own teams together using the same strategy.

Patrick brought in some talented former Sfuzzi people, including Samir Dhurandhar, former executive chef with Sfuzzi New York and a graduate of the Culinary Institute of America, plus manager Joe Palladino, who was making a name for himself at the MGM Grand Las Vegas. They were already known commodities.

As a rule, I like to hire people who have already experienced the highs and lows of the business or those who have been in business for themselves. My favorite hires are people who haven't had a safety net under them all their lives and who relish the challenge of nurturing a concept to success.

I made it clear that the entire team was essential to Nick & Sam's well-being but that it was only through their outstanding individual personal efforts that we would succeed. Teamwork is fine, but I still needed my employees to think like individuals. On a basketball team, you have five people whose objectives are all to think the same. But I don't need restaurant staff members thinking the same. I need them to think differently. Teamwork is important, but it can inhibit creativity because a group mindset will invariably restrict creative thinking. It can keep people from thinking out of the box.

I also don't want my staff to be like me. I just want to be the guy who says "yes" and "no" to their ideas. I want employees to be able to lead themselves. I don't want employees to work for me; I want them to work *with* me. If I wanted all of my employees to be just like me, they would limit themselves to thinking only like me. From the get-go, individuality was our forte at Nick & Sam's.

We wanted to put the romance back into wines. We established a wide-ranging wine wall "cellar" at the restaurant that featured 450 different wines. Patrons would see this wall of wine as they walked into the lobby-bar area, and it would provide a relaxing—and suggestive— after-dinner setting for guests, as well as our waiting area.

People could read about the wines on monitors in the wine area. There were wine facts, the number of bottles produced of each vintage, and other details. Customers would be allowed to sample the wines before deciding which one went best with their dinner, and they could indulge in wine tastings.

We would also offer free caviar to all of our bar patrons. Some of my cronies told me I was crazy to give away something that was so costly. Hearing that, I knew I was on the right track. And the free caviar? It means we get talked about.

We knew which wines paired well with steak or swordfish and would complement which sauces, and we readily shared that information with our patrons. Wines, after all, are fermented grapes, and grapes are food. So, when we serve wine with dinner, we're putting food with food, and we have to make sure that certain food combinations don't assault the patrons' palate. We even had a price-negotiable policy on every bottle priced over $400, and I was certain that customers would have fun with that idea. The wine stewards and managers knew what we paid for each bottle, so they could approve a slightly lower price. Or patrons could just sip gratis port wine that we would set on their tables, if they preferred.

A baby grand piano would sit right in the middle of the open kitchen in full view of the diners. We thought it would be fun for patrons to hear an accomplished pianist playing classics and soft melodies while the bustling chefs flanking him doled out dishes to our servers, who then had to make a little side-jog to scoot past the piano. New waiters had to quickly acclimate themselves to this. There was also raw bar with a dozen seats adjacent to the kitchen and another smaller private room right off the kitchen. It was called the Chef's Room because it is dedicated to the great chefs of Dallas and features framed glossy photographs of many of them.

The stage was set; now it was time for the show. When we opened in the spring of 1999, we decided not to advertise and just let Nick & Sam's rely on its own momentum. That way, we could ease into the operation and concentrate on the food and service. We opened only for dinner to maintain that focus. I was in no hurry to become successful there because I already was successful.

Nick & Sam's was an instant hit, not only because of the food but also because of the atmosphere. The restaurant has a long main dining room, arched ceiling, and U-shaped kitchen. The ceilings have large rounded lights, and booths face out toward the dining floor. The décor is upscale but far from stuffy. There is a lot of art on the walls, some of it my own.

While other restaurant people tear their hair out over such issues as human resources and payroll, my mind drifts to more abstract areas like imagery, energy, color combinations, spatial relationships, and even the realization of dreams. These elements bring joy to the dining experience and help spur lively conversation. People welcomed this at Nick & Sam's because they were tired of those old, solemn steakhouse themes. If you want a nice quiet dinner, take one and go to a funeral home to eat it!

Nick & Sam's cost about $3.4 million to get up and running. I gleaned a big chunk of that because of the Republican agenda of late 1999, with its lowered capital gains taxes and other tax considerations. I was able to use the money I saved on a $14 million capital gain, which was equivalent to about an 8-percent tax break, to open Nick & Sam's. If I had paid Uncle Sam that money, it would have been wasted on one of the government's many giveaway deals. Instead, I'm paying sales taxes, liquor taxes, employee taxes, and income taxes on my restaurant's profit. I'm able to give people jobs and train them—we employ about 90 people at Nick & Sam's—and help advance people in their careers. In addition, I'm paying thousands of dollars to food and beverage suppliers. And those people, in turn, are investing that money in their businesses and in job creation. The Republican agenda of 1999 helped stimulate the economy.

Nick & Sam's has a din and clamor, with excitement and energy of cheerful conversation combining with the bustling clatter of plates that add up to a strong and successful life for a restaurant. *D Magazine* named Nick & Sam's the top new restaurant in the city in 1999. We got great reviews from every publication visiting us, and the place is always crowded today, even on those traditionally slow Monday and Tuesday nights. It's not unusual for Nick & Sam's to serve 700 to 1,000 dinners in a night.

Not long after we opened, Joe and Samir started talking about leaving because they weren't getting along with Patrick. It wasn't how they had envisioned things working out for them, they said. I told them that I really wanted them to stay because they were performing very well.

Samir's food was imaginative, and I liked Joe's management style. So I told Joe that he could buy out the 10 percent owned by Patrick, who had his eyes on other things, but Joe didn't have the means. Patrick agreed to the terms, so I personally financed Joe's buyout. As time went on, Joe paid it off, and I gave him even more of an interest. I did the same thing for Samir as well as our chief financial officer. Joe really understands the "show-biz" element of the business and keeps the place exciting and creative, and he makes everyone who works at Nick & Sam's feel like it's their place. Samir keeps the menu fresh, and his creative new offerings always sell well, plus he's created menus for some of my other concepts.

The accolades continued. Our wine list received numerous annual Awards of Excellence by *Wine Spectator* magazine and was winner of the American Academy of Hospitality Science's Five Diamond Award. Nick & Sam's was the most-searched Dallas restaurant on Zagat in 2013, according to Google. We've won so many "best steakhouse" awards since then that I can't keep track of them.

Surprise promotions have piqued customers' curiosity. At the end of our first year in business, we celebrated by giving out $50,000 in free meals to our best customers. That brought out some great reactions. On the day after 9/11, we handed out letters to our patrons telling them that we were proud of them coming out to do their part to keep the economy afloat, thanked them for their patriotism, and said the meal was on us. One table was full of New Yorkers who had been stranded here. Some of them teared up because they were so grateful. We also held a benefit dinner for the widows of cops who died in 9/11, raising $25,000.

Our negotiable-price policy on wines is still intact. We've had people negotiate a $2,500 bottle down to $2,000 or less, which is still a good deal for us since we typically buy such a bottle for $1,000 or less.

We finished our first year with over $6.5 million in sales, we did $7 million the second year, and today we are doing close to $16 million annually, and that's just being open for dinner. I can't begin to list the actors, professional athletes, and other celebrities who have dined with us.

Today, I still own the building and just over 50 percent of the business. Joe, Samir, and some of my other people own the rest. When I first opened it, I knew more about the steakhouse business than anybody there. Now, Joe and Samir know more about it than I do. They run it well, and I don't have to worry about it anymore. They worry about it because they have ownership.

It's been nearly 20 years since we opened. Nick & Sam's will always have a special place in my heart. Named after my son, this is one restaurant I'm going to keep in the family.

Points of Difference: It offers free caviar to bar patrons, has a wide-ranging wine "cellar" on the walls, with small monitors that brief patrons on wine availability, vintages, and food compatibility. Customers can sample wines before ordering. It is the steakhouse destination of choice for celebrities and professional athletes. There is a baby grand piano in the middle of the open kitchen and the bar has a lively atmosphere.

Customer Bill of Rights: Diners will enjoy prime steak and fresh seafood in an upscale and cheerful atmosphere. It will not be one of those solemn steakhouses. The top chefs and managers are part owners who have a vested interest in making every meal just right.

1999 Wild About Harry's, Dallas, Texas

When we lived in the Highland Park area in Dallas, my second wife, Lillie, and our son, Sam, became regulars at a little custard and hot dog shop that they had discovered on Knox Street. They raved about the place and told me that I had to go and check it out, so I dropped by the place, which was called Wild About Harry's, one afternoon for custard and a hot dog. The owner, Harry Coley, was there, serving dozens of different flavors of the rich and delicious frozen custard that he made using his mother's family recipe, and selling his popular giant beef hot dogs. Harry was a bubbly, customer-minded man who reminded me of the old microwave popcorn icon, Orville Redenbacher. I overheard people saying that this place was reminiscent of the ice-cream parlors they remembered going to when they were children. After a few more satisfying "reconnaissance stops," during which it became obvious that Harry had a good thing going, I finally introduced myself to Harry.

Harry told me he wanted to branch out and expand the reach of his trademark custard product, but he didn't know what steps to take and said he could use my help. I told him, "Harry, I don't want to do too much of anything unless I'm sure I'm going to have a fun concept going and have a good relationship with the people involved, and I feel comfortable with them." We had dinner a few times and talked more about expansion, and I liked what I saw of Harry and his operation, so I agreed to go into business with him and roll out some new Wild About Harry's locations.

We put together some fun ideas for the new stores. we decided to put the custard machine behind glass and have an employee in a white coat and hat in there making the custard in full view of the customers— "truth in feeding." This would help customers recognize that the custard was freshly made on the premises, unlike most ice-cream places. Each employee, male or female, would wear a name tag identifying himself or herself as "Harry." There would be pictures of famous Harrys throughout history, such as Harry Truman, Harry Connick, Jr., Harry Houdini, Harry Bellefonte, and Harry Carey. We sneaked in Harry Ass, a donkey. We even considered running Harry for president as a funny promotional idea.

We thought we would handpick MBA graduates and students from the Cox School of Business at Southern Methodist University in Dallas, where I was active on the board at the time, to operate the stores. That would help us with continuity and would provide smart managers who could eventually become executives.

The concept was setting itself up to be a perfect mom-and-pop-style franchise operation and for product distribution on the side. Harry could become a lovable icon for the brand, I thought, and would help generate some fun public relations promotions and positive word-of-mouth publicity. We'd get Harry's custard in stores, including Eatzi's, to further expand the brand and take the product, and the stores, nationwide. Norman Brinker even liked Wild About Harry's so much that he wanted a piece of it, and I couldn't turn him down. But he couldn't get the deal past Brinker's board because they still had no room for new concepts.

Then, unfortunately, Harry pulled out of the deal, so we never really got it going. Harry died at the age of 75 in 2014. But his Wild About Harry's lives on today with the same great product.

Points of Difference: It served rich, distinctive frozen custard that the founder made using his mother's family recipe and giant hot dogs. The custard machine was set behind glass and manned by an associate in a white coat and hat. Pictures of famous Harrys hung on the walls. Every employee wore a name tag that said "Harry."

Customer Bills of Rights: Customers will see that the delicious custard is made fresh on the premises and will enjoy "truth in feeding" and a fun atmosphere. All-beef hot dogs will be plump and juicy. Service will be friendly with some added humor.

2000 Wé/Oui, Oui/Wé—A French Eating Place, Dallas, Texas

I have been to French restaurants at home and abroad, and they have several things in common: tiny portions, high prices, snooty service, and pretentious surroundings. So, I decided to create a French restaurant that was the opposite of that: big portions, modest checks, gracious service, and a casual atmosphere.

A few blocks from Nick & Sam's was a French-looking building and a Dallas institution, The Crescent Hotel. It had just lost its restaurant anchor, Sam's Café, and needed a replacement tenant, and I had just the right concept.

I hired an up-and-coming chef from Seattle, Nick Badovinus, as my executive chef as well as a manager, plus another chef, and brought them on an extensive tour de France to devise my game plan, expose them to various French foods, operational tips, and new ideas. I had hired the former food writer for the Daily Herald of suburban Chicago, a frequent French traveler, to set up a restaurant and food-store visitation schedule, and it was a great learning experience for us all.

We put together Wé/Oui, Oui/Wé, with the tag line, "French Food Every Day." The accent over the Wé, but not over the Oui, was a fun little twist to see if people were paying attention. We'd have an Art

Deco motif and lots of red, black, and white; a giant wine rack that climbed the entirety of the wall next to the long, open kitchen; clocks that told the time in cities from Paris to Honolulu to Calcutta; and our ruby-red "lips" logo splashed about.

Our "show" was going to be a fun one. The waiters would be extra friendly and speak with French accents, some of them faux. The typical American meeting a typical French person may not have a very good time because of the language barrier, but if you go to a restaurant and the waiters and staff speak English with a French accent, it's kind of sexy. We had a long marble bar that was not far from the hotel's elevators that would attract guests, hotel and otherwise, for late-night and after-dinner drinks. In the restrooms, we'd have recordings of "common" English phrases that would be translated into French, like "Will you meet me here tomorrow night?" or "Have you tried the roast duck?" and, of course, "Do you come here often?"

We opened in late spring of 2000. There was no intimidation factor at our French creation and no attitude problems from the servers. People weren't compelled to dress up to dine with us, and they didn't need a magnifying glass to read the menu or to see the food, either. Ordering was a breeze. All of our $15 entrees were grouped together, as were our $18 items entrees and our "market price" items, all to help make things even more simple and straightforward. Truffles, mussels, pâté de foie gras, and capers found their way into an assortment of dishes. There were frog legs, crêpes, escargots, pommes frites, plus some American-French dishes, all served in generous portions, as well as baguettes and a wide variety of cheeses and wines. A mini-Eiffel Tower creation made out of caramel came with many of the desserts.

The bar drew a young and upbeat clientele. We were a lifestyle concept, and one of our distinctive promotions caused quite a stir. Late at night, we'd pass out little packets that looked like matches, containing our lips logo. The back cover said, "From Wé/Oui for your Wee Wee." Inside was a kiss-of-mint condom and a note that said, "We support the effort to eliminate the spread of sexually transmitted diseases. We value you as a customer.…" Admittedly, this was a little racy, and a few Dallas folks didn't get—or appreciate—the joke. Others had a good laugh and pocketed a bunch of them.

Wé/Oui didn't work out, despite its many points of difference. In retrospect, the place looked great, but the location, and perhaps the timing, were wrong. It didn't help that the road in front of the hotel was under construction for what seemed like an eternity. But I make no excuses.

We had a big closing party, and I invited all of my loyal customers. We had about 400 of them in attendance, and they helped me celebrate losing $2.5 million. We ate and drank through the remaining inventory, kissed the red lips logo goodbye, and I chalked it all up to an R & D adventure that didn't have a happy ending (despite the condoms). Nick & Sam's was hopping, and there were plenty of other things to do.

Well after my Wé/Oui experience, something that happened on our France fact-finding trip stayed with me. We had been in a Paris restaurant when a very bright young man who operated the place asked us what we were doing in town. We told him we were looking for new ideas and different kinds of foods. He said, "Oh, you're in the wrong country; new and innovative things don't happen in France anymore." I asked him what he meant by that, and he said, "The way the government is set up here, we can't make any money—there's too much taxation. We are not incentivized to create anything anymore. It's terrible. America is where everything is happening. That's where all the ideas are. That's where all the opportunity is. God bless America!"

I thought about it a while. I have seen things happening in the United States that happened in Europe, and it's scary, for example, "regulation without representation" that I talk about, with many different forms of taxation and other costs that are killing incentives for small businesses, which are the backbone of our economy. There are more small businesses closing than opening. I often think about what that man said back in Paris. Let's hope the current administration follows through on its promises to change that course.

Points of Difference: We served large portions instead of the traditional spare French portions. The atmosphere was informal instead of stuffy. All $15 entrees and $18 entrees were grouped together. Truffles, mussels, pâté de foie gras, and capers appeared in an assortment of dishes. We had a young and upbeat clientele, an Art Deco motif, a giant wine rack that climbed the entirety of one wall, an open kitchen, clocks that told the time in cities from Paris to Honolulu to Calcutta, and trademark ruby-red "lips" matches and condoms!

Consumer Bill of Rights: Unlike in most French restaurants, there will be no intimidation factor or attitude problems from servers. Customers will be encouraged to dress casually. Portions will be large, savory, and satisfying.

2002, Lobster Ranch, Preston Center, North Dallas

I've always had fond memories of the old Shuckers restaurant that I opened in Palm Beach in 1974. My first working name for it, in fact, was Mother Shuckers. I had wanted to open a similar casual seafood restaurant in Dallas for years, but didn't get around to working on the project until 2001 because of the time I was spending on other concepts. Though I was tempted to call my creation Mother Shuckers, I had another good name I'd thought about for a while: Lobster Ranch, which would feature a "buckin' lobster" as a logo.

Investor Luke Crosland called me and said he had a restaurant space open in Preston Center in North Dallas near North Park Center that he wanted to fill, and I thought it would be a good place to try out my seafood concept. We agreed on a 50–50 partnership deal and landed well-known chef Tim Fleming, who had worked at popular local haunts such as Lombardi Mare and The Riviera. So far, so good, although I was still waiting for Crosland's 50-percent contribution. I elected to be patient and moved forward without it.

On the design end, I put kitschy little touches around the place, such as wooden shutters on the walls, a wood stairwell with "timbers" for rails, and a giant tropical fish sculpture suspended from the ceiling. At the top of the stairs was a raw bar with shrimp and shellfish on ice and a serving bar that was made in part with wooden panels from liquor and wine crates. I also had giant lobsters that were visible in an oversized tank. We'd offer bibs to customers to insulate them from stray butter spatters.

We cast Lobster Ranch as a New England-style seafood house and opened it in March 2002. Entrees ranged from $6 to $25 and featured live Maine lobster, grilled or steamed. Customers could get a one-pound lobster with new potatoes, steamed broccoli, and corn on the cob for only $18. We also offered a lobster roll and a fresh "Catch of the Day," ranging from trout to salmon to grouper, and we also had a non-seafood menu with grilled Italian sausage, chicken, and pasta.

Lobster Ranch was caught in that gray area between a "down-and-dirty," no-frills restaurant and a "fancy" restaurant, and we struggled to find its niche. Some of our customers complained about the location, which could have been better. Crosland didn't help matters by coming in regularly and issuing orders to employees, even though he was supposed to be a silent partner. I asked him to stop, but he persisted, and I felt that he disrupted operations and lowered morale.

The topper: Crosland never gave me his 50 percent of the money, and that made it all but impossible to keep Lobster Ranch open. I closed the place in October 2002, just six months after it opened. On the last few days of operation, a herd of disappointed customers came by to say goodbye to our restaurant and our Buckin' Lobster, calling it their favorite seafood place. I told them, "I sure appreciate you guys, but I'm not going to pay you to come and eat." The lobster had pinched me hard for $600,000. What's more, I had to sue Crosland to get his share of the money that he owed me.

Points of Difference: We used a "buckin' lobster" as a logo and featured live Maine lobsters. Giant lobsters were visible in an oversized tank. We offered a one-pound lobster with new potatoes, steamed broccoli, and corn on the cob for only $18 and gave bibs to customers. We featured a raw bar, with shrimp and shellfish on ice, and a serving bar made from liquor and wine crates.

Costumer Bill of Rights: Diners will be served the best in fresh seafood in an informal and kitschy environment, at moderate prices.

2002 Who's Who Burger, Highland Park (Dallas)

I was talking with a friend in real estate who leases space in Highland Park Village at Preston Road and Mockingbird Lane, and he said he needed to evict a tenant after his leased had expired, and he asked me if I had any ideas about filling it, at least temporarily. It was a compact space, but I put my mind to work and invented Who's Who Burger, which would use beef from Wagyu cattle in Kobe, Japan. Called Kobe beef, the meat is an incredibly well-marbled and flavorful delicacy that requires special cooking.

Although patrons would pay a premium for a Kobe Burger (about $10), its flavor was unparalleled and its fat content was lower than any other ground beef. Who's Who also would serve hot dogs, turkey cranberry burgers, and a veggie portobello burger. I came up with the name Who's Who Burger because patrons could inscribe their autograph on the walls right next to an assortment of local and national celebrity signatures.

Who's Who opened in early 2007 and I kept it going until late 2010 when my landlord friend needed the space back for a retail store. Who's Who Burger was mildly profitable, and people loved the unique burgers, but the space was tough to work with, plus other Kobe burger joints were cropping up, so closing it wasn't a problem for me.

Points of Difference: We used premium beef from Wagyu cattle in Kobe, Japan. We also served hot dogs, turkey cranberry burgers, and a veggie portobello burger. Patrons could scrawl their autographs on walls right next to assorted local and national celebrity signatures.

Costumer Bill of Right: The meat will be a well-marbled and flavorful delicacy with unparalleled flavor and a fat content lower than any ground beef.

2004 Il Mulino New York, uptown Dallas

I've backed other people's business ideas over the years, but when it comes to restaurants, I prefer to use my own ideas to assure continuity, consistency, and dedication to those key points of difference and "bills of rights" needed to keep my concepts unique. However, I received an

offer in 2002 that I couldn't refuse from a New York Italian family. Il Mulino, the Greenwich Village landmark that Zagat has ranked as the top restaurant in New York City practically every year since its 1981 debut, has made an amazing amount of money, despite its cramped location and 100-person seating capacity. Its Old World cuisine from Italy's Abruzzo region is perfection, and reservations can take months to secure, despite its top-scale price range.

Brothers Fernando and Gino Masci had been approached dozens of times over the years about expanding Il Mulino elsewhere, but they were worried that another restaurateur wouldn't treat their distinct brand in the right way. Nevertheless, the brothers, along with investors Jerry Katzoff and Brian Gallagher, finally decided to license new franchises and contacted me in late 2002 to talk about being their first. I told them that I'd have to first seek out a suitable Dallas location. The Masci brothers said that aside from New York-area patrons, visitors from Texas had by far been Il Mulino's best customers.

We met, and for about a year, we talked about the Dallas Il Mulino location. The brothers came to Dallas, where they visited Nick & Sam's and Eatzi's, and met my Nick & Sam's partner, Joe Palladino, who was keenly interested in partnering with me on the deal. Because of our mutual Italian heritage, the chemistry was ideal.

A perfect site, the former Casa Dominguez restaurant building, finally became available in uptown Dallas at 2408 Cedar Springs Road, just a block away from Nick & Sam's. I estimated the building would seat about 130 people, considerably bigger than the Manhattan El Mulino. New Yorkers may wait an hour and a half to two hours for a table, but Texans won't, especially for a top-dollar, fine-dining experience.

I knew this would be a great restaurant for Dallas and would enhance the city's international fine-dining reputation. I also knew I could take my family, friends, and business associates there as often as I wanted, and we'd be assured of a fantastic dining experience each time. The Masci brothers were also excited at the prospect of having enough room in the Dallas location to demonstrate their skills with a little tableside cooking, something they couldn't do in the limited confines of their New York venue.

We all shook on the deal. The Mascis told us it was like keeping Il Mulino in the family. And it didn't take long to attract investors to back the Dallas location. We hired a young chef, Michael Abruzese, who graduated from a culinary school in New York, and sent him to meet the brothers. They soon realized that their families came from the same village in Italy. The Mascis took Michael under their wings, and he trained six months with them. We also sent about 20 other people to New York to train with the Mascis. To be credible, the food would have to be the same in Dallas as it was at the New York restaurant.

We would have still-life oil paintings, imported furnishings and chandeliers, high ceilings, ornate draperies, terra-cotta walls, large Roman-themed wall plates, white tablecloths, and marble restrooms. Costs would exceed $1.5 million. We'd be open six nights a week and serve -only dinners, jackets would be required, and waiters would wear white ties and carry little torches from table to table to illuminate the menu, which they would explain in detail to patrons. Entrees would range from $30 to $50, but portions would be huge. We'd offer complimentary garlic bread, Italian sausage, bruschetta, and fried zucchini to diners as soon as they sat down, plus fresh Parmigiano-Reggiano cheese. We would offer some of the best and most diverse wines in the world.

Anticipation of its opening was unprecedented for my restaurants. We had 6,000 reservations before we opened the doors. Il Mulino New York in Dallas debuted in February of 2004 to long-reserved full houses. Fernando and Gino, who had each spent months in Dallas to shepherd its creation, were there to make sure everything was perfect. Customers found the food to be every bit as good as in Il Mulino in New York and welcomed the additional elbow room. Diners raved about such dishes as homemade ravioli with black truffles in champagne sauce, veal scallopini, osso buco, chilled baby octopus salad, Zabaglione, and a special marsala-flavored custard prepared in copper cookware at the tables.

The reviews were five-star, with the curious exception of one written by *Dallas Morning News* food critic Dotty Griffith in April of 2004. The bizarre and conflicted facts cited by Griffith in her visit to Il Mulino just floored us. Dotty came into the place with Janet Cobb, who staffers recognized immediately as a very good friend of hers and the owner of the Cobb Restaurant Group and Ristorante Italiano. Janet had even taken Dotty to Europe to help her buy wines for her restaurants. I say that because Janet, a competing restaurateur, would apparently be helping Dotty form her opinions and observations at Il Mulino. They ordered a bunch of different things, including more wine after consuming a bottle at the bar, stayed a couple of hours, and left. Before that, Dotty had declined multiple invitations to meet the Masci brothers and tour the kitchen.

When the review came out on April 16, 2004, I hit the roof. Every other reviewer had given us sky-high ratings and had used superlatives like "divine" and "best I've ever tasted," but we merited only 3.5 stars in the paper's five-star food-rating system. The headline read, "It's a fabulous scene, but the food doesn't rate a standing O[vation]." Well, that's just an opinion, of course. I read on, expecting that opinion to be backed by basic facts, and it became apparent that she completely missed on her guesses about the contents of several of our dishes and the manner in which other food was prepared.

She observed that our porcini-stuffed ravioli with champagne truffle sauce "whispered of Gorgonzola." The ravioli couldn't have "uttered" such an ingredient because there wasn't a trace of it in there. She deduced that our risotto was partially cooked before it was even ordered. Wrong. No chef would even think of doing such a thing at a restaurant of Il Mulino's caliber.

Our people wanted to know why she hadn't called us to fact-check, but I had no answer for them. She also compared the Dallas Il Mulino with the New York version in her review, though she apparently had never set foot in the original Il Mulino. I say this because we made arrangements on repeated occasions for her to dine there, but she never showed up. It's inconceivable that she would have shown up one day and slipped in under the radar of the place's tightly controlled reservations list. Dotty went on to hammer away at other aspects of the operation. She did give the place an overall 4.0-star rating in addition to the baffling 3.5-star food rating, but based on her review, how could we have merited any stars?

Curiously, the *Morning News* had routinely given 5-star food ratings and reviews to Janet Cobb's defunct Salve! restaurant and her other restaurants. The *Morning News* regularly gave better marks to small strip-center pizza and burger joints and other small eateries that were not in Il Mulino's league. The *Morning News* star-rating system, along with the rating systems of many other publications, was rightfully maligned for its inconsistent nature and inability to distinguish between sandwich and pizza places and fine-dining restaurants.

I went over to the *Morning News* and met with the assistant arts editor, Mike Maza, who quickly acknowledged that there were problems with the star-rating system. He also said that Dotty's review sounded personal, and he asked me if someone at Il Mulino "had pissed off" the reviewer. "Not that I know of," I said. I explained what I felt was the real motivation: the cozy relationship between Dotty and Janet Cobb that extended into their Il Mulino visit had created an obvious conflict of interest. I also told him about the facts that she had gotten wrong. In my 50-plus years of experience as a restaurateur, I have never seen anything like it. Such actions directly violate the Code of Ethics adopted by the Society of Professional Journalists, which instructs professional journalists "to avoid conflicts of interest, real or perceived."

A few weeks after my visit to the *Morning News*, Mike Maza wrote me a letter saying that virtually all of my complaints dealt with matters of opinion and that he didn't see any errors of fact that required correction. The review infuriated several of my customers, who wrote letters to the editor in response, but the *Morning News* didn't publish any of them or run a correction of the wrong "facts."

I felt I had no choice but to do something virtually unheard of in the restaurant industry: sue the reviewer and corporate parent of the newspaper, Belo Corp. for malice, fraud, and defamation in their attempt to cripple one of Dallas' finest new restaurants. I didn't take such an action lightly. I wouldn't have even considered it, in fact, if had not been for the bizarre circumstances of Dotty and Janet's visit.

The media, in general, are the watchdogs of the world, and hold everybody accountable for what they do. But who holds them accountable? Someone had to stand up to them. It's true that they have inalienable first-amendment rights, but that doesn't give them latitude to abuse their powers and smear an honest business.

I've never been a big fan of the way most food critics operate, even though my restaurants have been well received by them. Reviews can be lethal and their observations, subjective, especially if the reviewers don't have a discerning palate and an in-depth knowledge of specialty foods and spices. Even if they don't want to give themselves away as a reviewer during their visit, then all they need to do is call back the next day and ask for details about the preparation of the food.

My lawyer, business-litigation attorney Steven Stodghill of Fish & Richardson, deposed Dotty. He asked Dotty if drinking when she came into review a restaurant was unethical. She said, "Yes." He asked her if she thought bringing in Il Mulino's competitor to help her review my restaurant was unethical. She said, "Yes, that's unethical." Steven then asked her if she thought it was unethical for her to state things without substantiating the facts. She said, "Yes, that's unethical." Then we went back to the newspaper and told the paper's lawyers that I was personally going to take out billboards all over town saying that the *Dallas Morning News* Guide and food reviewer admitted to engaging in unethical practices.

One of the paper's lawyers said, "We'll settle it. You win. What do you want?" I said, "I don't want money. I don't need money. I want this thing re-reviewed, and I want her fired—or put in another department.

She shouldn't be reviewing." They agreed and asked for a month to relocate her to another post. Eventually, someone else from the paper came in and wrote another review, which was much more accurate.

Oddly enough, when I first sued the *Morning News,* all the other restaurants turned their backs on me and didn't want to join me in my outcry, and I was ostracized by fellow restaurateurs. They didn't want to take a chance angering the paper and were afraid that if they did say something, Dotty would start knocking them. Ironically, when I prevailed, in late 2005, I suddenly was their hero. It turned out that the other restaurant owners weren't too fond of her either, but they felt that they had to put up with all the crap she doled out. I feel I did a good thing for the industry. I guess I just needed to make a point about reviewers that was long overdue.

Sadly, Il Mulino New York shut its doors in Dallas at the end of June 2006. We won multiple awards for our food and serving staff, and national accolades in our short life, and we were booked solid for the first three months of 2006, but it started slowing down. We came to the conclusion that the cowboys and other local yokels would not pay our prices for Italian food in Dallas. They might pay it when they visited New York, but not in Dallas. However, I couldn't change the prices because of the licensing agreement I had with Il Mulino in New York. Further, changing the prices in opposition to the licensing agreement would have hurt my reputation, so I just closed the place. People have told me that they still have lasting memories of Il Mulino's food and long to dine there once again. But you won't see another Il Mulino in Dallas.

Points of Difference: We served superb and authentic Old World cuisine from Italy's Abruzzo region, modeled after the famous New

York location in Greenwich Village. The restaurant featured still-life oil paintings, high ceilings, imported furnishings and chandeliers, and other ornate touches. We offered table-side cooking, large portions, and complimentary garlic bread, Italian sausage, bruschetta, and fried zucchini. Waiters wore white ties and carried little torches from table to table to illuminate the menus.

Customer Bill of Rights: Customers will find the food every bit as satisfying as in the New York location, which has been a top-rated Zagat restaurant since its 1981 opening. The atmosphere and table-side cooking will help provide a fantastic dining experience each time, and the wine selection will be among the best and most diverse in the world.

2006 Coal Vines Pizza, Pasta and Wine Bistro, Dallas, Texas

Coal Vines is a chef-driven, coal-fired pizza concept that my Nick & Sam's partner, Joe Palladino, Il Mulino chef Michael Abruzese, and I originated in 2006 at 2404 Cedar Spring Road in uptown Dallas, and it has since expanded to the Prestonwood area on Belt Line Road next to Look Cinemas and the Shops at Legacy in Plano, and other area locations that have been licensed to different owners.

Coal Vines features an à la carte menu with signature New York-style pizzas cooked quickly and perfectly by the anthracite coal oven's intensely high heat (900 degrees). Whether topped by Italian sausage or a selection of other ingredients, or simply served with Bolognese sauce and tomatoes, the oven produces a crust that is crisp but also is chewy. Besides its signature pizza, Coal Vines serves other Italian entrees, sandwiches, appetizers, and salads.

Points of Difference: It serves New York-style pizzas that are cooked in an intensely hot anthracite coal oven at temperatures of 900 degrees.

Customer Bill of Rights: Food orders will be served quickly, and the pizza crust will stay crisp but chewy.

2009 Nick & Sam's Grill, Dallas, Texas

In 2009, Joe Palladino and I jumped on a lease space on a prime spot that had become available at the corner of Fairmount Street and Cedar Springs Road in trendy uptown Dallas, where we opened a casual off-shoot of my Nick & Sam's concept, called Nick & Sam's Grill. The place was an instant hit: it was jam-packed its first week.

With this concept, we felt we could attract the millennials and start cultivating future diners—something we call "raising our customers" — for Nick & Sam's original restaurant only a few blocks away. The opening was highly anticipated, and we attracted a lot of young people who were already in the area to dine and patronize trendy bars along Cedar Springs Road. Our longtime Nick & Sam's executive chef and partner, Samir Dhurandhar, designed the menu, which he called "international comfort food."

We featured an open kitchen and served steaks and such delicacies as Kobe beef sliders, pork ribs, brisket, pan-roasted redfish, chicken waffles, steak eggs rolls, lobster Cobb salads, crispy shrimp rolls with salmon, and a weekend brunch that was very popular, featuring $10 carafes of mimosas and "cinnamon crunch" French toast.

The numbers continued to be good, so we added a second Nick & Sam's Grill location at 8111 Preston Rd near Northwest Highway in the Park Cities area in 2011. With the advent of several new bars in the area, we closed the uptown Nick & Sam's Grill and reconceptualized it. Nick & Sam's Grill at the Preston location has a broader menu, including some of the Nick & Sam's steakhouse favorites, and remains open.

Points of Difference: This was a grill-concept version of the Nick & Sam's original restaurant geared to millennials, featuring steaks, ribs, brisket, fish, and comfort foods such as Kobe beef sliders, chicken waffles, steak eggs rolls, and lobster Cobb salads.

Customer Bill of Rights: Customers will enjoy high-quality food and service just like at the original Nick & Sam's but in an informal environment.

The following concepts are profiled in my Trinity Groves chapters later in this book:

2013 Trinity Groves restaurant incubator, Dallas, Texas

2013 Hofman Hotts, Trinity Groves, Dallas, Texas

2014 Potato Flats, Trinity Groves, Dallas, Texas

2015 Saint Rocco's New York Italian, Trinity Groves, Dallas, Texas

2017 The Network Bar, Trinity Groves, Dallas, Texas

6

Hunger Busters: Giving Underprivileged Kids a Crucial Third Meal

Enhancing the nutrition of food-insecure kids improves both their health and their school performance.

I am well into the third stage of my life. The first was about making money, the second was about doing things for social recognition. The third stage, which I think is the most important one, is about making a difference in as many lives as I can. To me, finding solutions to human problems is far more important than all of the pasta, burgers, and steaks I've sold at my restaurants. In fact, as I went into my 60s and 70s, giving back became a top priority, although my drive to create restaurants and other businesses didn't let up. The two worked hand in hand, in fact. So I remain extremely busy.

Back in 1999, I had a revelation that also served as a catalyst. One afternoon I was reflecting on my life with a good friend of mine, who happened to be a priest, Father John Waggoner, the same man who gave my father the last rites and who baptized my son. We talked about the legions of people whom I have fed in my career and how gratifying and challenging that has been. Then the conversation turned to people in this country who aren't being fed—or fed often enough—and the countless thousands of homeless people.

Homelessness is a huge problem in Dallas, we agreed, much like in other major cities, and the problem is worsening. The government has obviously not found a solution. I often wondered how I could make a difference in the lives of the homeless, I said. I had long thought about opening a soup kitchen where homeless people could eat free, but where the general public could eat also, to help support the place. I played around with that idea and a few others, but nothing seemed especially meaningful or practical. Before I finished my talk with Father John, however, I vowed I would do something.

I realized that the homeless population was one "customer" type I had never served, yet it is an important one. As I researched this group, I discovered that many homeless people won't go to soup kitchens and shelters because they're typically associated with faith or sobriety organizations that make people sit through a lecture or a religious service before they're fed. The meal they get is often not an adequate trade-off, Dallas homeless advocate Clora Hogan once told me. Others won't go to shelters because of the constant noise, because mentally unstable or potentially dangerous people are there, because pets aren't allowed, or because they're afraid that their belongings will be stolen, among at least a dozen other reasons. Those folks need food brought to them.

After much consideration, my second wife, Lillie, and I resolved to create a soup kitchen on wheels to feed them and take it to the streets. Thus, "Hunger Busters: The Food Foundation" was born. We were setting out to do for the city what it couldn't do for itself, I remember thinking at the time. Our chief motivation would simply be to keep the local homeless alive and fed until they found a way to turn their lives around. We bought a former UPS truck and started working on the permits and retrofitting it, and we put out calls for volunteers, recruiting several conscientious and kind helpers.

Starting in late 2000, Hunger Busters made runs from about 4 P.M. to 7 P.M. each Wednesday, bringing food directly to those folks who shunned the city shelters and, instead, would congregate near City Hall and in other downtown enclaves, usually under bridges. They wouldn't be eating the tasteless fare that they were accustomed to; we gave out sandwiches that were whipped up fresh that morning at Eatzi's or Nick & Sam's, by an executive chef, plus tasty and highly nutritious soups, such as sweet potato corn chowder, and fruit and treats. The homeless were at first skeptical that we had some kind of agenda and that they would have to pray or grovel for their food, but we slowly assured them that we wanted nothing but for them to tell their hungry friends about us. We just wanted their dignity to remain intact as we fed them. "What's the catch?" I often heard. "No catch," I'd say. "Just fill your belly."

Meanwhile, our volunteer base grew, and so did the number of days we ran routes. Our son Sam often rode along; his job was handing out spoons. At first, it was a little shocking for him to see how these less fortunate people lived, but it did help plant a seed about helping others. So far, so good.

Several things happened, however, that would eventually cause us to change the direction of Hunger Busters. Things had run relatively smoothly for the first year or so of operation. But in 2002, after Mayor Ron Kirk vacated his post to run for the senate, local columnist Laura

Miller was elected mayor, and we soon started getting harassed. She had pushed a new ordinance through the city council limiting the feeding of street people to designated areas because she thought we were enabling them and keeping them away from shelters.

So, there we were, serving nearly 2,000 meals a week to the homeless and obviously meeting an important need, and suddenly our serving sites under the bridges and near City Hall were off-limits. "What this community is doing isn't working because there are a lot of hungry people out there and they're not getting fed," I told the mayor at a council meeting. "Most of these people won't go to the shelters. We're just trying to help them."

Soon, Laura sent the police to give us warnings and even tickets. Fines could be as high as $2,000! I remember telling friends that we should ignore the tickets, get arrested, and see what the public said about that. "Maybe we should just try this in the court of public opinion," I told them.

To circumvent the new rules, we persuaded one of the downtown property owners to let us use his lots. But the city continued to give us citations, saying the downtown merchants didn't like having us around. Then the health department came in and said our truck had to have a bathroom if we were going to continue to feed people. By the way, those food trucks you see everywhere today aren't ever required to have bathrooms.

Although we weren't cooking anything on the truck, the health department gave us a long list of requirements that we had to meet in order for us to continue, from refrigeration to a sink to hot water, and then later, to a spigot. I was really angry. "We are trying to help people, and here you are asking for things that will cost us at least $50,000," I told the local press. "We're just handing out food that has already been prepared!" We finally met with someone higher up at the department who was able to grasp what we were doing, and she gave us her tentative blessing, imploring us not to make anyone sick. (We never did.)

Meanwhile, however, crusader Laura and the city had all of the homeless camps bulldozed, citing public sleeping ordinances. She also clamped down hard on panhandling and things like the personal use of shopping carts and even public smoking by the homeless in front of the downtown Day Resource Center. Dozens of street people were ticketed for these things and later thrown in jail because, surprise, they couldn't pay. It was like a war was being waged on the homeless. Thanks largely to the mayor, Dallas climbed up to sixth on the National Homeless Alliance's list of "America's Meanest Cities" and got national attention for it. While Hunger Busters was trying to help paint Dallas in a more positive light, Dallas was doing just the opposite.

Laura more or less harassed us for three years until I could take no more. Finally, I turned to the city's new homeless czar, my friend Mike Rawlings, who had been brave enough at the time to accept the chairmanship of the Metro Dallas Homeless Alliance. "Mike, here's what I'm trying to do here, but if you want me to stop it, I'll stop," I told him. "But if I do stop, you should know I am going to take out a full-page ad in the *Dallas Morning News* and tell everyone what the mayor has been doing and how it has hurt, not helped, the city's homeless and that there will now be a gap in feeding all these people." Ever the peacemaker, Mike got up in front of the city council and said that, while those ordinances may have been well-meaning "they can also criminalize somebody trying to do something good." But he also promised he would do something about the situation, and he delivered—in a big way.

Mike devised a long-term plan to ease the Dallas homeless crisis, and the centerpiece of this, he said, would be the type of safe haven that this population has been telling us for years that it needs. Mike consulted with me for several months on what the new complex should include, and he worked very hard to secure millions in city and private funding in order to build what would go on to be called "The Bridge Homeless Assistance Center."

The Bridge became a reality downtown. It can house and feed up to 1,400 "clients" (yes, that's what they're called) and is open 24 hours a day. It has dorms and an outdoor sleeping pavilion for those who are uncomfortable sleeping indoors, plus mental-health facilities, a fitness center, child care, counseling, and a support program designed to help the homeless people there find permanent work and permanent housing. It is a place of promise and dignity and is a reasonable solution for many of the chronically homeless, especially those who truly want to turn their lives around. Hunger Busters was a catalyst for change in the Dallas homeless community, and we're pleased that we were able to play a role. Now, Hunger Busters was ready for a change.

Besides the aforementioned bureaucracy, we had many other frustrations during our nearly seven years of operating our mission. The biggest one, ultimately, was the fact that was no end to the homeless population. We did see some progress from those who'd been just a paycheck away from being homeless and found themselves on the street after losing their jobs. Many of them managed eventually to get back on their feet. But most of the homeless population, sadly, consists of alcoholics, addicts, and the mentally ill, and they were going nowhere. Many of the same folks we saw when we started the feeding program were still on the streets when we made our last run.

— — — —

With The Bridge's opening, the downtown Dallas homeless would be getting fed (and housed), and they didn't need our help anymore. That phase of Hunger Busters was over, we realized, though my resolve to help wasn't. So, I met at length with Mike about how we could further address the growing problem at its roots. Soon, I got my answer. Most of the homeless had an unstable childhood and were often insufficiently fed, making them unsuccessful or less-successful students—and ultimately, unsuccessful people. The streets, or the jails, would often become their fates. What we really needed was a program that would start when the kids were young and went on to prevent the genesis of this perpetual poverty cycle. We couldn't get into these families' homes, but what if we could get into their schools?

I looked into the nutrition situation of local public schools and came across some sobering information. More than 137,000, or 87 percent, of all children attending the 160 schools in the Dallas Independent School District relied on both school-subsidized breakfasts and school-subsidized lunches as their only food sources. Most of these kids were picked up from after-school care in the early evening and would usually go without dinner because there was nothing to eat at home. That meant that they weren't getting anything substantive to eat from noon during lunchtime at school until they ate breakfast at school the next morning—a period as long as 19 hours.

Hungry kids, our research found, were twice as likely to be absent from school than their peers who weren't suffering from hunger. They also had two to four times as many health problems. It was apparent that enhancing the nutrition of food-insecure kids improved both their health and their school performance and would give them a far better chance to grow into productive, civic-minded adults. I wanted to address that, I said to Mike. So, in 2007, Hunger Busters transitioned to becoming a provider of that all-important third meal that kids could eat at school or take home so that they wouldn't have to go to bed hungry at night. It was a big challenge to launch this phase of the charity and considerably more time-consuming than you would think. There was quite a bit of administrative red tape and background checks and so on, but we persisted and finally earned approval, which was quite an achievement in itself, we were told. We brought a nutritionist on board to help us determine the type of well-balanced portable boxed meals that would best nourish the kids and fit our budget.

We settled on a hearty sandwich with meat and cheese, juice, fresh fruit, a cookie, and applesauce or a fruit cup. In the meantime, we started lining up vendor discounts and product donors, including my own Eatzi's and Nick & Sam's, and finding volunteers and administrators for what we'd come to call our Hunger Busters "Feed the Need" program.

We launched the after-school initiative at one test school, James Bowie Elementary School in an impoverished section of west Dallas. Eatzi's and Nick and Sam's produced the lunches and bagged them up, and we sent them over to the school. The program was very well received, and teachers reported positive changes in the overall performance of those kids who participated.

This gave us the green light to expand the program. By 2010, we had grown to providing meals in 11 Dallas public schools, serving 3,300 meals each week, or about 160,000 meals per year. Teachers and school administrators in all of the schools were uniformly reporting a positive difference in the participants, who entered the program on a voluntary basis with their parents' permission. At Botello Elementary School in the Oak Cliff section of Dallas, we were feeding nearly 100 kids when the principal called one day and said, "Can you please bring 25 more meals?" A few weeks later, the principal called again, asking, "Can you bring us 25 more meals?"

As the program grew, it was apparent that we needed to centralize the operation. So, we presented the Hunger Busters program to the Dallas philanthropic group, Crystal Charity Ball, and they gave us upwards of $600,000, which enabled us to retrofit a building on Sylvan Avenue near Trinity Groves with its own kitchen commissary to prepare the food. In 2017, we went to Crystal Charity Ball again, and they gave us another $1.2 million, all of which goes directly to purchasing the food.

Since Hunger Busters costs us about $600,000 per year to operate, we've expanded our fundraising with our Hunger Busters Corporate Program, in which we encourage companies to adopt a school for $40,000 to $45,000 a year to feed the kids. Participants often dispatched volunteer employees to help at the commissary and elsewhere as well. It's good to get the private sector involved like this because it allows local decision makers and their staffs to see what we're trying to accomplish, and it creates more discussion about the program. Banks, insurance companies, and other businesses also help sponsor us.

Our major fundraiser is the annual Hunger Busters Golf Classic, which raises about $400,000 each year, with local celebrities participating. This funds our administrative and overhead costs and much of the food, clearing the way for other donations to go straight to the kids' dinners. More than three-fourths of all dollars raised go directly into school meals that we produce annually.

My company throws in funds when needed, which is frequently. As of 2018, the cost to produce each meal was about $1.75. We'd like to reduce that going forward with additional donations and economies of scale, but it's still a small price to pay for filling these kids' stomachs. One of our promotions features a fork, and under the fork there is a pencil. It says, "Without one you can't use the other."

We hired a sharp, conscientious executive director, Trey Hoobler, who oversees a network of 350 volunteers as part of his duties. He goes out to private schools to enlist more privileged kids to help Hunger Busters by working through their community-service obligations, both as volunteers and as fundraisers. Trey, who is bilingual and previously worked at the Center for the Advancement of Human Rights at Florida State University, is really igniting these kids and our cause.

Today, Hunger Busters operates at 11 Dallas Independent School District schools and sponsors six after-school programs, providing nearly 400,000 meals annually. To date, more than 2 million meals have been delivered, with millions more to come. We're going to keep doing this, and we will expand it when practical and may add such services as volunteer tutoring. There are still plenty of unmet needs across the school district. Texas ranks fourth in the nation, with the highest rates of food-insecure children. Hunger Busters is always open to accepting donations and volunteers (214.220.0031, www.hunger-busters.com). We also encourage other communities to start similar programs to feed their communities' growing needs.

After nearly 20 years of heading Hunger Busters, I have turned the organization's day-to-day operations over to a board of directors, which is comprised of about 75 percent young and smart millennials. They run it well.

I hope more programs like Hunger Busters catches on around the country. Hunger Busters is not just giving these kids a meal; it's also giving them hope. And that goes a long way in nipping homelessness in the bud and creating a better future for them and our inner-city communities.

7

APPLAUSE FROM
THE GALLERY

To all entrepreneurs: We're all artists when you think about it. That doesn't mean that we're all Rembrandts. But we all have the capacity to create something unique, whether a restaurant, a musical composition, a building, a painting, a book, a sculpture, just to name a few possibilities.

I am a frustrated artist at heart. I love to create restaurants, but when I'm between concepts, I still have to do something to keep my creative juices flowing, so I paint. Unlike in the restaurant business, I don't have to buy, build, or lease a building to do this. I just buy a canvass and start creating something. The things that I see in the world, I put on canvass. The same goes for restaurants. The things I observe out there that I think need to be in a restaurant, I put into a restaurant.

When I was young, I got marketing ideas for my restaurants by going to the movies. When a movie was jam-packed with excited people, what kind of movie would it always be? A high-energy movie, not a love story. People just naturally gravitate to high energy. So I was determined I was going to infuse my restaurants with high energy. And I am also going to put high energy into my art, I thought.

Even as a young man, I loved art, and I was inspired by dozens of museums and art galleries at home and abroad, especially when I visited Europe. I've learned that I can project different types of energy using one color or another, both on canvas and inside my restaurants. What really turns me on are vivid colors. When I see a great piece of art, it just captures me and shouts "Wow!" I also like black-and-white paintings, which make a strong artistic statement because of the way those two simple colors contrast and complement one another. I always want to know how a great painting was done: what paints and techniques the artist used and how those indefinable elements that drew me in came to life.

I get my inspiration from some of the greats: Vincent van Gogh, Jackson Pollock, Salvador Dali, Peter Max, Mark Rothko, Robert Motherwell, and Gerhard Richter. I saw their works and thought, "That's amazing; a human being did that!" I found myself thinking, "If that artist could do it, maybe I can, too."

So, when I was in my early 30s, I bought paints, canvases, and brushes, and just jumped right in. I never had formal art classes at any point in my education, but I felt like a natural at the easel. I'd work on several paintings at a time—some abstracts and some realistic. Most of my art was crude at the start, but I just kept painting. I could go months without picking up a brush when I was creating a new restaurant, but I always returned to it.

I painted at home for a long time and then finally rented a little studio in the late 1990s near my Nick & Sam's steakhouse in uptown Dallas. There, I could spread my artistic wings without distraction and introduce my young son to art, and he'd paint with me. Back in 2000, *Dallas Observer* arts writer Patricia Sharpe saw some of my works and called me a "frustrated abstract expressionist," with paintings that are rich with "dramatic colors, grand gestures, high energy, and a penchant for painting outside the lines," much like my restaurant concepts. She was right: my paintings were a window into my creative mind and my soul.

The more I painted, the better I got. I even started liking my own work. I hung several pieces in my homes in Dallas and upstate New York. Over time, my paintings got more and more professional look-ing, and they got bigger and more plentiful. "If a little bit is good, more is better," I thought. I loved working on large canvases, includ-ing 78-inch-by-78-inch monsters, and people seemed to appreciate the added dimension a little more.

As happy as I was with my progress over the years, I felt that my work could benefit from a little added pop to really bring out the "wow factor" that I seek in my creations and move it to the next level. I stuck with using mostly acrylics and other water-based paints, steering away from the oil-based paint, in part because of the strong fumes, the mess, and the solvents needed to clean the brushes, and the fact that I was bringing my son Sam to paint alongside me.

In 2008, I met an artist, J.D. Miller, who owned a gallery down the block from Nick & Sam's. I liked his art, and as we started talking, I told him that I was also an artist, "at least I think." I brought him to my house and to my studio to look at my work. He said, "Wow, I like these."

At the time, J.D. just used oil paint and I just did acrylics. He said that if I was able to do my paintings in oil, it would add another dimension to them. I didn't know anything about painting with oils, so I went down to J.D.'s studio, and he was kind enough to show me the ropes. So I started adding oil to my paintings, but I kept an acrylic base. J.D. said that he really liked the effect I achieved by doing that, and I enjoyed the fact that I could actually mix paints on the canvas as part of the process.

I had been thinking, "What am I going to do with all my art?" My walls were getting full, so I kept giving paintings away to friends, who were putting them in their offices and homes. Then I suggested to J.D. that we open a gallery together. I owned an old building right next door to Nick & Sam's and said, "J.D., let's open up an art gallery there." We'd be partners in the business, and I'd renovate the place, I said. But the more we looked into it, the more we realized that it wasn't the right place for a new gallery. It should be over on Dragon Street, in the Dallas Design Center neighborhood near Oak Lawn, around other galleries.

I bought a former warehouse building at 1105 Dragon St. in the middle of the new "gallery row," where we would jointly display our works alongside other contemporary artists. I invested about $2 million in the renovation of the 11,000-square-foot building with the intent of making it the best art gallery in town. J.D.'s work, which is now displayed around the world, has a three-dimensional look because of his use of thick "impasto" strokes, or strokes with a brush and palette knife that create a three-dimensional effect and texture reminiscent of the old masters. He named the style "Reflectionism" because it is based on the belief that the universe mirrors each of us in a unique way. He said that his goal is to interpret that phenomenon through the multidimensional reflections of life that he puts on canvas. We also call his work

3D art, because when you stand away from one of his paintings, you get a deeper perspective of the 3D effect that it creates, with dimension and depth, and oil paints.

As we talked, I encouraged J.D. to make his work more contemporary. He was still doing some still lifes of floral arrangements and the like, and selling them to repeat customers, but I said, "That's good for old people, but you've gotta get modern." He took it well. The truth is, all of his works are amazing. But his contemporary "Reflectionist" pieces, I think, are catching fire in the art world and may someday be akin to the shift to Impressionism in the nineteenth century. It is a lively, new movement, much like a compelling new brand.

We needed a distinguished name and settled on Samuel Lynne Galleries, a combination of my son's name, Samuel, and J.D.'s daughter's name, Jaime Lynne. I thoroughly reshaped the interior and installed a 30-seat high-definition movie theater toward the back of the building where we could host lectures, educational panels, artist video screenings, and the like. We also added a wine and espresso bar there. We built a customized painting area for J.D., but I decided to retain my own studio since I did big paintings, used oversized easels, and needed more space than the gallery could comfortably accommodate. I also like to spread out and work on several paintings at a time.

Alongside our own contemporary work, we decided that we'd display paintings and sculptures from a mix of new, blue-chip and mid-career contemporary artists. We agreed to not only keep an eye out for emerging artists but also to help support them, as well as cultivate strong relationships between ourselves and our collectors.

This isn't just a pastime or a frivolous hobby for me. It is a retail business, and we both knew that we would need to actively sell art and augment our exhibitions frequently in order to keep the place relevant—and open. Our market is an expanding one. Dallas and its surrounding area continues to grow—the Dallas-Fort Worth region will have 7.5 million people living there by 2019—so there will be a lot of walls in new upscale offices and homes that will be in need of art.

We opened Samuel Lynn Galleries in September 2008, just nine months after I met J.D. Though Dallasites have historically gone to New York, Santa Fe, or elsewhere to buy art, J.D. asked the gathering at our grand opening to strongly consider Dallas as an art hub now as well, because our flourishing local artist community had grown in size, scope, and quality.

I sold my first piece of art for $15,000 at the age of 68! I learned that how much you charge for your art tells you what caliber artist you are, and I say that with a little irony. Who you're hanging with is who you are, as they say, and I'm in good company. I tell people that I'm too old to develop into a good artist, so instead of becoming one, I'm just going *to be one*. Do I want to be a world-famous artist? Hell, no. Do I want to be a recognized artist around my home base and in my country? Hell, yes. Soon after we opened, I landed my first commission piece for a private residence in New York. More recently, I did a huge horizontal painting for the University of Nevada at Las Vegas for the William F. Harrah College of Hospitality's new building. It was installed in April 2018.

Our roster of artists and sculptors has included the likes of Bernie Taupin (a great, creative visual artist in addition to his role as Elton John's longtime songwriting partner), fellow Reflectionist Lea Fisher, sculptors Hans Von De Bovenkamp, Lidia Vitkovskaya, and John Henry, plus sculptor/painters Fletcher Benton and Phil Gleason, and photographer David Yarrow, whose works are on display at my new Trinity Groves concept, The Network Bar. We've also housed the collections of photographer Tyler Shields, pop-art painter James Gill, fiberglass artist Tom Holland, funk-art painter Robert Hudson, painters William T. Wiley and Denis Mikhaylov, and the watercolor and mixed-media works of Incubus vocalist and front man, Brandon Boyd, to name only a handful.

Some might argue that people who buy my art do so because of the novelty of owning a piece by "that famous restaurant guy." But many buyers who don't keep up with the business community have absolutely no idea who I am other than as just an artist, even when I am introduced to them as Phil Romano.

When I buy art for myself, I always have to meet the artist because I need to like and understand its creator. After all, I'm going see this work hanging in my home daily. As an artist, you paint your feelings onto a canvas and project your vibrations into it, and those vibrations are important. I don't want an evil person's vibrations in my home; I look for a pleasant and positive feeling, something that projects good energy. That's what good art does. It just grabs you and pulls you in.

Consequently, I want to meet every person who's going to *buy* my art, to be sure that it's going to have a good home and so that the buyer can see who created it. If I don't like the buyer, I won't sell it, because I don't need to. I sell my paintings at my discretion. The money is just applause.

As galleries go, Samuel Lynne Galleries does more business now than any others in Dallas, selling between $2.5 million and $3 million in art annually. To date, I've sold well over $1 million worth of my paintings. Nearly all of the money, by the way, goes either to my

Hunger Busters charity or back into our gallery to make it better and bigger. I sell a surprising amount of my art out of Nick & Sam's, too, where I've had dozens of pieces hanging over the years. Artists who come there often comment about the art without knowing it is mine. After I identified myself as the artist, one of them told me, "When you have your art in the room, it takes over the room."

Samuel Lynn Galleries continues to build its patronage and draw local, regional, and national press. We're always trying to broaden our appeal by participating in major art fairs and organizing off-site showings to expose our collection to a variety of markets.

Of course, viewing art is subjective. Not everyone likes contemporary and modern art. In my long career, in fact, I've learned that you can make most people happy but not everyone, no matter how hard you try. That reminds me of the old Jewish grandmother who took her grandson to the beach. She was sitting under her umbrella while the boy was playing near the surf with his pail and shovel, wearing a little floppy hat that his grandmother had bought him. Suddenly, a huge wave hit the shore and pulled him out to sea. The grandmother jumped up and looked to the heavens, tears streaming down her cheeks, and cried out, "Please, God! Please! Bring back my beautiful grandson, my only grandson. He had his whole life before him. I've been a good Jewish lady all my life. Please, God!" Suddenly, another giant wave crashed ashore and deposited the grandson, still holding the pail and shovel, safely on the beach. She ran over and picked him up, hugging and kissing him. She called out, "Oh thank you, God, for bringing back my beautiful grandson. Thank you!" Then she paused and said, "But didn't he have a hat on his head?"

Joking aside, it's been my good fortune to possess more creativity than just about anybody in the restaurant-creation business, and I'm happy I can project that with my art. As I get slower and older, young people will be passing me by in the business world, but I won't fight it. I'll embrace it as the natural evolution of things. I'll just go to my studio and paint all day and again be king of my craft. I enjoy making art for two other reasons: First, I'm breathing life into something that never before existed, just like with each new restaurant concept I created, and there's nothing like it in the world. Second, I've got something I can do the rest of my life. When I *really* get old, I'll still be able to toddle down to my studio and create, and that's something few if any of my younger restaurant-industry colleagues can or will do.

My art is one more way for me to leave a lasting mark on the world, another way to be MAD, or Make a Difference. Philosophically, painting is not unlike the way you I create a successful restaurant or any other business. It has the same ingredients of creativity, color, finesse, charisma, and heart. Conversely, entrepreneurship is like art: it's a creative force. The same way in which I pause and absorb what is going on around me in the world and then reflect that in my restaurant creations, I pause and reflect and put that down on canvas.

Anyone can be creative—some more than others, of course. Anyone can play baseball, for example, though some play it much better than others. Creativity to me is a gift from God and using that creativity is a gift back to God. I'm often asked, "When are you going to retire and stop doing all these new things." I always respond that I will stop doing things when I am no longer creative. To not use the gift of creativity, no matter what my age, is a sin.

To all entrepreneurs: We're all artists when you think about it. That doesn't mean that we're all Rembrandts. But we all have the capacity to create something unique, whether it's a restaurant, a musical composition, a building, a painting, a book, or a sculpture, to name just a few possibilities.

I will be remembered by the things I've done in life, the people whom I've helped, and the differences I've made in this world, with my restaurants, the inventions that I have backed, and the charitable work I have done— those things that make people happy and well, full and fulfilled.

And now I have my art that's going to live in people's homes for decades. Anytime people see it, they'll think about me as its creator. Hence, I'll leave behind a creative energy that will remain indefinitely in people's lives and, hopefully, their descendants' lives.

As I've noted, I'm really not going to need a tombstone. I will live on in the art, restaurants, the 90-acre Trinity Groves development, and the medical devices I've funded. Like my paintings, I'll still be hanging around long after I'm gone. But my biggest and best creation I am leaving behind for mankind is my son Sam. I hope—and believe—he will contribute his share.

Chapter

8

AN Rx FOR THE WORLD'S ILLS: THE ART OF MEDICAL INVESTING

"It's not important how much money you've got; it's how you made the money and what you do with the money."

I was fortunate enough to make a lot of money when I was a young man. By the age of 40, I had $30 million in the bank. But I always remember what my father told me: "It's not important how much money you've got; it's how you made the money and what you do with the money." He was saying, in effect, "Make a difference with it, son."

How right he was. The best investment I have ever made occurred nearly three decades ago and ended up saving hundreds of thousands of lives around the world, as well as my own.

Here's how I saved my own life. On a warm morning in 2013, I was beginning my daily run, testing myself on some tough hills near my summer home of Skaneateles in central New York. I had charged up those same hills, located a few miles from my birth town of Auburn, dozens of times, but it was a real struggle that morning; I felt like I was running up Mt. Everest. I eased up but still couldn't catch my breath.

Still sucking air, I finally gave up and started walking home. At 73, I thought, maybe age was finally catching up with me. But something else was different—and bothersome. My shortness of breath came with a side of heartburn, and that condition is a rarity for me—a guy who spent a half-century in the restaurant business creating, selling, and devouring all kinds of rich and spicy dishes. I returned home to rest, puzzled and more than a little worried. Maybe I was just having a bad day, but maybe there was more to it.

It was as if my gut was literally telling me something was wrong. So I called my cardiologist friend in Dallas, Dr. Mark Jenkins, and told him, "Doc, I think I need one of my stents." *My stents.* I described my symptoms, and the doctor's tone grew serious. Mark was concerned that I might be having a cardiac episode and persuaded me to hop on a plane for Dallas the first thing the next day for an exam. While there were good physicians in the upstate area of New York near Syracuse University where my son now attends college on a lacrosse scholarship, I trusted Mark, who was not only a friend but also a product of the great Johns Hopkins University School of Medicine. He said he didn't want anyone working on me other than himself.

If this was what I thought, it would be my second brush with mortality. On my red-eye flight to Dallas the next morning, I flashed back to 1990, right after my 50th birthday. I was riding the wave of success I enjoyed with the creation and sale of Romano's Macaroni Grill, the country's first national, chef-driven Italian concept, which I founded in the outback of San Antonio in Leon Springs, Texas, in 1988. I had sold it for $6 million in stock in 1989 to publically held Brinker

International, and the Dallas-based company was starting to roll it out. They asked me to stay on month-to-month as a consultant, but I ended up being a joint-venture partner with them, creating Cozymel's Coastal Mexican, Spageddies (now Johnny Carino's), Rudy's Country Store and Bar-B-Q, and Eatzi's.

Life couldn't have been better. That is, until I developed a sharp pain in my side. "Appendicitis," I thought. "Well, they can just remove the appendix can't they?" After examining me, the doctor agreed with my assessment and scheduled an appendectomy a few days later. In the meantime, though, the pain subsided. Baffled, the doctor ordered a battery of tests. It was a swollen appendix that was the source of this on-and-off pain alright, but it wasn't appendicitis. Pressing on my appendix was a huge cancerous mass the size of an apple, and from the glum look on the doctor's face, the prognosis was grave. "It's malignant lymphoma," the doctor told me. I asked, "What is that?" He said, "It's a form of cancer." Well, you haven't really lived until you sit in front of someone who tells you that you have cancer and that you might only have months, or maybe just weeks, to live.

He told me they were going to operate and to go home and get my affairs straightened out because they didn't know what—or how much of it—they we were going to find. His words sounded like code for "you're dying." I had watched cancer take my dad, so hearing the word *malignant* was a punch in the gut. I was more pissed off than scared at the thought of going out this way with so much I wanted to do yet. A few days later, surgeons took out the massive tumor along with my appendix and six inches of intestines. By a quirk of fate, this ordinarily aggressive cancer was fully encapsulated and hadn't spread to my lymph nodes. It was a manageable large-cell cancer, which is aggressive, so it tends to try to attack chemotherapy and kill itself in the process. The doctor put me on chemotherapy for six months. I said goodbye to my signature ponytail and shaved all of my hair before the chemotherapy could finish it off. I looked like a six-foot dildo. Except for my wife and my attorney, I didn't tell anyone the truth because I didn't want people to think I had one foot in the grave. When people commented on my bald head, I said I was trying to win a bet. Little did they know that the real bet was whether or not I would live. Thank God I won that wager and have had no flare ups since. I had dodged a bullet and a big one at that.

I emerged from that episode fully realizing that we all have an expiration date, and it strengthened my resolve to produce and create—and to waste no time doing it. I told myself whenever I was inspired by an idea, "A thought just went through my head. I'd better do it now'; I can't when I'm dead."

Now there was this apparent cardiac episode. I was growing a little nervous as my flight got closer to Dallas. I couldn't help but wonder, "Is my expiration date nearer than I thought?" After touching down at Dallas/Fort Worth International Airport, I went straight to the cardiologist's office, not even bothering to drop off my bags at my Dallas home.

By midmorning, Mark had me on the examination table. By late morning, I was prepped and on the operating table for an extensive exam, which turned into surgery. The bad news: doctors found blockages in two of my arteries. The good news: Mark had inserted a pair of "my" coronary stents to keep the clogged arteries open. Fortunately, he liked what he saw when he examined me the next day and released me.

Bam! I was on my way back to New York that afternoon after my release. Easy in, easy out. As I settled back for that return flight, some profound things occurred to me. First, I had nearly died where I was born. Second, I had saved my own life. How so?

While most people assume I made the brunt of my fortune creating national restaurants, my main source of income came from one specific medical investment, and it was the best money I ever spent. Back in 1986 in San Antonio, I got a dinner invitation from a physician friend, Dr. Richard Schatz, who was an interventional cardiologist at Fort Sam Houston. He told me about an innovative young doctor of vascular radiology, Julio Palmaz, from the University of Texas Health Science Center at San Antonio, who had invented a tiny mesh-tube contraption that he would later call a "stent" that would prop open clogged arteries. A surgeon could attach this stent to a mini-balloon, deliver it to the site, and deploy it, I was told.

Richard even roughed out a drawing of one on a dinner napkin, and I remarked that it looked like a Chinese finger puzzle. The problem was, Julio had another kind of puzzle to figure out. He couldn't generate the funds to bring his invention to fruition, much less to market. As part of ongoing budget cuts, the university was about to shut off his R & D funding, and potential "angel" investors weren't very interested. But I was interested!

Though I had been a dedicated restaurant guy, funding this handy little device seemed like a no-brainer, even with my limited medical knowledge. As an investor, I thought it had what I call "sex appeal." That is, everybody has a heart, everybody abuses it, and there's really no remedy for it. But if this project worked, it would revolutionize health care and keep people alive for years longer, if not decades. My instincts told me that Julio would deliver.

As fate would have it, I was flush with capital after selling off my majority interest in Fuddruckers, which had gone public. I had more money than I could spend but not more money than I could lose, as the saying goes. And I was open to parking some of that bankroll in someone else's idea if the right idea came along.

My friends, my lawyers, my accountants, and my other advisors all said, "No, Phil, don't do it." Restaurants were my sweet spot, they said. But I told them, "I am going to do it." To this day, I say that if I didn't do what people had told me not to do, I wouldn't be where I am today. And if I had listened to them about the stent, I might be six feet under.

I agreed to put up $250,000 for Julio's continued research, clinical studies, development of the idea, and whatever else he needed. I would own 30 percent of the stent, Richard would own 20 percent, and Julio would own 50 percent. For his part, Richard would test the stent on animals and I would handle the negotiations with the pharmaceutical companies and other business matters. I talked with 10 different companies that were anxious to buy it and finally picked Johnson & Johnson because it had tentacles in markets around the world.

Needless to say, the stent took off, home and abroad, and hasn't stopped. Between our sale of the patent to Johnson & Johnson and royalties, our stent partnership has earned us more than $600 million. In fact, the stent was recognized by *Intellectual Property International* magazine as one of "Ten Patents That Changed the World" in the last century.

On that flight back to New York after getting my own stents, the irony of what had just happened was hitting me. More than a quarter of a century after I brought the stent to market, I now had two of them inserted in me. It was like eating my early food creations, only 27 years later. "I'm heavy into lateral integration," I had often joked with my customers and friends. "You eat my hamburgers, you get high cholesterol, and then you get a couple of stents." Now I was a living part of that joke, and I didn't mind a bit.

Not long ago, a person with my condition would have simply succumbed to arterial disease, and probably after much suffering, but no longer. Today, in fact, it's hard to find anyone who doesn't have a friend, a loved one, or coworker with a stent—or have one themselves. Over the years, as gratifying as it was to hear that my food was good or that my restaurant creations helped revolutionize the industry, it's nothing compared to, "Phil, you saved my mother's life," or "Phil, you saved my son's life." Or, better yet, "Phil, you saved *my* life."

I smiled, realizing that not many people can claim responsibility for bankrolling an invention that would save their own lives over a quarter of a century later. Now, with two stents holding open my previously clogged arteries, I was heart-healthy and free to keep creating and investing in new restaurants and new medical innovations. My son was only 15 years old at the time, and I still wanted to be able to help him through life. Now I would have more years on earth to do just that.

I also realized that all the working out I'd done through the years had helped save my life. If I wasn't active and in good condition, I don't think I would have suspected that I had heart problems because I wouldn't have been pushing my body with vigorous exercise. When I noticed a difference I took action.

I was feeling "new" when I got back to Skaneateles. A couple of days later, I was charging up the same hill like I was 21 year old. While

I felt a huge sense of relief to be alive, I also felt that familiar sense of urgency, much like the epiphany I experienced in San Antonio after learning I was cancer-free and then moving to Dallas to do bigger things.

— — — —

How did the stent come about? Dr. Palmaz, who was born in Buenos Aires and earned his medical degree at the National University of La Plata in Argentina in 1971, didn't see himself as an inventor. He started practicing vascular radiology at the San Martin University Hospital in the city of La Plata before moving to the states, where he did his U.S. residency in diagnostic radiology at the University of California—Davis.

By chance, Julio attended a 1978 medical seminar in New Orleans where Dr. Andreas Gruentzig, the inventor of the balloon angioplasty, was speaking. To his surprise, Gruentzig talked more about his invention's limitations than its merits and how once-clogged vessels and arteries could still "occlude," or close up, in patients after the procedure.

Julio is a guy who likes to figure things out, so he set out to find a solution to the problem, wondering if some sort of collapsible miniature scaffolding inserted in the balloon might keep the vessels open. He wrote a paper on that possibility, and in it he said that it might be possible to find a way to insert the tiny scaffolding into the artery to expand it.

To document his idea, Julio created rough drawings that would later reinforce the fact that this was his idea. Julio began playing around in his garage with wires, pliers, and a soldering gun, trying to create a prototype that could solve that occlusion problem. He would bring home angioplasty balloons and expand them inside rubber tubes to get a feel for what logistical issues he would face.

Julio tinkered around with his invention in his spare hours as the years passed. One day he found a piece of metal lathe—the kind that masons use to apply plaster—lying on the garage floor. An came on to mind. Julio realized that the lathe was made with a pattern of staggered openings and that a device made of such material might be the solution to building the necessary scaffolding. When Julio cut off a small piece of the lathe, folded it in half, and then pounded it with a hammer on his work bench, he saw that the staggered openings became staggered slots. This closed lathe created an interlaced structure, or a "mesh," with evenly spaced holes. It would serve as a crude model of what would become the expandable stent.

Julio accepted a post at the University of Texas Health Science Center at San Antonio in 1983 in part to gain access to the resources and the funding necessary to further his development of the stent . He eventually succeeded in creating a scaled-down, stainless-steel mesh prototype that could be expanded once it was inserted inside a blood vessel or an artery to allow blood to flow more freely. In the meantime, he worked with cardiologist Dr. Schatz to help with testing, designing, and funding the device. The device was showing promising results in animal tests, so they started contacting medical companies, but the response was tepid.

That's where I entered the picture, in 1985. Julio and Richard told me that the University of Texas system had turned down Julio's request for a patent filing on the stent and was running out of patience with its development. A federal grant to assist the stent's development was also nixed. I had turned down many entrepreneurs who sought funding for their inventions, but I sensed that this was something special because of its enormous potential to combat heart disease, the number-one killer of mankind.

The doctors needed $250,000, as I noted, and I was happy to oblige despite being warned off by those advisors who were concerned about the length of time required for the U.S. Food and Drug Administration (FDA) approvals. I didn't think about making a lot of money on the device. Instead I thought, "What are we going to do if this thing works?"

We formed our company, EGP (Expandable Graph Partnership), for further research and development, and I received a 30-percent partnership for my role. I handled the business end of EGP, including negotiations with the different manufacturers, and I helped negotiate a technology release from the University of Texas at San Antonio on the stent. (Today, that would be impossible because universities are so tightfisted that we don't even bother dealing with them on other medical innovations.)

Within a year, we had licensed the intellectual property of the device to a Johnson & Johnson subsidiary called Ethicon for $10 million, plus a lucrative 17-year royalty stream. This was before the stent even got its FDA approval! Another one of the big medical-products companies, Boston Scientific, passed on it, which would later come back to haunt them. Boston Scientific tried to lowball us by appealing to our idealistic nature, saying we should consider taking less money because the device would help humanity. Of course, I already knew it would greatly benefit humanity, but I told them that I wasn't a doctor, so I wasn't interested in the philosophical part. I said, "But aren't you going to charge for this thing?"

The more far-seeing Johnson & Johnson put $100 million of its own money into development of it. Julio and Richard did some feasibility studies in the United States and in Europe, for both a coronary version and a periphery (peripheral artery) version, and then a trial was approved by the FDA. In October 1987, Julio placed the first peripheral stent in a patient at Freiburg University in West Germany. Later that year, a patient in São Paolo, Brazil, was the first recipient of the new coronary stent. Both procedures were successes. Nearly one decade had passed from the idea of the stent to its being inserted in the first patient.

In 1991, the FDA finally approved the peripheral stent for the treatment of atherosclerotic obstructive disease, and it quickly became the product of choice for the interventional-radiology community around the world. The coronary stent was approved in 1994. Both were the first stents ever approved by the FDA.

It would become a monumental investment for the firm. In 1994 and 1995, Johnson & Johnson was the sole supplier of the product. We thought that maybe 20 percent of patients with clogged arteries would receive the stents, but that jumped quickly to 30 percent and then 40 percent of patients. Before we knew it, it became 75 percent. We were thrilled.

While Johnson & Johnson held the original patent, that didn't stop several other medical companies from jumping into the game. By mid-1996, there were three of them: Medtronic, Guidant, Cook Catheters, and Boston Scientific, which had passed on it at first. Johnson & Johnson's market share shrank. To defend its stent market, the company developed a systematic approach to suing the firms that appropriated its stent patent. The litigation with Boston Scientific dragged on for 12 years until they finally agreed to pay $716 million to Johnson & Johnson in 2009 and an additional $1.73 billion in 2010—the largest such awards ever granted.

We settled with the other companies. In its case against Cook Catheters, Johnson & Johnson called me as a witness. Fortunately, I had the foresight to keep the little drawing of the stent on the dinner napkin that Richard had given me before I met Julio, the one I said looked like a Chinese finger puzzle. It and some of Julio's early jottings and drawings also came in handy in proving Julio and our team were first to create the stent.

By 1996, the stent had earned our group $450 million. But with their market share down due to the competition, Johnson & Johnson wanted us to change our royalty deal. I said, "No. Why don't you just buy the patent from us?" They did, for about $150 million more. That's a pretty good return on investment. With my 30 percent of the company, I made almost $200 million alone on the stent out of our group's $600 million.

Within four years of its FDA approval, the stent was used in over 80 percent of percutaneous (done with a catheter through the artery) coronary interventions. No medical invention in history compares to it. New versions of the stent have since come out, including the drug-eluting stent, which prevents clotting and releases immune-suppressing drugs to help keep peoples' systems from trying to reject the stent as a foreign body.

Some of those early artifacts from Julio's research on the device are now part of the Smithsonian Institute's permanent medical collection, and the stent has grown to a $6 billion-per-year industry. I always wondered what would have happened if I hadn't funded this amazing little device. Hundreds of thousands of people might not be alive today—and that includes me.

— — — —

One thing the stent did was to signal to medical inventors, entrepreneurs, and friends that I was an angel investor who just might bite on a worthy idea. In fact, people came to me in droves with all kinds of different ideas and inventions. I guess they thought I knew what I was doing in the medical-device industry, but, in truth, I didn't. I just exercised good common sense with the stent and did the right thing.

Flash forward now to 2004. At a cocktail party at my house one evening, I met a cardiologist named Dr. Fred Maese and a surgeon named Dr. Richard Benavides. They were talking with me about lapband surgery, more formally known as laparoscopic adjustable gastric band (LAGB) surgery, which had just been approved by the FDA about six months earlier.

Part of Dr. Maese's practice was to get people to eat right and to lose weight, as he was dealing with a lot of obese people in what was becoming a growing epidemic. He'd basically evaluate the patients for the surgeon, who would then perform the lap band surgery at local outpatient surgical centers. At the time, the two had teamed up for more of these surgeries than anyone else around, but the surgical centers were making most of the money.

The two doctors wanted to continue performing these procedures, but they told me that they wanted to base their operations in their own outpatient surgical center. I told them I'd investigate this, and I took it to my attorney and dear friend Cecil Schenker, who I grew up with and had been my attorney and a partner in many of my ventures for 40 years. Cecil, by the way, had started out in a humble three-man practice and moved on to become managing partner of the high-powered Dallas law firm, Akin Gump Strauss Hauer & Feld. Cecil and I investigated and came away thinking that this was another one of those timely "sexy" ideas that would work because it addressed a pressing need: the lap bands were adjustable and safer than stapling and would no doubt save lives.

What we needed to do, we thought, was merge the cardiologists' plans to buy or build our outpatient surgical center or centers. There was already such a facility in Richardson where the procedure was being performed, run by a bright young MBA named Peter Gottlieb, but Gottlieb wasn't making much money.

Through Peter, we approached the owner with an offer to buy the center for about $1.6 million, and he accepted. I put in $800,000 and was the controlling partner, and the two doctors put in $400,000, each on individual loans I helped them arrange. We talked Peter into coming on board for a nice salary and a piece of the deal. We opened the first of our centers there and called it the American Institute of Gastric Banding (AIGB)—True Results. As far as I know, it was the first center of its kind dedicated exclusively to lap-banding. As part of our marketing, the doctors gave speeches to groups of about 30 people and explained the procedure. The doctors stood to make money from both the center and the patients.

Gastric banding, by the way, was replacing a more invasive and irreversible procedure called stomach stapling, or gastric bypass, after which patients had to be hospitalized for four days and could never eat a full meal again. Stapling cost more than $30,000 and had a significantly higher mortality rate of around 2 percent.

Gastric banding could be done cheaper—for less than $20,000—using a small laser incision and on an outpatient basis. The process consisted of wrapping an inflatable silicon band around the bottom of the esophagus to create a small pouch that served to limit the amount of food intake. Patients would eat less as a result, in part because it would increase the time it took for food to digest, suppressing their hunger. Later, depending on the patients' progress or level of comfort, the "keyhole" opening the doctors created could be deflated or inflated by adding or removing fluid through an easily accessible "port" that had been placed under the skin in the initial procedure. Most patients could go home the same day of surgery. The procedure really made a difference in people's lives and gave them both a physical and psychological boost that made them more productive citizens.

We opened additional locations in Houston and Fort Worth. Between the three locations, we made about $26 million in profit in the first two years and had almost no debt. But by 2006, there was a lot of compression and competition in the industry, and prices were dropping as a result. Also, insurers were starting to cut back on covering such weight-loss surgeries, despite their high rates of effectiveness.

We hired an investment banker to sell the business. An outfit out of Salt Lake City, Sorenson Capital Partners, a spin-off of Mitt Romney's Bain Capital, offered us $90 million for 60 percent of the company, and we took it. My son, Sam, who was 10 years old at the time, wondered why I didn't hold onto the company. "Dad, how many places do you have?" he asked. I said, "We have three places." He responded. "Why don't you keep them and build more places and sell it for twice that much." I said, "That's a good idea, son. I like the way you're thinking, but timing is important, and you've got to sell while it's hot." The profit on my $800,000 investment was $45 million.

A consistent problem with companies buying my businesses over the years, whether they're restaurants or medical companies, is that new owners go out of their way to put their own stamp on them to the detriment of the business. We had a perfect, profitable model when we sold EGP (Expandable Graph Partnership). But the new owners came in trying to use more of the lasik-surgery model without partnering with local doctors like I had. The business quickly went south. We never did profit on the back 40 percent, but we did well on the front end.

Like the stent, gastric banding met my personal medical-investment parameters: it filled both a big need and a big market niche. But there would be many more niche opportunities coming along for me to keep making a difference in medical investing.

— — — —

One of the offshoots of the gastric band venture was a weight-loss shake we called AmazeRX. One hitch in lap banding, we had found, was that the swollen livers of some morbidly obese people had to be moved out of the way to complete the procedure, and those livers tended to be fatty and easily damaged, so we developed a 30-day liquid protein diet designed both to help heal livers and jump-start the weight-loss process. It worked. Their livers were pink and healthy looking after a few weeks, but the shakes, frankly, tasted awful, so I ended up bringing in a flavor creator from Baskin-Robbins to conceive four different palatable flavors, with Divine Double Chocolate being the most popular, and we even made an infomercial for AmazeRX, which sold pretty well.

AmazeRX was the impetus in 2006 to form a small venture capital business called Scientific Health Development (SHD), in partnership with Stuart Fitts, who would also become my Trinity Groves partner later on. Thanks to my successes in the medical field, I was getting inquiries from other friends and investors seeking opportunities.

As we looked around, there were many opportunities out there to help nurture small health incubators and inventors. While health-care "venture investment" had grown into a big industry, most venture firms required at least $5 million from investors for the investors to get in the door. That made our investor niche of less than $2 million easy to identify.

We would become a "boutique" venture firm and create small investment funds—there are three at present—and apply the money from those funds mostly to American life-science companies with promising medical devices or new cutting-edge pharmaceuticals. The big venture funds tend to ignore these small medical start-ups because they find them too risky, so, consequently, many potential game-changing inventions are lost. We could help bridge that gap and find more companies and, again, make a big difference in people's lives in the process.

We chose to take the incubator with what you call "garage technology" and grow it to a point where larger medical funds would buy it. At the same time, we'd be given a lot of opportunities through these larger medical funds that saw inventions in which they'd like to invest but couldn't because those inventions weren't big enough for them. They'd show them to us, we'd put our money into them and help them grow to a point where the larger medical funds would want to buy them. Sometimes we'd sell an invention to them, and sometimes we'd take it on ourselves. The larger medical funds would have the right of first refusal.

We wouldn't monopolize the profits or charge management fees like other funds did, which were two other factors that were in our favor. We didn't want to form a company that was dependent on fees for income. These tend to make investment firms complacent because they provide an income stream that makes the investment firms less motivated to actually perform. We had also decided that we'd only take out money from the fund to pay the rent and minimal staffing costs at our modest offices on Cedar Springs Road in Dallas.

Individual investors, including Stuart and me, would invest no more than $1 million and no less than $100,000 in each of the first two funds, SHD I and SHD II, which would top out at about $15 million each. Those funds, in turn, would invest $1 million to $2 million in each medical start-up venture and try to have it ready to sell in two years, which we called our "two-plus-two philosophy." Our third fund, SHD III, which was created in March of 2015, has a $5 million-per-investor limit and has grown to over $30 million. One of the problems in dealing with the medical-research field, by the way, is that scientists and doctors never want to stop researching and making their products better, which is good, but it really slows down the process.

To get started, we hired Carter Meyer, a "recovering lawyer" at the time—his term. He had been a transactional attorney for the Dallas-based firm of Vinson & Elkins and came aboard to set up and operate SHD. Carter already had substantial experience making investments in both the public and private sectors. He joked that Stuart and I were dumb enough to hire a lawyer to do a job and that he was dumb enough to go to work for two guys without a fund yet. About a year later, though, the first fund was going at full speed. We later brought in Andrew Offer as chief financial officer. He was an expert in the business valuation of health-care companies and a senior analyst at Value Management Group (VMG Health) of Dallas.

I might add that I met Stuart, who earned his MBA at Southern Methodist University —he attended on a golf scholarship, at a children's soccer game when our children were each about four years old. He had been a partner in an intellectual-property partnership that owned a portfolio of more than 150 patents, and he had operated TV and radio properties in Palm Springs. Our team quickly established a pipeline of ideas and built a network of doctors, analysts, and other health-care experts to provide a perspective on them. We didn't need to beat the bushes to solicit investors; most of our deals came from referrals, and some of them came from larger funds. Over the years, we'd met dozens of innovative people in the medical industry, and several of them either came to us or brought other people to us. There isn't much early-stage capital available out there in the venture capital world, so word traveled fast in medical-entrepreneur circles. My track record with previous medical investments, which had netted me more than $250 million, didn't hurt either.

As a venture capitalist, I want to see three things before I invest in someone's idea: a distinctly different concept from anything that exists in the marketplace, a person behind it who has the ability to execute that concept, and a product that will not replace one that the doctors or the principals involved already own. We looked for these qualifications in all of the small companies whose owners we interviewed. The products they made would have to be innovative and be backed by clearly defined goals and would have to make sense to develop from a cost position. They shouldn't require an enormous amount of financing to get them into the market, and they should solve medical problems that will benefit society. That goes back to my premise: don't think about making money; think about servicing a need, and you'll make twice as much money.

The first fund had eight companies under a pretty broad umbrella of general health care, and the second fund had seven companies. Through our first fund, we determined our venture capital "sweet spot" was life-science products, diagnostic medical devices, and pharmaceuticals.

Among our many successes were Loma Vista Medical of Burlingame, California, which created a dilatation balloon made from high-strength materials. It's resistant to the catastrophic ruptures, punctures, and tears that are common with other balloons inserted during heart-valve implant procedures. The product, called the TRUE Dilation Balloon, also has a capacity for fast inflation and deflation, which further improves its stability. It's the first time any company has been able to produce something like this. We put $2 million in Loma Vista Medical from SHD II and tripled our money, selling it off for $6 million.

Another of my favorites was Anterios Partners, a biopharmaceutical "aesthetic-medicine" company that has developed a Botox-like cream that we believe is destined to replace a lot of the injectable versions. It not only reduces wrinkles but also works on acne, and it provides a remedy for people who sweat profusely, called hyperhidrosis, by paralyzing their sweat glands. The remedy is used like a deodorant. They rub it on in places where they sweat, and it deadens the muscles under the skin so that the sweat glands aren't squeezed. The cream lasts for 30 days and is a good alternative to getting shots every 30 days. We helped the company fund their all-important clinical trials. Anterios Partners is also producing a new ready-made Botox preparation that will save doctors the hassle of mixing freeze-dried botulinum toxins in their offices before they give injections. Anterios Partners was sold in early 2016 to Allergan for $90 million plus milestone payments.

We also assisted Sight Sciences Inc., an ophthalmic medical device start-up, with funding both a minimally invasive surgical-product line and a breakthrough dry-eye treatment device. Sight Sciences Inc. was founded by Mack and Tommy Hicks, the sons of Tom Hicks, former owner of the Texas Rangers baseball club and the Dallas Stars hockey team. Their company, Hicks Equity Partners, came to us in 2011 to tap into our industry due-diligence expertise.

We tend to own 10 percent to 20 percent of companies with our fund investments. By its nature, venture capital can be risky because there are a lot of start-ups that fail: Venture capitalists are doing very well if they have a 50-percent success rate, and that's where we stand. That's also why we try to keep each fund so diversified.

As for AmazeRX, we hung in there until 2014 with it, when annual profits dropped below $5,000, so we finally pulled the plug on the weight-loss protein shakes. Carter liked the chocolate blend so much that he had the remaining inventory unloaded into his garage before the balance was liquidated. However, that shake is an example of what we *don't* do now.

SHD has supported or is supporting development of a cryoablation (extreme cold) treatment to kill cancer cells, clinical trials of a drug to help women suffering from heavy menstrual bleeding, emergency preparedness-and-response software, technology for early detection of Type 1 and Type 2 diabetes, a treatment for central nervous system disorders, and a catheter-deployed micropump for the heart. A fourth SDH fund is certainly a possibility in the next few years.

The problems we're trying to solve with the start-up companies we support are significant, and the products invented by the people we deal with are fascinating and on the cutting edge. SHD is another way for me, along with my partners and investors, to make a difference in the world. The good health of our country is at stake.

9

PHIL'S ORGANIZATIONAL CHART FOR A SUCCESSFUL LIFE

"Honesty must come first in everything of value"

I have never been big on the confines of organizational charts. I'm not a corporate kind of guy, even though I have launched dozens of companies. I just don't fit that rigid corporate mold. In fact, when Norman Brinker of Brinker International, then called Chili's Inc., tried to talk me into coming on board back in 1989 after I agreed to sell Romano's Macaroni Grill to him, I told him I'd ruin his culture and that I'd be a dark splotch on his organizational chart.

I can be headstrong, un-PC, and I never do anything by the book, I told Norman. Doing something "by the book," I always believed, is usually just a way of saying you can't figure out a better way to do something. Plus, I'm a crowd-pleaser, not a crowd follower, I said, and I had a ponytail and didn't wear socks (I still don't). Much like now, I spend very little time in the office because I can't get inspired sitting behind a desk. My office is in my head.

How much nonconformity could Norman deal with, I wondered? Yet he persisted, and I agreed to join him on a month-to-month basis as a consultant to help make sure that he was doing the right thing with Romano's Macaroni Grill. After six months, I told Norman I was giving him my 30-day notice. Norman, along with his right-hand man, Ron McDougal, asked me what I was going to do, and I said I was going to go out and create new and different concepts. Norman asked me, "Why don't you create them for us? I had some reservations, but he and Ron persuaded me to become the industry's first concept-creating "intrepreneur," with some autonomy to do my own thing if I wanted to.

The truth is, I find most corporate structures stifling because they're too systematized, which just kills creativity. Most systems tend to make people afraid to step forward with fresh ideas or to offer solutions to problems for fear of stepping on someone's toes. So naturally, I've never used a pyramid organizational structure in my businesses or anything resembling one.

My concepts' organizational charts are structured so that my people can quickly react to changing customer demands, new challenges, and customer feedback. They're more like wheel charts, with me in the center and various spokes—marketing, finance, real estate, construction, and so forth—extending out from me. Although I make the major decisions, I have a handful of trusted people in each "spoke" advising me independently. When the organization gets too big to operate, I create a standard operations chart and let someone else run the organization.

Over time, I started conjecturing about what my personal organizational chart would have looked like if my Sicilian-born parents, Rose

Chapter

and Samuel Romano, and my grandfather Philip, who helped raise me while my dad served in World War II, actually had drawn one up. As I pondered this, I came to realize that most of the values instilled in me to make me a better human being were the same values that I lived by in my restaurants. Those values—truth, integrity, honor, responsibility, imagination, passion, and generosity—give my concepts a point of difference and usually a long and productive life span.

With my son growing up quickly, I had another thought: why not create an "organizational chart" for Sam? Wouldn't it be better for him to have all these guidelines on paper—besides just hearing me repeat them all these years—than to lose sight of them later? I also wanted to put his "organizational chart" on paper as a reminder to him of his obligations to himself, to his family, and to other people. After all, Sam has always been a receptive kid who's been open to my advice, which I doled out as I drove him to school every morning. So, I started jotting down the qualities that made for a happy, successful person, and worked up a "human organizational chart" for my son. I think this could apply to just about every kid.

At the top of chart is the "CEO," the governor of us all, "Health." Like me, Sam has endured his share of health issues, and we both have emerged with a great appreciation for the importance of good health. Sam had ulcerative colitis as a kid, which is the chronic inflammation of the large intestine, and he did everything he was asked to do by the doctor to heal, taking his medicines and complying with a special diet to reduce the inflammation. He recovered without having surgery and has no problems with the condition since then.

Later, in his mid-to-late teens, Sam went under the knife twice for labrum tears in each of his hips, which are not uncommon in lacrosse, which requires a lot of repetitive cutting and twisting. Each time, he did everything he was asked to do for rehabilitation. For an active, athletic young man with a lot of energy, he showed commendable patience. As one of the top high school lacrosse prospects in the nation while he attended Episcopal School of Dallas, he won a scholarship to Syracuse University and decided to have his second labrum tear repaired during his first year there, sitting out as a "redshirt" during his freshman year and coming back the next year with his four years of playing eligibility intact.

For my part, I suffered through an initial diagnosis of malignant lymphoma at the age of 50 and went through intensive chemotherapy, followed by a cardiac episode at age 74 when I became the recipient of the miracle stents that I bankrolled back in the 1980s. Sam and I know that you have everything when you have your health. These challenges taught us both to be survivors.

Under "Health" on the organizational chart are five "spokes" (areas) that have great importance: Parents, Academia, Girlfriend(s), Athletics, and Friends. Ideally, parents are responsible for instilling these essential traits under the "Parents" heading: Principles, Responsibility, Integrity, Communication, Patriotism, Charity, and Spirituality.

I taught Sam as a young boy that Principles are sticking to any deal you make with others and doing what you say you are going to do. Responsibility is about owning up to the choices you make and accepting the consequences of the wrong choices you make. Integrity is about being honest with others in all dealings and being honest with yourself. Honor your promises and your deals. (I've done many deals on a handshake.) "Above all, don't lie to yourself," I would tell him. "And think for yourself; don't let your peers or others do it for you."

I also told him not to be afraid to tell others how he feels and to commit to effective Communication in all his matters. "No one will know how you feel unless you tell them," I said. "But don't let people tell you how you should feel."

I also impressed upon Sam the importance of Charity and how good it feels to help others. When he was small, Sam would ride with me on our Hunger Busters route when the program included a mobile soup-and-sandwich van that would roll out to points around Dallas where the homeless congregated. Seeing that aspect of life left an early impression on Sam about the less fortunate and how we can help the needy—and do so without being judgmental. When he was six years old, he would say, "I'm worried, dad. Where are all these people going to go to keep warm? It's cold out."

I told him he could employ this same charitable process later in his life by first helping out people he knows and making a difference in their lives. As it turned out, a few of his buddies were struggling to afford college; another had a family financial crisis. We talked about each case, and I asked my son what he wanted to do about them. Each time, he said he wanted to help, so we did. Sam discovered how gratifying it is to make a difference in other peoples' lives.

Because Making a Difference (MAD) has been the theme for my entire life, I'm confident Sam will carry on that tradition. As the years went by, I told Sam he would be able to identify ways he could help even more people. He can support my Hunger Busters organization, of course, and/or other charities, or he could create his own.

Sam is already conservative about money and lives by the "One-third Rule," which I taught him when he was a young boy. One third of what he earns must go to charity, the second third must go to savings (and later to investing), and the final third can go to anything he wants. So, if he wants something that costs $100, he has to earn $300 to get it. By the way, the "Value System" entry under the "Parents" column on the chart includes several key components to life success, so I broke them out at the bottom as a constant visible reminder. They are Principles, Responsibility, Integrity, Communication, God, Patriotism, and Charity. I've long reminded Sam that he needs to show loyalty to God, to himself, to his commitments, and to his country in everything he does.

Academia, which heads another column, is not only for a place to learn but also can help teach him how to think critically and creatively, as well as to better understand different cultures and walks of life, I told him. He will get functional knowledge there for his career. "Learning is your job when you're young," I regularly told him. But I was careful to add: "Education is a great thing, but it's not the only thing. Life is the best teacher of all."

Having a Girlfriend is also a crucial learning experience. It will help teach the joy and sometimes the sorrow of affection, love, and the expression of feelings, plus the establishment of trust. "This shows you how to get along with someone you care for in the long term, and, eventually, it lays the foundation for having a family of your own someday," I told him.

Sam grasped the merits of Athletics early on, enjoying team sports from the time that he was a young boy. This does so many things, he found, including bonding with like-minded people, gaining pride and prestige from winning, and humility from losing, plus the realization that he can change outcomes by adjusting and adapting new strategies. Athletics also teaches us how to read our bodies, which gives us a better sense when something is wrong because it's reflected in our performance. My own lifelong dedication to fitness probably kept me from having a full-fledged heart attack, which the doctors said was probably coming, since I realized that my unusually heavy breathing and heartburn during the workout that day signaled that something was wrong, maybe very wrong. If I hadn't exercised daily, I would have had no such gauge, and the worst might have happened.

Athletics can also be an avenue to bigger things, and it was for Sam. While he was good at football and other sports, he seemed to gravitate to lacrosse, and he practiced it relentlessly. When he was in the sixth grade, his history teacher made Sam write a letter to himself about his future plans, which she would keep until he graduated from high school, and then she would send it to him. Sam, who had decided to attend Syracuse University as a high school sophomore, read it with me when it arrived. "When I graduate from high school," it said in part, "I want to go to Syracuse University and play college lacrosse." Talk about knowing yourself! I thought, "Wow, maybe my human organizational chart is paying off."

Of course, Sam worked very hard for his success. He didn't use drugs, he listened to his coaches, he ate healthy, and he kept up his grades. He was ranked the No. 1 lacrosse player in Texas and the No. 3 lacrosse player in the Southwest. On his wall full of honors there were Nike All-American, *USA Today* First Team All-American, Adrenaline All-American, U.S. Lacrosse All-American, and StickStar Lacrosse Player of the Year. He also broke his high school's single-season points record. Sam is shrewdly self-promoting (I wonder where he got that?) and has used his considerable computer and social-media skills to put himself out in front of the sport's decision makers. He maintained his own Sam Romano Lacrosse Blog during high school, with a personal lacrosse highlight reel that received 100,000 hits.

Sam was focused and had a goal, and he worked hard to achieve it. He had ulcerative colitis and got over that. He was privileged and got over that, resolving not to let that privilege affect his character, his work ethic, or his ability to relate to all kinds of people. He had labrum tears and got over that. I told him, "You worked hard to do the things you had to do to get there, and you worked hard to avoid the things you knew you couldn't do to get there. You did it. I am proud of you."

Along the way to Syracuse University, Sam made a lot of Friends, which is the last area on the organizational chart. I told him in heart-to-heart talks when he was young that that's where his Camaraderie and Bonding and some of his best Memories and Enjoyment of life would come from. As for his friends? "I trust you because you're my son," I said. "But I don't necessarily trust your friends." He should choose friends who have the same values, I suggested. "Don't choose friends who lie to you, who have questionable principles, who are lazy or disrespectful, who use drugs, or who don't believe in God; people who have good values are also going to choose you for a friend. After all, you're going to go to their weddings and their funerals." Parents would become less and less important to him because they would already have done their job of instilling good fundamental values in him.

Our environments and role models are very important in our lives. I was lucky enough to grow up in a stimulating environment with strong, positive values, thanks to supportive parents and grandparents. Outside the home, if you associate with respectable people who work hard and have good habits, that's how you will act, I told Sam.

I've tried to offer Sam the same type of supportive home environment that I had growing up and to help steer him to an arena where he would find the right kind of people, and there's no doubt in my mind that he's there now. He continues to build on that nucleus. Yes, he's privileged, but we've worked hard at not letting that privilege affect his character and his ability to build a work ethic and to relate to all kinds of people.

We are all "human concepts" who need rules to live by to be successful. With a little modification, the approach to life using this organizational chart can also apply to businesses, communities, and other entities, as well as to kids. It's flexible. The areas of importance can change, but the elements of responsibility, ethics, principles, and integrity should always be included.

I always applied this sort of chart, at least mentally, to my restaurants. When I create a concept, it's as if I am creating a person. I see how this "person" operates, how strong this person's constitution is, whether this person has a clear operating framework, and how I can help this person remain faithful to the core principles. Just like a person, if a concept's constitution is weak or flawed, then poor and inadvisable decisions can follow. I see the latter happening all the time throughout the restaurant world and in other businesses, and I can usually tell when a business is doomed.

To me, the management and employees of a good concept need to understand its constitution from top to bottom and stay true to its founding principles, regardless of outside forces. They should feel that they have a responsibility to do the right thing and to be responsible for what they don't do right. Honesty must come first in everything of value. A good concept needs to make its brands stand for something good. As an entity, it needs to communicate openly with customers and employees, and maintain a running dialogue.

Every restaurant I do has its own Bill of Rights. Furthermore, in every concept I create, I ask myself, "What is sacred to this concept?" I give it a constitution and a personality. People are attracted to a strong personality, but if that personality changes, people may not like that person anymore. The same goes with a restaurant. If its personality changes, it won't be the same, its atmosphere won't feel the same, it won't be perceived the same, and its food won't taste the same or be liked the same. It's not enough to say the food is fresh; you've got to show it. And you have to make a Bill of Rights to stay true to your founding principles.

For example, following is my Customer Bill of Rights for Fuddruckers.

1. Meat: Only the best

2. Buns: Only the freshest

3. Cooking: Cooked to order

4. Condiments: Whatever customers want and as much as they want

5. Atmosphere: Truth in feeding and fun

The following shows how the Customer Bill of Rights were fleshed out as the concept evolved.

1. Meat: We ground our own meat, bought beef by the quarter, deboned it in-house, and used no additives. It was grilled the day it was ground, and it was never frozen.

2. Buns: We baked the buns fresh in-house all day long using our recipe. They were hot to the touch when served to customers.

3. Cooking: We cooked burgers on cast-iron griddles to the customers' specifications, searing the meat first and then cooking it to order. The cooks focused only on the meat; the buns and condiments were handled separately.

4. Condiments: Customers took their perfect burger and bun to a convenient condiment bar that was so big and full that it looked like a supermarket produce stand. It also had a pot of melted cheese. Customers could layer on as many condiments and as much cheese as they wanted. They weren't at the mercy of the chef.

5. Atmosphere: We put people right in the middle of the space where the World's Greatest Hamburgers (our trademark) were being made. Everything was prepped and cooked openly, including the meat. We had a glassed-in butcher shop where the meat was visibly ground. The walls were lined with displays of our premium supplies, including bins of produce and cases of ketchup and mustard, and beer. There was a separate, highly visible bakery where the buns were baked from scratch. Customers could smell the baking bread and could watch as bakers carried trays full of hot buns across the eating area, yelling "Hot buns, coming through." Because we were in high-density areas where apartment dwellers didn't have backyards, there would be a patio in the back where customers could sit and enjoy a burger and a six-pack.

Most of the original Bill of Rights for Fuddruckers remained well after I sold it off but others didn't, such as the visible butcher shop. But it still translates well in today's demanding restaurant climate and serves a great burger.

As for the best "concept" I've ever created, my son Sam, I have full confidence that he will stick to his founding principles—those that are listed on his own personal organizational chart. I am a good father only because he is a good kid. His personal organizational chart is essentially his own Bill of Rights. "You have all these values spelled out for you so that you won't be a rudderless boat in the water," I told him. "That's your life in a nutshell; these are your guidelines. You have all these expectations that you're going to do a great job at life. You don't have to be super intelligent. But I do want you to be super smart."

Value System

Principles – Responsibility – Integrity – Communication – God – Patriotism – Charity

<u>Principles</u> – Stick to your deal. Do what you said you were going to do.

<u>Responsibility</u> – Be responsible for making the right choices and be responsible for the consequences if you don't. Know right from wrong.

<u>Integrity</u> – Honest...Truthful...Trustworthy...Don't lie and don't lie to yourself.

<u>Communication</u> – Tell people how you feel. Don't let them tell you how you should feel. Express yourself. Show leadership.

<u>God</u> – Believe in God

<u>Patriotism</u> – Love of your country

<u>Charity</u> – Giving Back

Grade School to College

Health

Parents 20%	Education 20%	Girlfriend/ Boyfriend 20%	Athletics 20%	Friends 20%
Foundation	College	Feelings	College	Companionship
Independence	Job	Companionship	Enjoyment	Camaraderie
Value System	Reasoning	Affection & Love	Teamwork	Fun
Human Dignity	Thinking	Understanding	Friends	Enjoyment
Role Model	Future in Life	Enjoyment	Bonding	Bonding
Education	Succeed	Trust	Winning	Memories
Support	Be Functional	Memories	Fitness	Networking
	Culture	Bonding	Prestige	
	Career Choices		Health	
			Self Confidence	

YOUR VALUE SYSTEM

Principles – Responsibility – Integrity – Communication – God – Patriotism - Charity

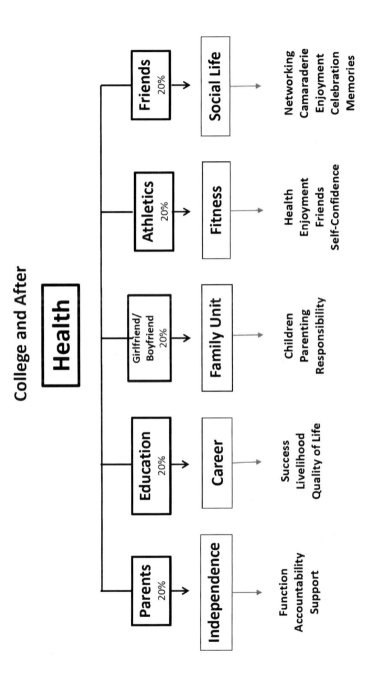

College and After

Health

Parents 20%

Education 20%

Girlfriend/ Boyfriend 20%

Athletics 20%

Friends 20%

Independence

Function
Accountability
Support

Career

Success
Livelihood
Quality of Life

Family Unit

Children
Parenting
Responsibility

Fitness

Health
Enjoyment
Friends
Self-Confidence

Social Life

Networking
Camaraderie
Enjoyment
Celebration
Memories

YOUR VALUE SYSTEM

Principles – Responsibility – Integrity – Communication – God – Patriotism – Charity

10

A BRIDGE TO SOMEWHERE

"Let's create the world's first restaurant incubator."

Though I've been a lifelong restaurant inventor, I have seldom dabbled directly in the real estate end of the business, even though my creations occupy millions of square feet around the country and the world. In the past, when people started talking to me about the subject, I'd usually brush them off with an off-color joke with a double meaning: "Real estate? All I know is that you need to get a lot while you're young."

For the most part, I've left all the details of negotiation, due diligence, land planning, development, and the like to the professionals. But I made a vow decades ago that I'd never stop adapting to the changing world or miss out on any great new opportunities. Sure enough, a great opportunity presented itself to me at age 65, which made me a full-fledged developer for the first time and cast me in a variety of other new roles.

In 2005, Dallas politicians started talking about building a signature bridge over the Trinity River to connect downtown Dallas with the city's economically challenged west side, part of the Trinity River

Corridor master plan that was designed to provide better flood control and new amenities along the river. Hating to miss an opportunity, I got together with a couple of my far-seeing friends and associates, Stuart Fitts and Butch McGregor, to start hashing over investment and development possibilities for the "poor" side of that planned bridge, in what was a destitute part of town.

While no clear development idea came from that meeting, we decided to start buying up land there anyway, and we formed a new company, West Dallas Investments LLC, to move forward. We bought every tract of land that we could on the north and south sides of Singleton Avenue at the foot of the future bridge, the first property that motorists would see as they crossed the bridge. Early on, we were paying as low as $2.50 per square foot for our hodgepodge of tracts, and we just kept on buying. Most of the properties were underutilized commercial and industrial parcels with aging warehouses. Their owners, for the most part, were more than glad to unload them. Some of our purchases were time-consuming and challenging due to poor public-record keeping, title issues, un-platted lots, hard-to-locate multiple owners, abandonment, unpaid tax bills, and a few holdouts.

The process dragged on, but we persisted over the next few years, and when we had accumulated about 25 to 30 acres, we invited Tom Leppert, then Dallas mayor, to come over to our site and talk with us about his thoughts on potential uses for it. We explained what we had done so far and told him that we'd like to buy more land but feared that we would have to fight City Hall all the way when it came time to develop the properties.

Tom could see the potential impact of our project and got very excited about it. "Whatever happens here is going to dictate what happens in the downtown area for the next 100 years," he said. "Go right ahead and keep on buying; if you can park it (build enough parking), you can build it. You're not on any flight pattern or under any other restriction," he told us. "We're very interested in this sort of thing with the bridge coming in. The city will cooperate; we don't want to build a bridge to nowhere."

When Tom said that, I responded, "Then let's call it a bridge to somewhere." The mayor nodded and smiled. So we kept on buying. And buying. But then, all of a sudden, after we had accumulated over 80 acres, it felt like we were the proverbial dog chasing a car. What do we do with it when we catch it?

We bought up a few more tracts but then realized we needed a definite plan. Through the University of Texas architecture department, we organized a charrette, which, in real estate circles, is basically an intense planning period that brings together design and development professionals who propose ideas and solutions for a property's stakeholders.

Half a dozen of some of the world's top urban planners, including the designer of the 2012 London Olympic Village, came to Dallas for the charrette and sketched out their visions of what the site could become. We also brought in city managers and other officials so they could better understand the potential of what could happen there, given our strategic location and great access to downtown. Dallas Area Rapid Transit light rail would be coming, and this development could evolve into the crossroads of Dallas at some point, they said. "It's the only place the city can grow to its west, toward Fort Worth," said one official.

Most of the local moguls weren't very excited about it. "This is west Dallas, and it has a stigma," we were told. "There's really nothing of consequence down there other than Ray's Gun Shop." Others said, "It's downtrodden; there's crime and chop shops all over there" and "I'd be afraid to go down there at nighttime," I also heard, "No! What are you doing, Phil?" People thought we were absolutely crazy. They said we should do this thing in North Dallas, if anywhere. But at $35 to $40 per square foot, how much higher could values go from there? Plus, it was becoming apparent at the time that redevelopment was going to continue to push back into the city's urban core, much as it has around the country.

On the whole, we bought into our west side development for about $10 to $11 per square foot. For comparison sake, land on the downtown side of the bridge was going for $275 to $300 per square foot at the time. What does that tell you? Given the right project, we felt that our land could be worth $250 to $300 per square foot someday. We had 100 acres in total by then—and that was after selling off 25 acres that we weren't going to use to other investors and developers at a handy profit. Once more I realized that if I didn't do things because people told me not to do them, I wouldn't be where I am today.

We wanted to do something trendsetting and long-lasting. There were three different plans we talked about with the urban designers. One was trying to turn the area into the new financial district for the United States and even the world. We thought it could become a new financial hub. It was centrally located, and the Federal Reserve Building was just across the river and would be just a few minutes away when the new bridge was built. All the banks in the United States and even the world could put their iconic buildings there and talk about how they were adapting for the future. It was a good idea with maybe a 20-year horizon or longer. At that time, however, Wall Street was headed for disaster.

Another idea was to make the development a green noncarbon energy capital. We could try to get all of the new high-tech sustainable energy companies to come in, since Dallas was already the power capital of the country, and have them show off all of their next-generation bells and whistles. Every major green company in the United States that wants to make a statement about their business could put up iconic buildings there; it could become a Silicon Valley for green energy. We could create a greener model for the world and make Dallas famous for it. Again, this was a sound idea but with at least a 20-year horizon.

We also thought that we could come up with a short-term plan that didn't interfere with our long-term plan, sort of like putting a golf course on a property for cash flow and land-banking it until we came up with a permanent use for it. We all began thinking about these ideas.

Sometimes the long-elusive solution to a problem has been staring you in the face all along. One day I went to Stuart and said, "You know, my industry needs fresh restaurant concepts. This new generation has been going to the same chain restaurants with their parents for 20 years, and they're looking for something different. They want their own clothes, their own way of shopping, and their own restaurants run by their own people. What better place than here?"

I had already done some test-clustering of restaurants in the San Antonio area in the little town of Leon Springs and had put together some very successful concepts, including the first Romano's Macaroni Grill, Cozymel's Coastal Mexican Grill, and Rudy's Country Store and Bar-B-Q plus a dancehall, and people were going to them in droves. "Leon Springs quickly became a little entertainment center," I told

Stuart. "I think we could do that here but a little differently. We could bring in promising young millennials who are short on money but want to be entrepreneurs and control their destiny, and help them create brands." I call millennials "new people," and who better to create new brands for new people but new people?

Millennials are the consumer group you hear so much about, making up the largest part of the American work force. Born from the early 1980s to the year 2000 or so, they're more ethnically diverse than previous generations, and logically they have more diverse tastes. We'd need to offer a wide diversity of food options to stay ahead of the curve. Millennials are also finicky and can feel a little bit entitled, and they get bored quickly with the "same old, same old." Because their attention spans are shorter, restaurants and retailers have started tailoring their products to them in ten-year cycles as opposed to those defunct 30-year models. That's why pop-up shops—and now, pop-up restaurants—have become so popular.

Stuart loved the incubator idea and the target demographic, as did Butch. And the location was perfect for it, we agreed. I told them that one of the lessons I had learned from Leon Springs was that people would go just about anywhere for an extraordinary restaurant, and that the "just about anywhere" in our case was a short jaunt over a beautiful new iconic bridge. Our research confirmed that this was an original idea and that there was no such incubator in the country or world. There were business incubators in the technology world, but all they did was lease space with only minimal assistance from the project's creators. We could provide both capital and guidance. "Let's create the world's first restaurant incubator," I said to the partners. "We'll have new brands for the millennials, the new people."

We came up with a name: "Trinity Groves," for its location along the Trinity River Corridor, with the "Groves" piece reflecting the 1,500 trees on the property, which we realized that we could illuminate at nighttime with twinkling lights.

Millennials, we came to find, also like to patronize independent and local businesses more than they do established chains, and we vowed there would be no national chains recruited for our restaurant complex. We wanted to *create* national chains.

Millennials also want "wrap," meaning they lean toward services, products, and businesses wrapped around a good cause—a little extra "feel-good" bang for their buck. And they like "ethicacy" in the businesses they patronize, a term used for those companies that do the right thing the right way, that is, with more of a service motivation than a profit motivation. That's always been my operating principle anyway. It's why I split with my very first restaurant partner at The Gladiator: he just wanted to soak the customer and I wanted repeat business. These days, if you really want to succeed in business, you need an ethical purpose, a value system that will help you stay successful. You need "wrap."

The opposite of their parents, many millennials have fled suburbia for city living and are moving downtown or to other urban spaces. Due to our do-nothing government bureaucrats, much of this demographic is still renting, thanks to their enormous student-debt levels and underemployment due to the imploding economy of the late 2000s.

Although they may not be able to afford to live in New York City or the handful of other large cities that are "alive" 24/7, millennials are more than happy to live in 18-hour cities such as Dallas, especially if they can take mass transit or walk to work, while living a short jaunt from night spots, entertainment options, and imaginative eating places. My partners and I soon realized we would be wise incorporating a mix of uses with residential components at Trinity Groves, as well as offices and retail spaces. But, in our case, we would first build the amenities—the restaurants—which is the opposite of how most developers proceed.

Dining out is one of the main vices of millennials, and they're more prone to supporting unique homegrown start-ups than are baby boomers and genXers. They like to "eat local," opting for locally sourced foodstuffs when given the choice, and generally eating healthier than previous generations, although they do leave room for indulgences.

Our homework, in fact, told us that millennial consumers spend money on four major categories in this order: clothes, eating out in restaurants, alcohol (mostly craft beers), and electronics. Also, they are on the lookout for new opportunities and prefer to work for themselves. Because millennials think so differently, we had a group of college kids who interned locally come in to participate in a focus group and talk about what they thought would work at this complex and what wouldn't. We gained a lot of additional insight this way.

Because of the Dodd–Frank Wall Street Reform and Consumer Protection Act, which makes it far more expensive for start-ups to raise capital and create jobs, would-be millennial entrepreneurs have been hard pressed to obtain loans from banks these days in order to strike out on their own. The borrowing public would have to take all the risks. If you are established, banks will, in effect, loan you some of your own money, but woe to the young entrepreneur with a good idea who walks in the door. So, we set to work laying out a funding formula for our cash-strapped millennials ("incubatees") that would not bog down their creative minds as they built their businesses.

When we put out our ads and social media feelers for prospective entrepreneurs, we got a huge response: over 400 prospective entrepreneurs came to us. We handled the screening process much like the *Shark Tank* TV reality show, in which entrepreneurs give their business presentations to "shark" investors, who then decide whether or not to invest in their business, except that our format was more practical and less exclusive.

We formed a Food and Concept Advisory Committee that interviewed a wide assortment of aspiring restaurateurs, from chefs and operators to people who never worked in the business but had good ideas. We listened intently to determine if their concepts were what we were looking for and would fit our format. We also wanted to see in them a passion for their ideas and a commitment to working extremely hard. As we narrowed the field, we had the finalists cook in our kitchens, where we tasted their food two or three times. We had them create a five-page business plan and meet with our designers and architects. There was one other important factor: not only did their ideas have to work in a 2,500 square-foot space that seated 125 people (plus a patio), but also their ideas had to "have legs" meaning the candidate and concept had to be imaginative enough in the eyes of the committee to eventually be rolled out at different locations.

To finance our "incubatees," we put together an entrepreneurial fund of $12 million. I put some money into it, as did Stuart and other investors in the community, including law firms, accounting firms, vendors, and friends of ours. Our partnership gave each restaurateur up to $500,000 for finish-out, equipment, furnishings, and so forth, with no investment required from the tenants unless they wanted to add some of their own money, in which case they'd get a higher percentage of the ownership. One of our stipulations was that the restaurant always had to be owner operated.

The entrepreneur would own 50 percent of his or her restaurant concept. Trinity Groves, in turn, would own the other 50 percent of the restaurant, and we would serve as the general partners. The incubatees would have no financial liabilities in our deal but no guarantee on the lease, either. They would pay us a portion of total sales as rent. The restaurants would have to offer a creative and distinctive concept and gross about $2 million in annual sales.

A separate management company that we formed would charge a 5-percent management fee, that is, 2.5 percent from the incubatees and 2.5 percent from us as co-owners, to run the back of the house, which would include handling the money, accounting, profit-and-loss (P & L)statements, invoices, tax payments, and economies-of-scale purchasing. We negotiated a great deal with U.S. Foods, which offered us a huge volume rebate on food and drink.

We told our incubatees, "You must listen, work hard, and have a passion for your concept." For that effort, the tenants would receive a $60,000 yearly draw against their profits. At the end of the year, if the place made a $300,000 profit, the fund would get $150,000, the tenant would get $90,000 plus a $60,000 salary, or $150,000, plus the potential to become a chain. That wasn't a bad deal for someone who didn't have a job but had a great idea. Where else does this sort of opportunity present itself in North America? We're doing what our government hasn't been able to do for itself: create new jobs, opportunities, and brands in the city; recapture land and expand the tax base; and give people a place to go that's new and different. That's what Trinity Groves is all about.

We also reassured our incubatees that we were there to help them be successful, because some haven't owned or operated a restaurant before and they don't know how to run a business yet. Every month we sat down with the incubatees to go over their P & L statements, address any challenges they faced, and tell them what they were doing wrong and what they were doing right. We also worked together with them on marketing to teach them how to keep their concepts successful, how to grow them, and how to replicate them somewhere else. We're basically built-in consultants. If the restaurant fails to perform, however (we usually give our tenants 12 to 18 months to establish themselves), the tenant gets booted out. There were always 25 other owner-operators ready to come in there. We will never have a shortage of available tenants.

If a concept really takes off and expands or is bought by a national chain, the owner and investors stand to make a bigger chunk, franchising or growing it themselves around the region and country. When they take their concepts elsewhere, Trinity Groves still owns 50 percent of those concepts.

— — — —

Meanwhile, the Trinity River Corridor bridge, which was becoming a huge priority for the community, was moving along as scheduled. Designed by Spanish "starchitect" Santiago Calatrava, the $182-million bridge was in the process of getting topped by a 40-story, curved center-support arch that would be visible for miles in several directions. It would become, planners believed, one of the city's top landmarks. And the bridge would open up that part of town to countless thousands who hadn't visited West Dallas in a long time, if ever. Our job was to give these folks a reason to drive across that bridge.

Visitors and locals alike who'd see this signature piece would immediately want to see where it led. You could tell people who were interested in Trinity Groves that it was at the end of the bridge—a giant and eye-catching span that you could point to from just about anywhere in town. I told city leaders that I thought our project would be the most recognizable destination in Dallas.

We were excited about the opportunities Trinity Groves would create and the new entrepreneurial blood it would attract. For years, I had been beating the drum about how more businesses were closing than starting up and that we needed to do something about it because the future of our economy was at stake. The reason for this situation, at least in part, was oppressive government regulations, an overall bureaucratic attitude that trumped reality, and high corporate taxes, which have thankfully dropped in the current administration. The regulatory hoops you need to jump through to get a restaurant open today have gotten ridiculous. Yet, it's these same aspiring entrepreneurs who are responsible for all the new small businesses in the country that the government has practically been shaking down. I often wonder why our government doesn't understand this.

It comes back to my term, "regulation without representation." Governments tend to make rules without having any understanding of how they're going to affect the people they regulate. In the United States, we have career politicians making all these self-defeating laws when what we really need are more business people rewriting them or getting rid of them entirely. This would be fairer representation. People who have actually done something in business know what it takes to run a business and know what it takes to hurt one.

How bad is the problem? America used to rank first in business start-ups among developed nations. Where are we now? Second? Fifth? No, try twelfth. This is a serious economic illness. There are more businesses dying than businesses starting every year in America, and this is really only a recent development. There are about 400,000 new businesses springing up annually, according to the census, with 470,000 per year dying. This is tragic because our nation's economy and financial future depend on the velocity of small businesses being created.

Legislatively, the federal government treats small businesses like major corporations, though this is changing in the present administration. The same regulations they put on major corporations, they put on small businesses and it's just killing them. Since the Great Recession, small firms have created two-thirds of net new jobs in the United States, and they're responsible for 13 times more patents than large firms. Besides being tax-prohibitive, it's very risky, if not cost-prohibitive to open a business today. Start-ups should have access to low-interest loans and should be given more of the advantages, incentives, and credits that are given to the big firms. Fairer tax structures and smarter and less onerous regulations would give start-ups a better chance of survival.

At Trinity Groves, we addressed this problem by supplying our incubatees with seed capital and a physical space for those who couldn't afford to do it themselves. This would create opportunities for talented young people to build their own businesses, to control their own destinies, and to become an asset to their communities. It doesn't matter what brand you talk about, it still has to have its first location, whether it's Starbucks, Bed Bath & Beyond, or Fuddruckers, and it has to have a smart, ambitious operator and adequate working capital. Let's give some of these people a chance.

Stuart, Butch, and I knew our plan would appeal to millennials in a variety of ways, especially if we added a strong "mixed-use" element to the complex with residences, retail shops, a hotel, and offices. The sum total of that would give millennials something new, homegrown, and unique—just what they are seeking. We would have a wide variety of concepts, categories, and retail shops throughout the development to help satisfy the diverse tastes of these "new people." As for the "wrap," we'd set up a program so that a percentage of each restaurant's take would go to benefit a worthy charity.

The project would also give me latitude to create some new concepts that I'd been dreaming up for a while, and to have a leasing program for unique permanent spaces. Some of the naysayers thought this sort of thing would be tough to pull off in West Dallas, but I love a new challenge, especially if it's something I was told not to do but persist anyway, and Trinity Groves is another shining example of that recurring theme.

We briefed our then-new Dallas mayor, Mike Rawlings, on our ideas, and he practically turned cartwheels. Mike was elected mayor in 2011, and he came into that office already knowing what we were trying to do. We were already friends, and he'd worked with me in repurposing the charity I founded, Hunger Busters. It is common knowledge that I am a dedicated Republican and that Mike is a Democrat, but I really like him because he knows what it takes to succeed in business.

Mike has much more of an entrepreneurial spirit than others who've held his post and has an impressive business pedigree to boot. He's been good for Dallas. He's the former CEO of Pizza Hut and former chief executive of the high-profile Tracy-Locke advertising agency in downtown Dallas. Soon after his election, I met with him, and he vowed to get behind our project and help us gain access to any relevant city incentives and resources available. Mike clearly appreciated the economic potential of this project; he gets it. Mike is now vice chairman of a private-equity firm, CIC Partners, which provides counsel and capital to entrepreneurs growing small and mid-sized businesses.

A boon for us and for the city was Mike's decision to include West Dallas in the GrowSouth initiative he created, aimed at incentivizing and renewing the city's struggling south side. He knew that a lot of Dallasites typically wouldn't venture to economically challenged South Dallas, but with a future bridge spanning the Trinity River, they could actually see what it was we were doing in our neck of the woods in West Dallas. They would understand firsthand that we were taking an impoverished part the city and rejuvenating it, creating hundreds of jobs, improving the neighborhood, making it a safe area, and creating a bigger tax base. Rawlings said the transformation of the old industrial area over just a few years was "remarkable."

We were also able to access some incentive money for infrastructure as part of a municipal management district called Trinity River West. The city also linked us into the same tax-increment finance district (TIF) it used to develop the American Airlines Center arena, home to the Dallas Mavericks and Dallas Stars, and the area surrounding it, in part thanks to Mike's help. At one point, I told Mike he ought to really take advantage of what he was able to help do with Trinity Groves as an illustration of a successful private–public endeavor that worked and created jobs and opportunities. I told him Trinity Groves would put a feather in his cap and would be instrumental in making it happen if he were to run for the Senate. We'll see what he does.

As the incubator started to generate a buzz, some envious investors who'd otherwise never have taken a second look at the property started bitching that we got the jump on the land and were tipped off about it ahead of time. Frankly, by the time we made our move, plans for that bridge were no secret. Some commercial investors came in later to the game and bought land near us, kicking themselves that they hadn't acted sooner.

Meanwhile, the city was ecstatic that someone was taking the initiative to activate such a run-down area and that we were starting our project well before the bridge even opened. While city planners and Dallas citizens were optimistic that some economic development would occur there, they never expected anything as productive as what was happening. The Margaret Hunt Hill Bridge, named for the late philanthropist from the prominent local Hunt family, was now becoming the "bridge to somewhere," and Trinity Groves was becoming the gateway to the city's resurgent west side.

— — — —

For decades, this deteriorating West Dallas neighborhood had been plagued by abandoned storefronts, warehouses, and crime, and it needed major infrastructure upgrades and some land leveling. The city asked us if we might buy out four beat-up, problematic drug houses on an adjacent tract in the modest La Bajada neighborhood, and we complied, tore them down, and left the land vacant. The *Dallas Morning News* picked up on this and started interviewing people who accused us of trying to kill the residential part of the neighborhood by buying out every house there, even though that was never our intent. We already had the acreage we needed. The only changes we intended to make to owners' homes was fixing their porches and fences and cutting their lawns, if need be because it was our neighborhood, too. We did this only for owners, not slumlords.

Still, a local architect and self-proclaimed activist, Brent Brown, pushed hard to designate La Bajada as a conservation district, and he eventually got the city to approve a restrictive Neighborhood Stabilization Overlay there. The overlay would prevent construction of buildings higher than 27 feet, among other controls such as disallowing the joining of multiple lots to facilitate commercial construction. Brent is founder of the City of Dallas's CityDesign Studio, so that may be why the city stood behind him and just let him go ahead with it. (I also suspected that he might have had a conflict of interest there, since he was taking the old houses and renovating them for a living.)

For all we were accomplishing in this once-downtrodden neighborhood, the city sided with Brent, not listening to our warnings and not realizing the long-term consequences for homeowners. So, instead of the remaining owner-occupiers (about two thirds of La Bajada's residences were owned by landlords) having the potential to sell their properties to commercial or other investors at a substantially increased value at some point in the future, they were stuck. Over the last few years, in fact, residents have been coming to us, practically begging us to buy their homes in La Bajada, but we don't want their property and never have wanted it. "We can't get anyone else to buy it," they have told us. And why is that, Brent Brown? Because you tied their hands.

The neighboring land that we bought for as little as $2.50 a square foot is now selling for between $30 and $40 per square foot, and it probably will sell for more by the time this book goes to print. Sadly, those homes will never be worth that price. The Neighborhood Stabilization Overlay took care of that. What Brent did, in effect, was freeze these owners' property values and make it much harder for them to sell their property. To top that off, Brent acted like he had the authority to tell us what we could and couldn't do with our own property in our planning stages. I still don't know where he got the impression that he could do that.

Once, one of his CityDesign Studio lieutenants got up in front of the Dallas City Council in the guise of giving an economic-development presentation, saying that the studio wanted this and that in our development. Finally, a frustrated councilwoman asked him, "Do you folks have any money in this thing?" He replied that he did not. "And have you ever been in this business before?" she asked. Again, his answer was no. "Then leave these people alone," she continued. "They are entrepreneurs, and they are trying to build something here for the west side. They're trying to create jobs." Exactly.

Though we did our best to recycle and renovate existing buildings for the initial phase, of which was a former truck terminal loading dock was the first, some new construction would have to occur at Trinity Groves, but we did our best to reincorporate everything there.

Meanwhile, work on the bridge, which started in earnest in June 2008, was progressing well. In 2010, its 40-story support arch was finally topped with the anticipated dynamic curved span. The bridge opened on March 29, 2012, seven years after we first started our land speculation. Now, the pressure was on us to keep our project moving toward a planned 2013 opening in order to capture all of the new bridge traffic.

Despite my air of brashness and confidence, the fear of failure that first took hold of me when my dad mortgaged his house for me remained firmly intact as Trinity Groves took shape. There were times when Stuart and I would call each other up at three in the morning because we both couldn't sleep, worrying about what was happening at the site.

Of course, this wasn't the first time I had created a cluster of restaurant concepts. Back in San Antonio, following my cancer scare at the age of 50, I had felt the need to create again, and I started eyeing property in the sleepy little town of Leon Springs, about 10 miles from San Antonio along Interstate 10. I long maintained that if you served outstanding food and marketed yourself in the right way, you could put restaurants in the middle of nowhere and people would still come. And I was right. Three national concepts, Romano's Macaroni Grill, Cozymel's, and Rudy's Country Store & Bar-B-Q, all were in Leon Springs, which the local press nicknamed "Philville."

Trinity Groves, however, was a far different animal than "Philville," with a lot more moving parts and an ever-changing master plan. We were aiming for a spring 2013 opening that would eventually turn into a fall opening. It was a strategic delay that would give more tenants a chance to settle in and have their own individual openings, which would be staggered, instead of our original plan of unveiling everything at once.

There was an even bigger buzz going on about Trinity Groves than I had anticipated. We were flooded with 400-plus inquiries and about 75 business plans, initiated by word of mouth and our marketing efforts. The best of the best were going to set up shop at Trinity Groves, and the project was evolving well beyond our imagination.

11

TRINITY GROVES GOES LIVE

"The American Idol of incubators."

When we first started planning Trinity Groves, we thought about pulling together all the famous chefs in town to put restaurants there, but then we realized that millennials and the rest of the general public might be a little tired of seeing all those famous chefs. They were wonderful chefs, but there was nothing new with them—it was the same old, same old. Also, they tended to be prima donnas. After a while, we realized what we really needed were young chefs, who could introduce new ideas and new food. With them, we would get the benefit of the "wrap" and of making these young chefs successful and famous rather than making famous chefs wealthier.

We opened in the fall of 2013—a few businesses at a time. We signed some deals for our lease spaces, including a business called 3015 Trinity Groves, which was the brainchild of cooking instructor and caterer Sharon Van Meter, who uses the 10,000-square-foot space as a site for catered events, cooking, and corporate team-building exercises.

She was joined by brothers Mike and Bob Babb, who opened the fast-food and casual BBQ & Blues on Bedford Avenue as our inaugural incubator concept, offering Kansas City-style smoked meats and live music. I opened a gourmet hot dog restaurant called Hoffman Hots, serving the same brand of dogs I ate when I was growing up in Auburn, New York. I'm a partner in a group that bought out a 135-year-old manufacturer of Hoffman hot dogs, with plans for an eventual national rollout. We commissioned top-flight artist Shepard Fairey to paint two beautiful murals in Trinity Groves for our opening.

We created a pop-up restaurant location called Kitchen LTO (Limited Time Only), an incubator within the larger Trinity Groves incubator, featuring up-and-coming chefs and artists for four- to six-month dining experiences. Contestants would take part in a tasting and design review, and a panel of judges would select the finalists. The community at large voted on the winners on the Kitchen LTO website.

Another inaugural incubator was Souk, a zesty Moroccan bistro featuring wood-burning ovens and rich colors, with live music and belly dancing on weekends, and Amberjax Fish Market Grill, a combination fish market and casual grill. Chino-Chinatown opened, a Latin-Asian fusion concept created by chef Uno Immanivong, ("Chef Uno"), who is known for her role on ABC's *The Taste* with Anthony Bourdain. Uno was the exception to our "no famous chef" rule. She is a source of never-ending creativity. Resto Gastro Bistro and Casa Rubia opened as well but have since closed, making way for other concepts. However, Hoffman Hots, which was performing well, had to be knocked down to clear a space to build apartments. Hoffman Hots will likely crop up elsewhere.

We've added incubatees Sushi Bayashi, with its authentic cuisine from owner-operator Yuki Hirabayashi's hometown of Shitimachi, Japan; LUCK (Local Urban Craft Kitchen), a craft-beer-inspired bar and kitchen promoting local craft beers; Tapas Castile, a fresh take on the Spanish tapas bar; and Off-Site Kitchen, a predominantly to-go gourmet burger joint that also serves brisket , all in a compact space with stool seating; 3015 at Trinity Groves, a flexible culinary event venue overlooking the Margaret Hunt Hill Bridge that can accommodate events drawing up to 500 people, including weddings, receptions, corporate meetings, parties, nonprofit events, culinary education classes, and more. Then there is The Hall Bar & Grill, Saint Rocco's New York Italian, V-Eats Modern Vegan, Beto & Son Next-Generation Mexican Food, and The Network Bar, all of which I'll touch on in the coming pages.

In a three-person partnership such as ours, you have to divide the responsibilities according to specialties for things to work properly. Since I am the restaurant guy, I am in charge of that segment, getting the units constructed and operating, and then overseeing them. Butch is the real estate guy in charge of buying and accumulating all the land and selling off parcels that we aren't using, while Stuart helps develop the property, negotiating with tenants and builders. It works. In a *D Magazine* article recounting Dallas/Fort Worth's top real estate stories in 2014, Christine Perez wrote of Trinity Groves, "Boy, do Stuart Fitts, Butch McGregor, and Phil Romano look like geniuses now." So much for those naysayers that I fortunately didn't listen to. I must also note the irony of three Republicans launching a project that was facilitated by a Democratic mayor, whom I made a pact that we wouldn't argue politics.

We also brought several key nonpartner team members into Trinity Groves, including Bob Sambol, founder of the world-famous Dallas-based Bob's Steak & Chop House chain. He created and runs our management company, called Trinity Groves Support Group. We needed someone to come in and oversee the restaurant concepts and to make sure they were working well and doing the right things within Trinity Groves requirements. Bob was an easy choice. We also added Jim Reynolds as the construction and development director for Trinity Groves; he handles our building contractors as well as zoning issues and other developmental dealings with the city. Luis Cruz came aboard as our chief financial officer, in charge of financing and accounting.

There have been some casualties, as we knew there would be, including one of my ideas, Potato Flats, a fast-food casual lunch concept similar to a build-your-own burrito bar. We would smash potatoes flat on a press—fried or baked, sweet or regular (or half and half)—and then serve them the way customers wanted, with vegetables, steak, chicken, ground beef, turkey, or seafood. Customers would walk down a line to specify what they wanted.

Potato Flats was a good, well-received concept, but it was in the wrong place. As Trinity Groves evolved, our customers overwhelmingly preferred wait service over the counter service that we had at Potato Flats. Also, Potato Flats needed to be "in the way," that is, in airports and colleges, and possibly in malls, where there was high-volume foot traffic, instead of "out of the way" at a destination location. We've had numerous investor inquiries about Potato Flats, and it too may resurface again.

One of my Trinity Groves concepts, Saint Rocco's New York Italian, took form at the prominent front corner space of the restaurant complex. It is our most visible eatery from Singleton Road, and it pulls people in with its theatric Broadway-style lights, which are visible from across the river.

People asked me, "What's New York Italian?" Well, most immigrants from different parts of Italy came through Ellis Island, much like my grandparents and mother and father did, and when they got there, they had no money to go anyplace else, so most of them stayed in the New York area. Their recipes, like their Italian dialects, differed from region to region of origin: different sauces, different tastes, different ingredients and different cooking styles. Over time, all of these different regional styles blended together and became a hybrid—a best-of-the-best melting pot. It's not northern Italian or central or southern Italian. It's New York Italian food, and that's what Saint Rocco's New York Italian serves.

Saint Rocco's New York Italian is also an ode to all the great food-and-family memories I had as a child as I sat around our big round table in the kitchen with my parents, friends, grandparents, and other relatives, drinking, dining, laughing, telling animated stories, and arguing. A fellow Italian, Jay Valley, is my Saint Rocco's entrepreneur. Jay has been with me for more than 20 years and was my Eatzi's executive chef. I put the concept together with him in mind (he owns half of it). Both Jay and I gathered up a lot of our old family photos to hang on the wall to create a family feel and Italian authenticity. Photos of my dear mother Rose and my father Sam, who met working in the old Dunn & McCarthy shoe factory in Auburn, are principal among them. There's one of me taking First Holy Communion. Such a reverent smile for a kid who could be a holy terror at times, especially at school.

The menu at Saint Rocco's New York Italian is a slightly modernized combination of Jay's family recipes and my family recipes. Talk about a homage: Jay even uses his mother's old hand-cranked pasta machine and ravioli cutter to make our lobster ravioli. We also serve wonderful flatbread pizzas with a crispy crust and generous toppings, and such things as an antipasto board with salami, prosciutto, aged provolone and Gorgonzola, roasted red peppers, and artichoke hearts, and a deconstructed lasagna like our moms used to make with tiny sausage meatballs. We offer Milanese, Bolognese, and Parmigiana cooking, all at a moderate price point.

To set the mood, there's ruby-red carpeting, black-and-white tile, and some large, circular, Italian "arguing tables." Loaves of bread are stacked near our domed oven, cans of San Marzano tomatoes line the shelves by the open kitchen, and there's a big wall of wine. In the background, the famed Rat Pack crooners serenade guests as white-aproned servers tend to the patrons at linen-draped tables.

Several of my lifelong Italian buddies flew to Dallas for the Saint Rocco's New York Italian opening in September of 2015, including lifelong cronies Major General Jack Leide, David Dellostritto, Joe DeLoia, and Johnny Reo. They joined my old pal Tony TaCito, a Dallasite who helped create Saint Rocco's New York Italian's atmosphere and organize the photos for the wall. Those guys told me they seldom eat Italian food outside their homes, but they felt like they were eating their mother's food when they tasted the breaded and sautéed Veal Milanese, which is one of my favorites there, and many of our other dishes.

We've since added an event space on the second floor called Saint Rocco's Event Hall, overlooking the Trinity River, Hunt Bridge, and downtown Dallas, which seats up to 200 people. It is proving to be a great place for wedding parties, especially Italian weddings. We also have a Rooftop Lounge that seats up to 150 people and may well offer the best view of Dallas that you can find at a bar.

And yes, there actually was a Saint Rocco (often called Saint Roch). He lived in Rome in the mid-1300s and was known as the "Protector Saint" because of the miracles he worked while protecting the people from the plague and other diseases. Italian communities around the world still honor Saint Rocco with annual festivals. And what would one of my Italian restaurants be without a little irreverent humor? The bottom of the menu says, "If Saint Rocco were here eating with us today, he would say, 'Jesus Christ, this food is good!'"

In the spring of 2016, our resident steak expert, Bob Sambol, put together a sporty little steakhouse and bar for another of our entrepreneurs, his long-time chef, James Rose. The Hall Bar & Grill has a club-like atmosphere and is dedicated to the history of college football. It features The Hall Wall, covered with 8-inch by 10-inch photos of former college football players living in the area. From the start, we always felt we were missing a steak component at Trinity Groves, and this place fills the bill.

The Hall Bar & Grill seats 100 people, has a classic-saloon feel, and is open for lunch and dinner, offering prime filet, sirloin, rib-eye, London broil, huge burgers, chicken, sandwiches, and a few surprises such as Creole strudel, plus a full complement of cocktails, beer, and wine. Among the first photos to go up on The Hall Wall were those of former Arkansas Razorback player and Cowboys owner, Jerry Jones; Mayor Mike Rawlings; and four U.S. presidents, all in college football uniforms, as well as former collegiate/NFL stars Neil Jeffrey, Doug Donley, and Matthew Sign. There are plenty of photos of regular guys who played a little college ball on display, too. The Hall Wall's website even offers a submission form on which "Hall applicants" can upload their photos and applications.

Another 2016 Trinity Groves opening surprised a few folks. Because I am a lifelong carnivore, people never thought they'd see the day that one of my businesses would be a vegan restaurant, but we did, in Trinity Groves, called V-Eats Modern Vegan. The entrepreneur, Troy Gardner, was running another Dallas restaurant with vegan offerings and was creating quite a buzz. I sent some people over there to try it out, and to a person, they said it was the best vegan meal they had ever tasted. Veganism is a fast-growing trend that appeals to millennials as well as other population segments, and I wanted to get in front of that tidal wave.

To make sure Troy has the proper credentials, we sent him off to one of Europe's top vegan cooking schools for certification. Over 80 percent of his menu is vegan, including such things as crispy tofu fingers, five-layer lasagna, baked potato soup, and tortilla-crusted "chicken" (actually tofu).

A restaurant that opened in late 2016, Beto & Son Next Generation Mexican Food, is packing them in like any Trinity Groves restaurant. Its founder, Beto Rodarte, and I have a history. In 1993, he helped me launch Nachomama's, which was later rebranded Cozymel's after Norman Brinker acquired it. Beto went on to become Brinker's "Innovation Chef" and served him well until he came aboard Trinity Groves in partnership with his son, Julian, who adds a fresh vibe to his dad's family cooking at Beto & Son. I remember going to Julian's first birthday party in San Antonio!

Beto & Son's ingredients are sourced locally, all of the sauces are made from scratch, and the meat and produce are brought in fresh daily. Beto & Son offers creatively reinvented classics, including tacos, enchiladas, and ceviche, plus pleasing table-side presentations. It's a new-generation concept that has become an attention-grabber. Beto's Barbacoa Enchiladas were named as a must-try dish by *Zagat, which raved about the place when it opened up.*

The retail program at Trinity Groves continues to grow, too. The Erin Cluley Gallery at Trinity Groves exhibits U.S.-based emerging and mid-career artists. Cake Bar, a dessert bar and retail shop specializing in mouth-watering, made-from-scratch, Southern-style cakes and confections, is actually our top performer per square foot. Incubatee-entrepreneur Tracy German opened Cake Bar in 2014 and is doing $1.5 million in annual sales in just 900 square feet. Instead of cupcakes, she sells cake by the slice in an assortment of flavors, including Italian Cream, Red Velvet, German Chocolate, and Pineapple Upside Down, plus a variety of pound cakes, quick breads, cookies, ice cream, and coffee. Tracy sold cakes out of her house for 14 years before getting her well-deserved shot at Trinity Groves.

By chance, Tracy met Babb Bros. BBQ & Blues owner Mike Babb on a stationary cycle at the Dallas YMCA, and he encouraged her to take samples over to Trinity Groves, where they quickly disappeared. A dessert place like Cake Bar is the perfect complement to Trinity Groves fare, as is Kate Weiser Chocolate, an artisan chocolate retailer complete with a chocolate café and ice cream in the summer. She specializes in hand-painted chocolates, which include such flavors as Hazelnut Latte, Peanut Brittle, Passion Fruit, Key Lime Pie, Raspberry, and Truffle Honey. Both of these places have generated a lot of great publicity. Kate has since opened a Fort Worth location and is planning to open stores in Austin, Texas, and at least one other location at press time.

Across Singleton Avenue from our Trinity Groves restaurants, about 35,000 more square feet of retail and dining space has opened on the ground floor of the development's newly completed an apartment complex. Inaugural retail and restaurant tenants included Steam Theory Brewing Co., K's Kitchen, a new Korean barbecue grill, Morgan Café from Chicago, and Bingbox Snow Cream Co., a shaved-ice dessert shop, plus Texas Capital Bank.

The first segment of the apartment complex, the five-story, 350-unit Cypress at Trinity Groves, is fully leased. The complex, which has about 1,000 residential units, was developed by a pair of talented ex-Dallas Cowboy players who knew their way around real estate. Selected to push the $100 million-plus residential portion past the goal line were Columbus Realty managing partner, Robert Shaw, and his NFL Hall of Fame business partner, Roger Staubach.

Roger, who got his start in the business during off seasons of his playing career, had quarterbacked his own hugely successful commercial real estate firm, The Staubach Co., for 21 years, recently selling it to the global real estate firm, JLL, where he's executive chairman. Robert, a Cowboys center whose playing career ended early due to a knee injury, went on to earn a degree in architectural design and management and would eventually found his own real estate investment trust. Robert is known for his innovative urban-style developments in uptown Dallas and in the suburbs.

A Class A hotel will rise next door to their residential development where an old concrete maker now stands. Redevelopment of an industrial site is never easy, but the 7-acre Argos concrete plant, which motorists see to their immediate left when they cross the bridge, had to go, we all agreed, so we cut a deal with the owner to move. Argos is relocating to a new spot about three miles to the west in an industrial park along Commerce Street.

With a hotel, offices, and other developments valued at more than $200 million in the works, the city voted to provide a $2.5 million grant to create a new rail spur and switch that will expedite the relocation. As part of the deal to buy the land from Argos and demolish the plant, we turned over the right-of-way to the city to serve as its West Dallas Gateway.

We have several potential developers and tenants for a 3.1-acre Class A office project at Singleton and Gulden Lane, next door to our incubator complex. Companies considering locating there are ecstatic about the resurgent community going up all around them.

The restaurant segment is still the catalyst, but it's just part of our flexible 30-year horizon. What's coming is anybody's guess because Trinity Groves is a fluid development designed to respond to changes in the market. Art-related retailers, a produce market, a sausage-maker and butcher shop, an artisan cheese maker, a winery, an off-Broadway theater, satellite branches for museums or arboretums, and supporting businesses like a bank, drycleaner, and convenience stores are all on our radar for future phases.

We passed the 1,500-job mark at Trinity Groves in 2017, including construction workers, no thanks to President Obama's policies. Dallas economic development officials tell me that Trinity Groves has already far exceeded the city's hopes of what would happen when the bridge opened and the city extended the TIF into West Dallas. All of the new rooftops will bring a captive audience of people who will patronize the restaurants as well as the banks, stores, and other things springing up.

We are delighted that we could raise the ante on progress there and help nurture the neighborhood back to life.

The entire west side is undergoing a transformation, much of it following our lead. Including our own multifamily housing development, more than 2,000 housing units are coming or have come on stream, including 340 apartments by Trammell Crow Residential at the corner of Fort Worth Avenue and West Commerce Street and 226 more units by Wood Partners across the street from Crow's development. A natural grocery store, Cox Farms Market, opened on Fort Worth Avenue, in the new Sylvan | Thirty development, which has space for community events, retailers, and 200 studios and lofts. Developer StreetLights Residential is doing a residential urban development that will have some restaurants and retail shops to the east of Trinity Groves. More new business is coming. Other things are happening at and around Trinity Groves. We are in the process of becoming a transit-oriented development with a station at the intersection of Herbert Street and a rail line just north of Commerce Street.

There have been a few failures at Trinity Groves. If entrepreneurs don't listen to us and aren't very successful, we send them packing, but we want all of them to do well and grow and expand to other locations. What has made the Trinity Groves work well is its diversity, including a tapas bar, a millennial beer garden, a sushi restaurant, a Mexican restaurant, an Italian restaurant, a seafood restaurant, a steakhouse, a vegan restaurant, a chocolatier and cake shop. As of early 2018, the incubator fund we created was yielding over 12 percent, which is not bad.

There are already signs that we are being "imitated." 1871, an entrepreneurial hub for digital start-ups in Chicago, launched a "food accelerator" of its own. Some major malls have created incubator programs to attract new chef-driven concepts by offering to run the back half of the business for them.

In December of 2015, Eddie Bernice Johnson recognized my business achievements in front of the U.S. House of Representatives, noting that Trinity Groves "will provide a community space for entrepreneurs to grow, businesses to invest, and people to enjoy." She went on to say more flattering things: "Whether it was a burger, a heart stent, a community, or a painting, throughout his life, Phil Romano has left a Texas-sized impression on Dallas, the city he loves that loves him back." Thanks, Eddie Bernice.

So, even in my late 70s, I have adapted. A master-planned real estate development, incubators, millennials, best-chef contests, even a vegan restaurant—they're all new to me. Around the world we see change every day in new technology, new concepts, new world events, new leaders. It's a continuation of our learning experience, and we have to adapt with it.

A good illustration of this is the story of two old guys sitting at a lunch counter complaining about the changing world. "You know, I'm getting old. I have to adjust, I have to adapt," the first guy said. "What do you mean?" asked the second guy. "Well, every day I have to roll out of bed at 7 A.M. to take a dump," said the first guy. "And it seems like I'm in the can all day long. It never stops. I gotta adapt to that, adjust my life to that." "Funny, I do the same thing at 7 in the morning," said the second guy. "But then I don't have to worry about it again until later that night or the next day. But I gotta adjust, too." "What do you mean?" asked the first guy. The second guy responded: "Well, I don't wake up until 10 A.M." The moral of this story? If you don't adapt, one day you're going to wake up in a big pile of crap.

We've adapted by resurrecting old buildings and vacant properties, using $75 million (and counting) in debt financing, and $30 million in loans in what was a run-down neighborhood, replacing it with a "new urban" development just a few minutes from the city's center. In the process, we increased sales tax revenues for the city and state, increased property values and the real estate tax base for the city, and we've served as a catalyst for other investment and renewal in West Dallas.

In a case study, the Urban Land Institute said that Trinity Groves "has reenergized this area of West Dallas, eliminated decades of neglect and blight, and reduced crime in the immediate area to almost zero." It also said that the model "is an innovative approach that deserves to be tested elsewhere."

When I think about it, we did Trinity Groves ass backwards compared to other mixed-use developments. We put our amenities in first to prove that people would enjoy Trinity Groves and patronize it. Now we're putting in the living units, hotel, retail shops, and soon, an office park. Usually, it's "community before amenities." But we took a calculated risk, and it's paying off.

In fact, we have economic development people coming to us regularly from cities around the country, saying things like, "We want this in our city; we have a rundown area where we could take old buildings and fix them up." Or, "We have all these entrepreneurs who would love to help create these kind of jobs; it would raise the tax base for this defunct area we have and give us an attraction for everyone from miles around to enjoy." Or simply, "Put one in our city, please!"

We gave very serious thought to that. But we realized there are also enough small cities in the Dallas/Fort Worth region, with a population of 7.5 million, far enough away from Trinity Groves where we could successfully put another development like Trinity Groves. It would take just 20 acres or so in the right location. That way, we wouldn't be completely reinventing the wheel in a new area. We already have tenants in Trinity Groves who are ready to expand, and we know their people and their abilities. To spice it up even more, we could put a small Eatzi's on one end and a Hoffman Hots on the other end to join 10 or more other restaurants, including some new entrepreneurs. For an added dimension, we could design rooftops for events and parties for some of them.

So, with the exception of one major new business there, which I will discuss in the next chapter, that's Trinity Groves, a place *D Magazine* would go on to call "the American Idol of incubators." We've created multiple new opportunities and brands, put hundreds of people to work, and given the public something they didn't know they wanted until they had it—one of my lifelong trademarks. The area is now a full-fledged business district, and we now call it Trinity Groves: West Dallas Business District on our website. There's more to come.

If I wasn't MAD, Making a Difference, this wouldn't have happened. And The Network Bar and the rest of Trinity Groves wouldn't be successful if it wasn't making a difference in the lives of young entrepreneurs and for West Dallas and the rest of the community, which now has a fantastic and unique place to enjoy.

12

The Network Bar

Every detail of The Network Bar has been planned out with the sole purpose of increasing members' ROR, or Return on Relationship.

In recent years, whenever I asked the last couple of generations of professionals how they network, they all responded, "online." That's a problem, because people tend to get stuck in their own circles that way, relying on texts, random online "friends" and other connection requests, and e-mails instead of real face time. It also makes it harder to build the type of authentic relationships that lead to better connections, greater opportunities, and more successful careers. Business people still need in-person skills and professional finesse to effectively connect with customers, clients, prospects, and even coworkers. Much like I've done throughout my entire life, I started seeking a solution to this problem—this market void. That's how the seed was planted for The Network Bar at Trinity Groves.

In 2016, I was kicking around a few ideas for the space beneath our new offices with my partner in Trinity Groves and in many other of my ventures, Stuart Fitts. I started reminiscing about The Key Hole, which I launched in 1969 in Palm Beach, Florida, while waiting for construction to be completed on a new office building across the street that would house another of my concepts, Romano's 300, which was a private club at lunchtime and a restaurant at night. I sold 300 club memberships for $100 apiece for those day-time business-use privileges. A lot of members were young businessmen who couldn't get into exclusive Palm Beach country clubs and were happy to have a comfortable, classy place where they could network, impress their guests, and conduct business.

In its previous ownership, the bar that became the Key Hole was run down and had a dicey clientele, and I didn't want those people coming back. The solution was to reopen the bar as a private club where patrons would need a key to enter. I fixed up the place, put a gold lock on the door, and sold keys for $25 each to preferred customers only. This made patrons feel more comfortable networking and hobnobbing there and also made them feel that they were part of something exclusive. When I explained the idea to Stuart, he thought I was just waxing nostalgic. But a few weeks later, I met with him again, this time toting an article about how most millennials really didn't know how to network beyond their online connections. I told him, "We need a new version of the Key Hole for these 'new people.'" He responded, "Phil, these millennials don't use keys; a lot of them don't even drive. And you can't give them keys. Anything you do has to be app-based, because the only thing they never leave behind is their iPhone. You'd have to make an app like a garage door opener where you press it and the door opens."

We were onto something. Stuart came aboard as my partner in the concept, and we started planning our "Network Bar" and its iPhone app. I knew that younger people wouldn't flock to a bar that an old guy had created. The concept had to be young, fresh, current, and on time, so we put together focus groups of professionals aged 21 to 35 and then hired a team of talented young people to help flesh out the concept. We hired an app developer to build a proprietary app from scratch, "an app that will be a bridge between the lost skill and the new skill," Stuart said. Since there was nothing like this concept already existed, there was no benchmark. We spent a year, and more than $250,000, developing our app from scratch. Since then, we have continued to invest in making the app better with a total investment nearing $1 million.

It would be a private club, as with the Key Hole. Those people who were 21 to 29 years old would pay $500 annually to join, while those who were 30 to 69 years old would pay $1,000 annually to join. Companies that were interested in grooming their personnel or promoting their services could buy bulk memberships at varying sponsorship levels. Couples would get a discount of 50 percent on the second membership. Those who were over 70 years old would get a free membership, with the caveat that they would pay $500 to sponsor a junior member and would be available as a mentor. The great thing about this arrangement is that the "mentor" members would benefit by meeting young, dynamic people in the workforce and investing in their entrepreneurial ideas, and the junior members would learn the ropes from a mentor who has "been there, done that."

The Network Bar opened in October of 2017, and members were quick to see its possibilities and how the concept can take socializing and networking to a new level. They were impressed with the app, the décor, and my signature service level. When one member joined, the member would invite guests that would jump at the opportunity to join, and the growth in membership took on a dynamic and member-promoted focus. This unplanned phenomenon was so effective that our membership numbers far exceeded expectations, and ten months into the concept we had over 1,000 members! Those first 1,000 members became our "founding members," and their membership rate was grandfathered in for life. Once we reached 1,000 members, the rates increased for both junior and mentor memberships.

Network Bar members need more than just a pulse to join; they must have a purpose. Membership is exclusive to business professionals who have something of value to contribute to the community, such as experience, new ideas, interesting projects, and more. Membership is comprised of some of the most accomplished and well-connected business leaders and entrepreneurs in the city from all walks of life, with varied skill sets and areas of expertise.

We strive for membership diversity and a balance in age groups and industry so that connections can be made on multiple levels. To gain membership, prospects have to be recommended by a member and accepted by a committee. As of summer 2018, the average age of Network Bar members was 42, with nearly 70 percent of them being Entrepreneurs or C-Suite level. There is a nice mix of generations, since 29 percent of members are in their 20s and 30s and 55 percent are in their 40s and 50s, not to mention that 30 percent of members are female. The top 10 industries represented are real estate, financial services, entrepreneurs, consulting, information technology, sales, legal, medical, hospitality, and marketing, in that order. A key component to the success of the concept is our Speaker and Social Series. Every Wednesday we host a professional speaker who gives a presentation on such topics such as cryptocurrency, emotional intelligence, and artificial intelligence, and from time to time we host Shark Tank-type events for investment opportunities. At least once a week we bring in vendors who are more than happy to have us sample their latest alcoholic offerings at no or minimal charge to our members to keep things a bit more lively and social.

Our goal was to make the 7,000-square-foot Network Bar a cozy place to be during the day and an ideal place to socialize at night. We built various private meeting rooms of different sizes, with their own TVs and speakers so that members could Airplay or Chromecast their presentations. Meeting rooms are available all day and for late-night deals as well, or for members who are just looking for a private space in which to socialize. The meeting rooms are more like living rooms than conference rooms. One wall in each meeting room is made of black metal so that it can be written on like a blackboard with chalk. There's an additional 1,000-square-foot fireside chat room that is used to host our Speaker Series or private member events.

We wanted Network Bar to have a speakeasy feel, so we decorated it with oversized Restoration Hardware furniture, ambient lighting, open ceilings, and brick walls that were sandblasted and stained. We brought in long leather couches, leather armchairs, low tables, and higher tables for members to work on. We put in numerous large-screen TVs, wood floors, and a great sound system, all designed around an end-to-end bar stocked with every alcoholic beverage imaginable. The walls were decorated with the world's largest collection of David Yarrow black-and-white wildlife photos. David, by the way, is an amazing worldwide photographer who has his work on display at my Samuel Lynne Galleries in Dallas.

Samir Dhurandhar, my corporate chef and partner at Nick & Sam's, designed the imaginative menu. Since opening, we have tweaked the menu numerous times to meet the needs of our members. We use only top-of-the-line ingredients, including prime meats from Allen Brothers, and we offer fresh sushi and seafood, all paired with a long, outstanding wine list, and appetizers such as deviled eggs with an andouille sausage and crunchy shrimp. One of the best mixologists in Dallas created our substantial craft-cocktail and barrel-aged alcoholic beverage menu.

One thing that makes the Network Bar unique is that the place is not a hook-up bar. With our app, members swipe up and down and not left to right. Men don't come in to chase women, and women don't come in to chase men. Both come in to chase business deals, so much so that if another member becomes overly friendly or obnoxious, the member can open the app, flag another member, and the manager will be immediately notified on his or her Apple Watch. Those serious offenders will be immediately "de-appitated."

When describing the app, think of it as LinkedIn one level higher. It includes photos of members and their professional achievements, interests, skills, and connections, and, once a member accepts a connection request, that member' contact information. It serves as a great icebreaker and helps take the intimidation factor out of networking. In addition, the app has an advanced search function to assist in making productive connections. If a business person is looking for, let's say, a patent lawyer, the person can search for "attorney" and the app will show which members meet the criteria. The app even has a special feature that shows who is at the bar so that a member can drop what he or she is doing and rush over to rub elbows with someone who meets a need. People can also post feeds to reach all members of the network at once with announcements, projects, questions, or ideas. Every detail of

Network Bar has been planned out with the sole purpose of increasing members' ROR, or Return on Relationship.

The Network Bar isn't just a one-off. Future possible applications of the concept and the app are plentiful. One or more hotel chains around the country could be licensed to have their own Network Bar. It could be paired with a coworking concept or expanded as a stand-alone concept. Who knows, maybe it will be sold to LinkedIn.

I have found that my MAD (Making a Difference) view is often the best way to start a concept, and the Network Bar followed that pattern. We created a space that provides businesspeople a central and exclusive go-to place that helps with "breaking the ice without breaking a sweat," as we say. Some call this act of network-building while eating, drinking, or sitting fireside "strategically mingling." Any way you look at it, we've struck a nerve. Network Bar is a concept that satisfies a need and a want—a type of LinkedIn country club but with affordable membership fees. I am not exactly sure where this concept will lead, but it sure will be, like most of my life, one hell of a ride!

The End (for Now)

Despite the many successes in my nearly 60-year career, I'm not finished. My body may be slowing down, but my brain is still in creation mode. As I'm given to say, creativity is a gift from God, and using that creativity is a gift back to God. (You may have noticed that I have emphasized some things twice in this book. There's a purpose for that: they are important!) Why should I try to shut down now? To me, that would be like a death sentence. I still have new ideas in the works, concepts to create and expand, paintings to paint, and interesting people to meet, so I will continue to be MAD, or Making a Difference, as long as the Lord lets me.

You're up next. One of the reasons I wrote this book so late in life is to pass along what I have learned about creativity, entrepreneurship, hiring, community development, customer service, and emotional intelligence, among many other aspects of my businesses and my life, to you.

Something I was fortunate enough to learn early on in my career I can't emphasize enough: don't wait to follow your dreams. Write them down and revisit them and refine them as you go. That way, your dreams will become your goals, and those goals, I've learned, can lead to amazing new concepts, new twists on old ideas, new inventions, and problem solving that can make the world a far better place.

Our society is in desperate need of fresh thinking and inventions. We all have the capacity to create something unique. So don't waste your God-given gifts.

I discuss my failures as well as my successes in this book for a reason. What I have learned about my failures is that they nearly always occurred because I have deviated from, or compromised, a concept's original purpose—the founding Bill of Rights I speak about so much. Even the greatest minds in the world failed, often repeatedly, before they changed the world. Instead of letting failure be a badge of shame for them, they made it a motivator to try harder and become smarter. They transformed their fears into action. The lesson is this: never let failure stop you from moving on and creating something new and different. Don't embrace the ordinary; let others follow the crowd. Create your own brand with a distinct point of difference and make that crowd follow *you*. Ask yourself (and others), "Why not? What if?" Embrace change, but realize that some core things never change, especially this truism: service is primary, and profit is secondary. This has never been more true than it is today. People want not only to be indulged and feel welcomed but also to be surprised and entertained along the way. They are always seeking out that "wow factor," especially finicky millennials. Wow them!

Put yourself in the customer's place at the customer's table. Apply empathy, discipline, and passion, and stick to the things that are making you and your brand successful: your Bill of Rights. Starting out, you have a great advantage that I didn't have. Today, there's a world of research, demographics, contacts, ideas, and customer feedback accessible on your mobile device. For most of my career, I had to rely on legwork, guesswork, and instinct to make decisions.

However, don't sidestep personal interactions on your path, as so many do today. Reach out to people, especially those who are already successful in your business and those you want to have as your customers. Nothing replaces that human touch.

I wish you success and prosperity in all your endeavors.